Journeys
and Journals
Five centuries of travel writing

For Sandra, Leïla and Mathis…

PUBLISHER'S NOTE: Where no author is given in the display quotes, these are taken from the diarists featured in the respective chapters.

First published 2004 under the title:
"Ces Merveilleux carnets de voyages" by Sélection du
Readers Digest
© Archipel studio, 2004

This edition © Kubik/RvR 2005
RvR Verlagsgesellschaft
Schulstr. 64
D-77694 Kehl
info@kubikinternational.de
www.kubikinternational.de

Design: Thomas Brisebarre

Editor: Juliette Neveux

English Edition
Produced by Silva Editions Ltd.
Project Manager: Sylvia Goulding
Translated by Jack Sims

ISBN: 3-938265-19-1

Printed in Slovenia in September 2005

Foreword
Titouan Lamazou

Text
Farid Abdelouahab

Translated by Jack Sims

JOURNEYS AND JOURNALS
Five centuries of travel writing

KUBIK PUBLISHING   RvR

Contents

'Strange travellers! What noble tales / We read in your eyes deep like the seas!
Open the jewel box of rich memory, / Show us precious stones of ether and stars.

We want to journey without sail or steam! / Lift the boredom of our prison,
Project your horizon-framed recollections / On to the stretched canvas of our minds.

Tell us, what have you seen?'

CHARLES BAUDELAIRE, 'The Voyage' from *The Flowers of Evil* (1857)

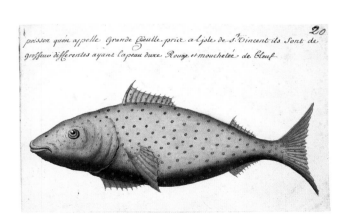

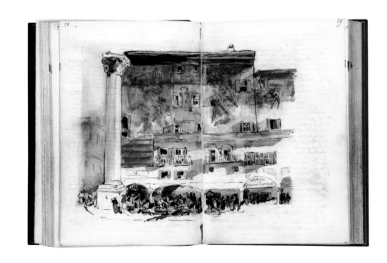

Foreword by Titouan Lamazou

I was sixteen and in my last year at school when I first really got interested in anything on the curriculum – Yvon Le Corre's art classes! They were also extra-curricular, though, because this art teacher operated off school premises, out of his studio on rue Stanco (Marseille) and outside of school hours, at night. His lessons were the highlight of my week and I drank in everything he had to teach.

At the end of the year Yvon left for the tropics on board the *Iris*, beginning work on his first 'travel diary', a precursor to contemporary enthusiasm for the genre. I was by far Yvon's most attentive pupil and I, too, now decided to abandon school life with the idea of heading off round the world to produce my own travel notebook.

Saint Exupéry, Conrad, London and Joseph Kessel may stimulate the young minds of future travellers but they certainly don't turn them into sailors. I was a complete innocent, neither sailor nor artist, yet I was both of them at the same time, and a pragmatist too! I drew a picture of how I wanted my studio-boat to be – it had neither poop nor prow! – and decided to hitch a ride on the first boat out. In fact, I got aboard a vessel in the Canaries and spent the next two years in the Caribbean. I drew portraits outside cafés to survive. I couldn't sell them – there weren't any tourists at that time – but I swapped them and bartered them, a system of exchange I'm still a big fan of now. I also proposed my services as a sailor and found myself going from one port to another, one vessel to another, until I was taken on board by the celebrated navigator, Eric Tabarly. He became my second teacher in the university of life and I spent the next

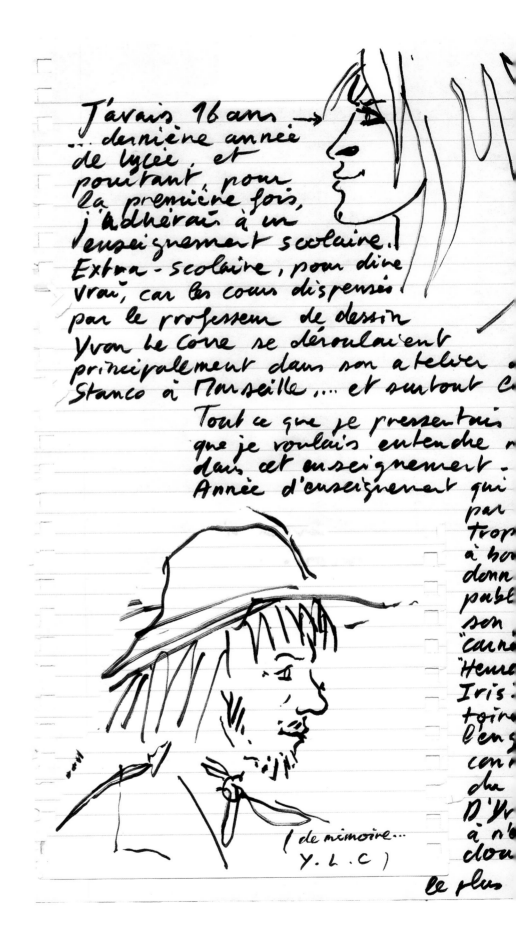

Cette année d'enseignement s'achèva aussi par l'abandon de mes études conventionnelles.
Je décidais, moi aussi, de partir autour du monde pour réaliser un ...
"carnet de voyage":
Saint Ex, Conrad, London, Kessel, Slocum .... bouleversent la jeune cervelle d'un futur voyageur, mais n'en font pas un marin...
Je n'y connaissais rien - Je n'étais pas un marin comme Yvon, ni même un artiste. Mais j'étais déjà les deux.
...et pragmatique. Je m'étais déjà dessiné un bateau-atelier, sans proue, ni poupe...
Je décidais de partir en stop... en bateau-stop. Je trouvais un embarquement aux Canaries. Je vivais deux ans aux Caraïbes.
Plutôt, je virotais de portraits aux terrasses des cafés (il n'y avait pas de touristes à l'époque) - Je troquais plutôt. Depuis, j'ai gardé le goût du troc... Et puis, je proposais mes services de matelot, de mousse,...
et je me retrouvais d'un port à l'autre .../...

Plan de bateau-Atelier 1973 (!)
chevalet (!)
atelier
banette
provisions

twenty years with him. When I won the single-handed round the world yacht race, the Vendee Globe, Eric threw a party in my honour and had me sit on his right-hand side. I had become a sailor! I had acquired legitimacy as a true traveller.

I took up my artist's notebooks and gouache paints once again and set off to finish what I had begun twenty years before. I travelled and painted to get my hand back in, working as if I were back at the art school I had never attended. At the age of sixteen, with Yvon, I had got up to Rubens. After the round the world yacht race I made it up to Gauguin. Maybe, one day, I'll manage a pastiche of a more contemporary artist!

My first notebook sold very well and no doubt contributed to the frenetic publishing activity that now surrounds the travel diary genre. The phenomenon often makes me think of the first pages of Claude Levi-Strauss' *Tristes Tropiques*, written as they were in 1955, the year I was born: "Amazonia, Tibet and Africa are invading our shops in the form of travel books […] in which a desire for effect is so dominant as to prevent the reader from appreciating the value of the account […], a very recent moral and social phenomenon particular to France, etc, etc." Travel diaries are one of the oldest forms of expression we have and remain invaluable today, so long as, both in terms of form and subject matter, they reflect the world we live in, or a personal perception of it. They should never become an extension to tourism marketing nor some kind of anachronistic transposition of it. The art of travel is still out there to be rediscovered.

[See also: www.titouanlamazou.com]

... et contribua sans doute aussi à cette frénésie de publications du genre qui m'évoque parfois les premières pages de "Tristes Tropiques" écrites ... en 1955, l'année de ma naissance : "...l'Amazonie, le Tibet et l'Afrique envahissent les boutiques sous forme de livres de voyages (...) où le souci de l'effet domine trop pour que le lecteur puisse apprécier la valeur du témoignage (...) Un phénomène moral et social, très particulier à la France et d'apparition récente, etc., etc." Claude Lévi-Strauss.

Le Carnet est une expression des plus anciennes et qui demeure, mais doit refléter, par le fond et la forme, le monde, notre monde, le monde d'aujourd'hui ou sa perception personnelle ., mais non sa transposition anachronique ou le prolongement d'un marketing touristique ...

Nuit étoilée à Tahaa

l'art du Voyage reste à inventer

Bon Vent Titouan

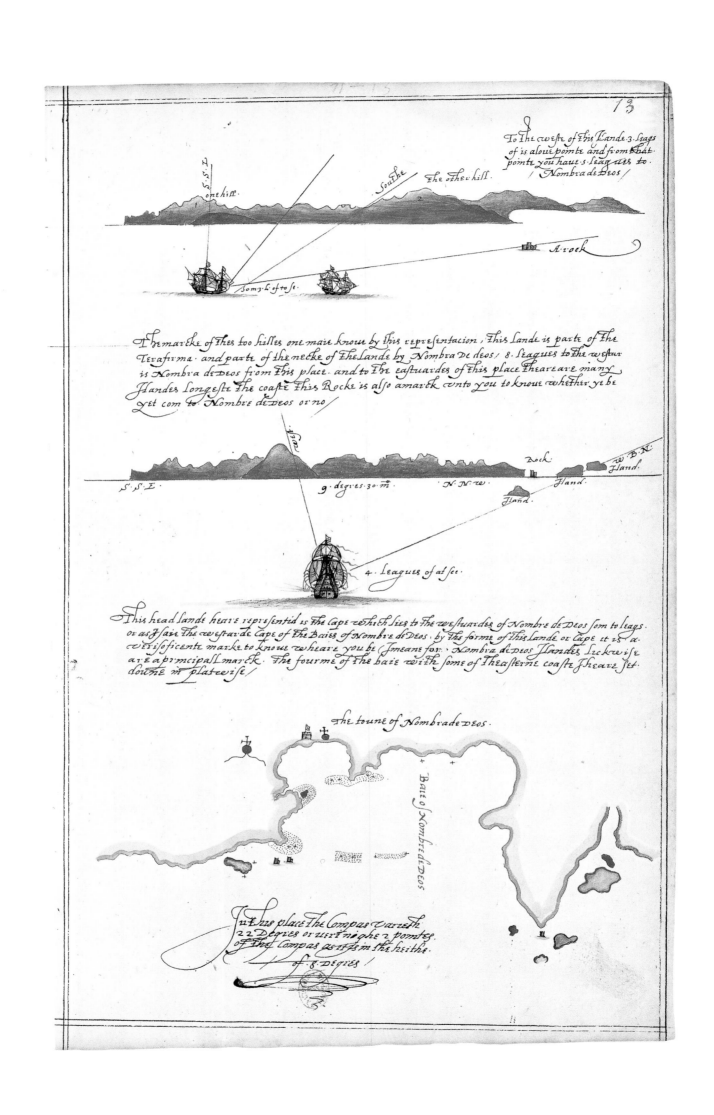

To The weste of This Ilande 3. Leags
of is aloue pointe and from that
pointe you haue 5. leag ues to.
/ Nombra de Deos /

S. S. E.   one hill.   Southe   The other hill.

A rock

Somz b. of to se.

The marke of thes too hilles one maie know by this representacion, This lande is parte of The
Terafirma. and parte of the necke of The lande by Nombra de Deos, 8. leagues to The westur
is Nombra de Deos from This place. and to The estuardes of this place Theare are many
Ilandes longeste The coaste this Rocke is also amarck vnto you to knowe whether ye be
yet com to. Nombre de Deos or no /

rock

Roch   w. b. N.   Iland.

S. S. E.   9. degres. 30. m.   N. N. w.   Iland.

Iland.

4. leagues of at see.

This head lande heare represented is The Cape which lies to the westunides of Nombre de Deos som to leags.
or as J saie The westarde Cape of The baies of Nombre de Deos. by The forme of this lande or Cape it is a
verisoficente marke to knowe wheare you be (Jmeane for. Nombra de Deos Ilandes Lickwise
are a principall marck. The fourme of the baie with some of Theasterne coaste Theare set
downe in platewise /

The toune of Nombra de DEOS.

Baie of Nombra de Deos

Jn this place The Compas varieth
22 Degres or veri nighe 2 pointes.
of The Compas as it is in The heithe
of. 8. Degres /

The Art of Travel

In the beginning there was travel. Or was there? True, the surface of the globe was peopled in successive waves of migration, but wasn't this simply what we call population movement? There is a difference between migration and travel. Imagine one of our early ancestors, of poetic soul, more curious than the rest, deciding one fine day simply to get up and leave. Maybe he was inspired by the comings and goings of migrating birds, or perhaps by a fallen tree trunk meandering its way down a river. We don't know. What we do know, however, is that this adventurous individual returned at a later date with a record of his wanderings. The proof lies in prehistoric art – paintings of animals found in areas that they never inhabited. The mammoths that decorate certain caves in the Dordogne, for example, lived at least five hundred kilometres away, and the anatomical detail depicted is proof that painters had observed them at first hand rather than drawing from third-person accounts. Pictures of these animals must therefore have been brought back from the artists' travels and reproduced in the caves.

Now, nomadic creativity is usually thought to have evolved as an oral tradition of music and song, inspired by nature rather than in competition with it. Graphic art, meanwhile is seen as an art form developed in sedentary cultures, representative art, whatever its form, automatically distancing itself from its subject matter. Travel, on the other hand, is seen as taking us back to the origin of things. In fact, Occidentals had to exorcise a world of make-believe before they could really observe the countries they were travelling through and catalogue their travels without simply finding what they were already looking for. Only then could they make their inventory and gauge value.

The first great chroniclers hardly described the landscapes they were crossing at all. For centuries biblical topography remained the only reference. Jean de Joinville, who followed the French king St Louis IX on the seventh crusade, described the Nile as 'a river that crosses Egypt and flows from paradise on earth', and for centuries afterwards landscapes continued to be described in the language of mythology. During his expedition to Brazil in the seventeenth century, Father Yves d'Évreux compared the native women he saw to Amazons, and the classical allusion stuck in the name given to the rainforest river.

◁ **NAVAL CAMPAIGN, FRANCIS DRAKE,** 1595–6
This plate, in ink and watercolour, is taken from the manuscript of Francis Drake's 'Colour atlas of twenty-two coastal views of the West Indies and the mainland, accompanied by explanatory captions'. Over the years 1577 to 1580 the celebrated pirate and explorer became the first Englishman to circumnavigate the globe, using Portuguese maps to guide him. Making maps and sketching views of the coast were ways of taking possession of land. They were also sources of information for future expeditions, and presaged the travel journal in terms of combining images and text. Here we see Drake's ship and the territory under investigation. In 1595 he set sail once again to lay siege to the Spanish ports in the Caribbean. He died of a tropical disease the following year in Panama.
Bibliothèque Nationale de France, Paris

△ STORM IN AN ALPINE VALLEY,
LEONARDO DA VINCI, 1517–18
The journals of Leonardo
would be put to diverse use
in anatomical, optical and
technical research: 'I
imagined all these machines
because, like all men of my
time, I was possessed by a
will to power… For me,
anything and everything
was worthy of study.
As a painter, for example,
light was the subject of
impassioned research.'
From the time of the
Renaissance onwards, his
journals would contain
different branches of
knowledge, including
studies of landscapes, to
which he devoted himself
when travelling. His
drawings of different sites,
done on the move, reflect
descriptions and
illustrations of the Great
Flood and the work he did
on perspective, which are

found elsewhere in his
writings and pictorial
œuvre. Of the painting
shown here he wrote: 'Let it
show the summit of a steep
mountain with a few valleys
at its feet, the layer of earth
on its sides and the small
roots of bushes appearing
to slide so that vast areas
are laid bare to uncover
surrounding rocks.'
Royal Library, Windsor Castle

**OVERLEAF: VIEW OF CHRISTMAS
HARBOUR, KERGUELEN ISLANDS, JOHN
WEBBER**, 22–30 DECEMBER 1776
John Webber completed
this drawing on Captain
Cook's third voyage.
The two ships *Discovery*
and *Resolution* have cast
anchor in the bay. In the
foreground we see a group
of penguins, a sea lion and
sailors coming ashore.
*Smithsonian Institution
National Anthropological
Archives, Washington*

In the first voyages of the sixteenth century, at the beginning of the capitalist age, expeditions began to include artists, scholars and talented literary men so that quality first-hand reports could be gathered. Once published, the works of these men were to pique the curiosity of their contemporaries, stimulating a desire for the exotic and a thirst for knowledge. The encyclopedic projects of the Age of Enlightenment pioneered new methods of work founded on precision and the necessity of proof, and a whole new visual landscape was born. Discoveries were observed, set down and compartmentalised according to areas of knowledge that were themselves being defined along the way. Through the development of the natural sciences, the mystery of existence was put under the microscope and the origin of man examined without recourse to God. Sketches of plants and animals began to appear and spread the knowledge gained from expeditions, proving to financial backers that money had been well spent and that it was imperative to set sail once again in quest of new discoveries. Although employed to record findings with straightforward clarity and detail, travelling artists were often overcome with emotion and astonishment when confronted with exotic landscapes, unusual creatures and people of strange appearance. Their encounters with tattooed Maori, for example, filled them with both wonder and uneasiness. Gradually, however, narrow working objectives were broken down and inspiration was nourished in the heady atmosphere of the new experience.

Whoever draws something for the first time also invents it. This is the privilege of discovery and is what makes the work of those early explorers unique. Some travellers became artists purely because of the strangeness and beauty of what they were seeing. Their work therefore expresses a naivety of extraordinary force, a totally original response.

The brothers Edmond and Jules de Goncourt were among the pioneers of the travel journal genre. Although they were schooled in the works of classical antiquity, their predilection was not for the path laid out by the academic world, and they rejected it both in form and spirit. With their journal of Italy (1855) they put their own imprint on the study of art history, which up till then had been viewed from a rather rigid perspective. Modern artists who made individual subjectivity their domain were able to clear new ground in which their emotions could be allowed free rein. Their search for truth led them to create new aesthetics in which they mixed their impressions with their own personal destinies and states of mind. Their expression became more conspicuously individual, and for artists such as Paul Gauguin the journal became a sort of laboratory of ideas, where, far more than on canvas, anything could be tried. Here experiments with forms and materials enjoyed a new synthesis. The travel journal became a place in which things could be added, cut out and stuck in. A photograph of a boat might appear alongside an ink

'*I saw marvels there and remain confounded with admiration for the ingenuity
of the men in those far-off countries.*' Albrecht Dürer

drawing of a fish, a watercolour of a flower, a pencil sketch of a man in action or a close-up portrait. Handwritten comments became an important element of journals, expressing passing thoughts, sometimes in a single word.

Although they went on to become outlets for philosophical or spiritual experiences, or places in which to record dreams, travel journals continued to have a role in further explorations of the globe. Their authors were often scientists who specialised in particular fields of research or concentrated on specific regions, their mandate and working methods clearly set out in advance. Others went with the aim of studying religion and the arts, perhaps to spread the faith or expand the empire. Still others aimed to conserve the memory of traditional civilisations threatened with extinction. In every case they confided their discoveries, and their feelings too, in the pages of a journal.

A diary is a wonderful travelling companion, giving the diarist an outlet for emotions and a way of surviving life in exile. By absorbing the fears and dangers of the here and now it helps to overcome them. Then, when the trip is over, it serves as a witness of what the traveller has been through, a sort of footprint. Whether exploring deserts, ice floes, jungles or, perhaps one day, planets, the writers of journals bear witness to their experiences, determined to share their knowledge in what Gauguin described as 'spare comment which, like dreams, has no sequel and, like life, is made up of many different parts'.

△ A VIEW OF BERGEN OP ZOOM, ALBRECHT DÜRER, 1520

In July 1520 Albrecht Dürer travelled to the Netherlands and to Aix-la-Chapelle to witness the crowning of Charles V, hoping that the king would continue to pay him the allowance he had been receiving. As well as keeping a journal of this year-long journey, Dürer also carried with him what he called 'My little book', a small sketchbook of rose-pink paper that measured 19 x 12 cm, in which he used the difficult but precise silver point, the precursor to the pencil. The scattering of quill pen drawings in this little book are probably taken from another sketchbook he dismantled. Larger-scale plates executed in various ways go to make up the rest of the journal. Dürer did portraits of acquaintances (such as his innkeeper's wife), studies of costumes, and views of towns. He also drew scenes from everyday life, and did detailed still life and animal studies. The journal unites disparate motifs on the same page, leaves room for the addition of afterthoughts, takes into account the need to economise on space and deliberately leaves drawings incomplete, the artist playing with space in a way that renders a feeling of remoteness and lightness of tone. This little book was to become a reservoir for inspiration, a source of the elements that were to become future works. His was one of the first journals to gain repute, and is as fine an example of the genre as it is of the tone that was later to characterise it.
Musée Condé, Chantilly

JOURNALS *of Great* VOYAGES and DISCOVERY

The manner of their attire and painting them selues when they goe to their generall huntings, or at theire Solemne feasts.

JOHN WHITE
In Conquest of North Carolina

In the spring of 1585 a military detachment left England on board a fleet of seven ships. Guided by Ralph Lane and led by the courtier Walter Raleigh, the expedition made straight for North Carolina. John White, who had an artist's training, was charged with bringing back drawings from this part of the world, which was still unknown to Europeans. He was to make illustrations of the flora and fauna, the inhabitants and their customs. The area to the south of Chesapeake Bay was at that time home to three Algonquin peoples: the Chowanocs, the Weapemeocs and the Secotans. The Secotans occupied the outer barrier islands for part of the year, and lived on the mainland for the rest of the time. This part of the Americas was not, in fact, completely unknown to the English. On an earlier exploration the previous year, also initiated by Raleigh, two small ships had sized up the strait, the lie of the coast and the islands protecting it, claiming possession of the land in the name of the English Crown. They named it Virginia in homage to the Virgin Queen, Elizabeth I. Granganimeo, the chief of the Secotans, who had given a friendly welcome to the English, did not imagine that they would return in a bloody conquest of his country.

In the heart of Secotan civilisation

At the beginning of July 1585, Ralph Lane and more than a hundred soldiers went ashore to explore the mainland Secotan villages. A bird's-eye view made by White in watercolour shows a perspective of Secotan, one of the shoreline settlements. Handwritten captions alongside the illustrations detail different aspects of the Secotan culture. White also recorded the cultivation of corn (three different varieties were grown, producing two harvests each year), culinary preparation techniques and areas dedicated to ceremonies (indicated by a circle of totem poles). He took great care to be precise in his descriptions and drawings, even those of everyday objects, such as compartmentalised chests and containers used for food. White did numerous portraits, including one of Chief Pomeiooc's wife and daughter in which they are wearing bead necklaces and holding gifts given to them by

△ **INDIAN DANCE**, 1585–90
During the summer the Secotans organised two agricultural festivals to celebrate the corn crop. These were the green grain festival and the harvest. Here, seventeen figures, some of whom are women, are dancing in a circle around totem poles on which masks with human faces have been fixed. In the centre three of the figures are embracing. Some of the dancers are wearing tail feathers and aprons, while others are shaking gourd rattles, spears and branches.
British Museum, London

◁ **AN ALGONQUIN IN NORTH CAROLINA**, 1585–90
The man's body in this watercolour has been painted, not tattooed. There is a crest of hair on top of his head, and he is wearing head feathers, a necklace, a bead bracelet and a quiver of arrows on his back.
He has a leather band on his left wrist to protect himself when using a bow. A suede apron is attached around his hips, and a puma's tail hangs between his legs.
British Museum, London

OVERLEAF: AN IGUANA, 1585–90
White's observations on his voyages to this new world were broad in scope. Pictures of the wildlife he came across, such as this iguana, were to provide precious anatomical information.
British Museum, London

Igwar
and

o . Some of thes are 3. fote in length.

ue on land .

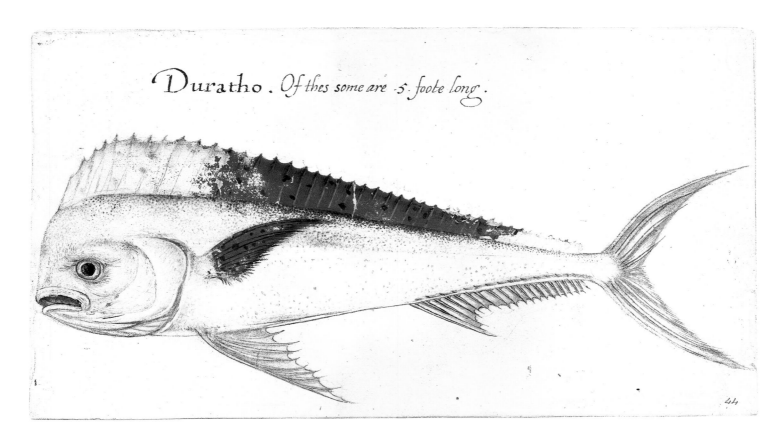

Duratho . Of thes some are 5. foote long .

△ **DRAWING OF A FISH,** 1585–90
Fish were abundant in the rivers and coastline waters, and the Indians hunted them with harpoons, caught them in nets, or trapped them by using dams made from reeds.
British Museum, London

▽ **A TURTLE,** 1585–90
The Algonquin fished either for turtles or shellfish, depending on the season. Some gathered nuts, wild berries and roots, while the hunters, armed with spears and bows, tracked deer, bears and small game.
British Museum, London

▷ **SECOTAN WOMAN,** 1585–90
This woman, who is posing with her arms raised to her shoulders, is wearing a suede skirt and earrings made from bone or polished pearl.
British Museum, London

one of the Englishmen on the expedition. A shaman (medicine man), whom the Europeans called a wizard and whom they suspected of having dealings with the devil, was pictured in the middle of an ecstatic dance. An effigy of a bird, its wings outstretched, is fixed to his forehead (this explains the title 'The flyer', above left on the drawing). Rituals, festivals and religious ceremonies were all of great interest to White, as can be seen in his representation of a group of Indians round a fire, singing and holding up gourd rattles. Thomas Hariot, who chronicled the daily life of the Secotans, noted that this occasion was to celebrate the safe return of a war party. You wouldn't know by looking at these images that the artist produced them in the midst of bloody events, as relations between the English and the Indians deterio-

'*[The Secotans] cook with care and eat in moderation...*' Thomas Harriot

rated. A potentially explosive situation was sparked off by scenes of reprisal following a minor theft from English stores. Lane, persuaded that the thief was an Indian, destroyed Secotan villages and fields of corn, forcing the Indians to leave their homes. Chief Pemisapan continued nevertheless to supply the English with provisions, and allowed them to build a fortress on Roanoke Island so that part of the garrison could spend the winter there while others returned to England in search of reinforcements and provisions. Lane continued to explore the region, sending a party to Chesapeake Bay, an ideal site for occupation, where it received a more or less cordial welcome

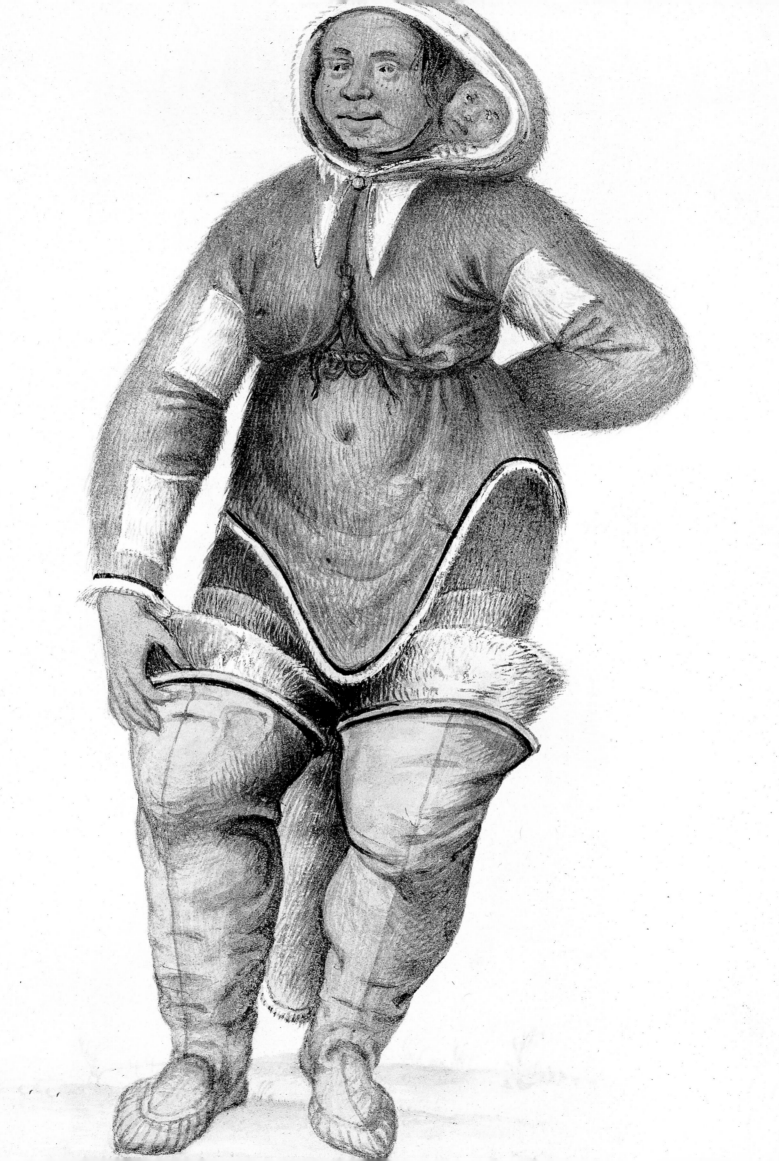

The manner of their fishing.

A Cannow.

from the Indians. The English continued to dip into Indian reserves of corn. Then, Lane decided to take the Chowanoc chiefs prisoner to obtain ransoms. In April a disastrous epidemic imported from England struck the local population and hundreds of Indians died. War seemed inevitable, especially when Secotan warriors sought the support of other tribes in rising up against the English. Lane's response was to lay a trap for Chief Pemisapan and assassinate him. The massacres had begun. Some days later, the fleet of the celebrated Sir Francis Drake arrived and put in at one of the islands. He evacuated the colonists from Roanoke Island and on 18 June 1586 the expedition set sail for England.

The lost colony

Despite the disastrous ending of Lane's mission, Raleigh dispatched a third expedition in 1587 in order to establish a permanent colony of English families. John White was named governor. One hundred and eighteen men, women and children headed for Chesapeake, where land to the north of Secotan territory was ceded to them. In mid-July they landed on the deserted Roanoke Island and reconstructed the fort and abandoned houses. Pregnant at the time, John White's daughter gave birth to a little girl on the island – the first English child to be born on North American territory. All too soon the colonists fell low on supplies, and it was too late in the year to hope for a harvest. White was forced to abandon his family and return to England, planning to come back with provisions three months later. Destiny decided otherwise, however. The Spanish Armada was lying off the English coast and threatening attack, so White was prevented from returning to Roanoke that year. Sir Walter Raleigh then lost the financial protection of the Crown, and White had to wait three years, until 15 August 1590, before he finally managed to reach the shores of the new colony again. On landing, he went to where the fortified village was constructed but found it completely deserted. Only the inscription 'CROATOAN', the name of an island village (today Cape Hatteras), suggests where the colonists might have fled. A raging storm made further search impossible, and the captain refused to land a second time, so John White was forced to return to England without having found his family. No white colony tried to settle these lands again for more than a century, allowing the Indian communities a period of respite. Numerous hypotheses have been put forward as to what happened to the vanished colonists, but the mystery remains intact and no one will ever know for sure what became of the lost colony.

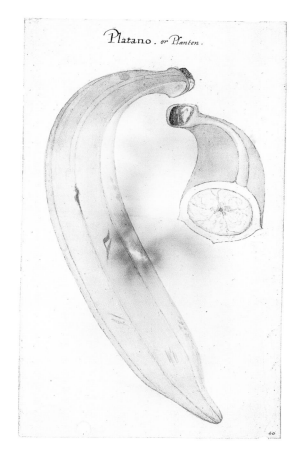

Platano. or Planten.

△ **A PLANTAIN,** 1585–90
Fruit and vegetables grew in abundance in orchards and gardens close to the villages, and were carefully tended by the Indians. Pumpkins, sunflowers, pigweed, tobacco and two different varieties of beans could be found.
British Museum, London

◁ **FISHING TECHNIQUES AMONG THE SECOTAN INDIANS,** 1585–90
White has grouped three different Indian fishing techniques in the same drawing. During the daytime the Indians used nets and spears. At night they lit fires in their canoes to attract the fish. They also trapped the fish in wooden pots or behind barriers of reeds at low tide.
British Museum, London

PRECEDING PAGES: ESKIMOS, 1577
Sir Walter Raleigh's second expedition to the Secotans (1585–6) was not John White's first experience as an artist accompanying a voyage of discovery. In 1577 he participated in Sir Martin Frobisher's second campaign on Baffin Island. The portrait on the left is of an Inuit captured by the English. He is wearing traditional summer clothing and is posing with his bow. The woman and child were captured at Bloody Point, a site the English wanted to colonise. The child has been injured by Frobisher's men and is seeking protection in his mother's cloak. White completed this full-length watercolour portrait shortly before the mother and child were taken away from their homeland.
British Museum, London

'They love to walk in the fields and along rivers, watching the deer-hunting and the fishing.' Thomas Hariot

ZACHARIAS WAGNER
The Book of Animals of Brazil

A native of Dresden, Zacharias Wagner left for Amsterdam at the age of nineteen to set sail for the New World. Once in Brazil, he joined the staff of Governor Johann Moritz von Nassau as cartographer, a position he retained until 1637. During this time he devoted himself to writing the *Zoobiolion* (or *Thierbuch*) – *The Book of Animals of Brazil*. Returning to Dresden in 1641, he pursued a career as a cartographer, and travelled to Southeast Asia, China and Japan in 1656. Six years later he was named governor of the Cape colony in South Africa. He returned to Amsterdam in 1668 and died there the same year.

The *Zoobiolion* is bound in leather and contains one hundred and eleven watercolour illustrations.

Most of the drawings are nature studies, labelled and numbered at the top, and accompanied by explanatory captions in elegant calligraphy. Zacharias Wagner shows a remarkable interest in flora and fauna. Birds are generally drawn in profile, standing on a strip of grassy ground, a branch or the stump of a felled tree. Fish, however, and certain kinds of seaweed or shellfish are rendered without context.

Wagner also drew detailed maps of harbour towns, pictures of exotic scenes and views of colonial settlements. During his trips into the interior, he completed numerous full-length portraits of the Indians in everyday settings, thus preserving a precious first-hand memory of the native inhabitants.

▷ FULL-LENGTH PORTRAIT OF A WOMAN AND CHILD FROM THE *ZOOBIOLION*, 1634–7
Wagner made numerous watercolour drawings of the inhabitants of Brazil – Amazonian Indians and slaves – as well as colonists. One drawing features the wife of a pioneer being carried in procession during an Indian ceremony, while another shows an almost completely nude cannibal woman carrying parts of human limbs.
Staatliches Kupferstich-kabinett, Dresden

▽ A PASSION-FRUIT FROM THE *ZOOBIOLION*, 1634–7
The artist often pictured the plant he was drawing from several different angles. This watercolour shows the exotic fruit slit open so that we can see its flesh.
Staatliches Kupferstich-kabinett, Dresden

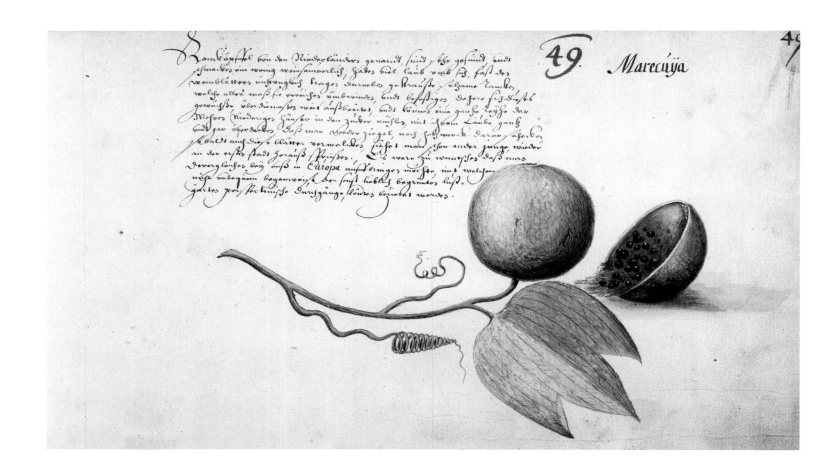

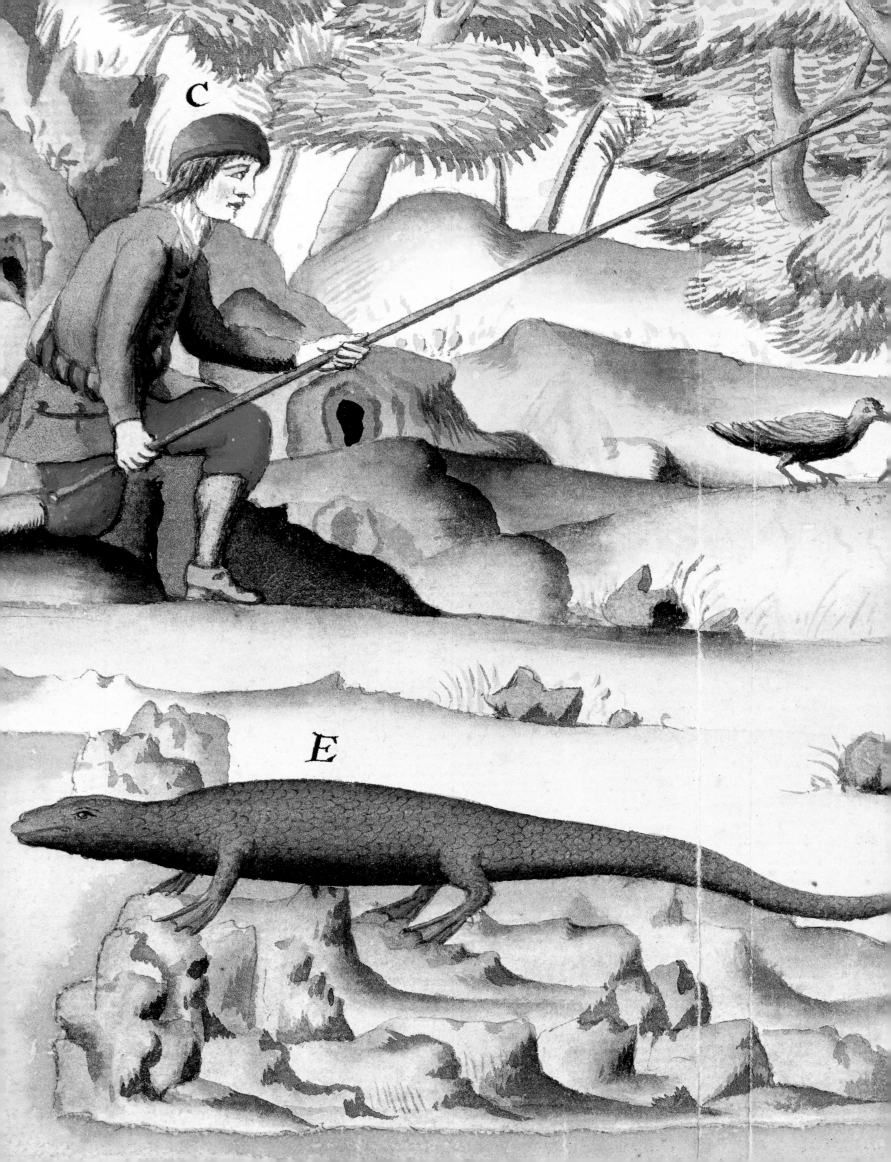

L'Ingénieur Duplessis
Voyage to the Galápagos

Early in 1701 the Comte-de-Maurepas sailed up the Brazilian coast from the Galápagos, crossed the Atlantic to the Azores and then returned to France. While on board, Duplessis [we don't know his first name, and he is always just known as 'l'Ingenieur (the Engineer) Duplessis',] was crystallising his ideas about the purpose of keeping a ship's log. On 28 February 1701, at the end of the voyage, he wrote, 'Why else keep a log if not to put it to use on future voyages back to the places already visited? If so much trouble is taken to write down everything considered necessary, is this not in order to sign the way for others or ourselves when by chance we are again confronted with the same regions and seasons? So much trouble [is] taken to write down,' he says. 'Write down and draw' would be more appropriate.

One hundred maps, watercolours and ink drawings, some of which are accompanied by detailed captions, blaze a trail through this large-format (35 x 23 cm) manuscript bound in Moroccan green leather. The scope of the work is impressive, showing Duplessis to be at once cartographer, naturalist and ethnologist – a man ahead of his time. In clear handwriting he gives a daily account of the voyage on the *Maurepas* under the command of Captain Jacques de Beauchesne, detailing its geographical discoveries and encounters from December 1698 to August 1701.

Commercial and geographical goals

In December 1698 the South Seas Company financed a fleet of three ships, including the *Comte-de-Maurepas*, with the aim of laying the ground for French annexation of new territories. In particular, the French wanted to supplant the Spanish monopoly around the Strait of Magellan. This was the first time Duplessis, a civil and military engineer, had travelled by sea.

On 17 September 1699, after a voyage of nine months, the *Maurepas* stopped off in the Cape Verde Islands. In the name of the South Seas Company, de Beauchesne took possession of a previously uncharted island and named it Louis-le-Grand. The quality of anchorages in its bays, its defendable position, and its sources of fresh water and provisions were all subjects of detailed investigation recorded by Duplessis in his journal. Of the

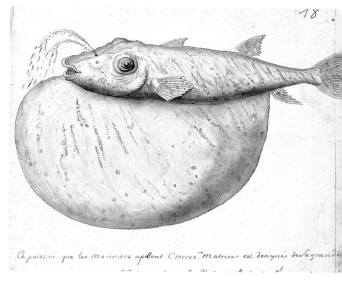

Ce poisson que les Mariniers appellent Crocros "Matrice" est designé de sa grande

◁ **DETAIL OF A DIPTYCH SHOWING A MAN HUNTING IN THE GALÁPAGOS,** 1700
L'Ingénieur Duplessis labelled the diptych using the letters seen on the drawing. The explanation reads, 'C shows a seaman killing turtles with a stick… E is…a huge sea lizard… of which there are many on the islands. They are black, covered in scales and live only on fish.'
The artist took care to give detailed descriptions of indigenous animals so that explorers would have helpful information about edible food to be found on the islands. Of the huge lizards pictured here he wrote, 'They are so hideous that none of us has yet felt the need to eat one'. This was in contrast to the enormous Galápagos tortoises, which, according to him, 'taste excellent'.
Service Historique de la Marine, Vincennes

△ **A FISH THE PETTY OFFICERS CALL 'CROCROS' OR 'MATRICE',** 1699
The author noted that the fish is drawn 'to scale'. He then records:
'We caught it with a hook and line in the natural harbour at St Vincent, Cape Verde… Some of our seamen assured us that it was very poisonous and that we should be sure not to eat it… [and] that the bladder you can see attached to the underneath of its stomach was full of water…'
Service Historique de la Marine, Vincennes

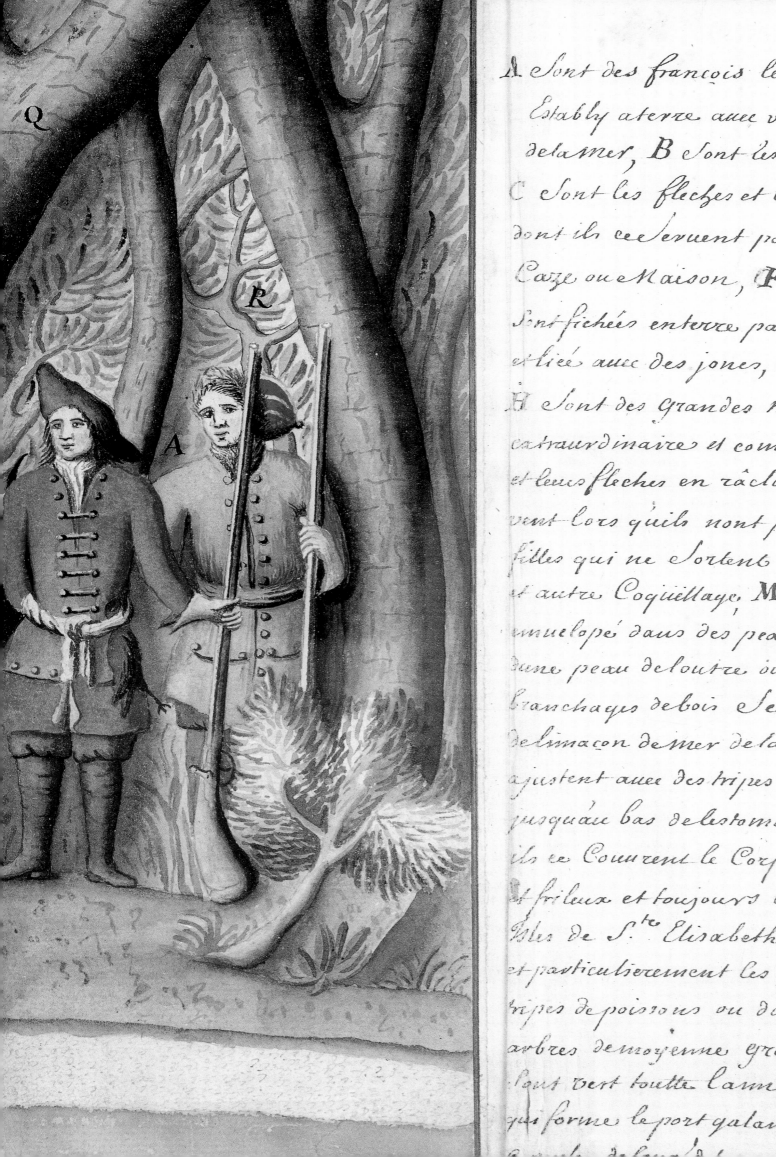

A Sont des françois les quels a[...]
Establ[y] aterre auec vne Caze
de la mer, B Sont les hommes
C Sont les fleches et l'arc d[...]
dont ils ce Seruent pour a[...]
Caze ou Maison, F Sont les [...]
Sont fichées en terre par le gros [...]
et liée auec des jones, G En vn [...]
H Sont des Grandes moulles q[...]
extraurdinaire et comme elle [...]
et leurs fleches en râclant, [...]
uent lors qu'ils nont pas dequo[...]
filles qui ne Sortent guerre [...]
et autre Coquillaye, M es[...]
muelopé dans des peaux et qu[...]
une peau de loutre ou de ping[...]
branchages de bois Sely pour [...]
de limaçon de mer de la grosseu[...]
ajustent auec des tripes de poisson[...]
jusqu'au bas de l'estomac, P S[...]
ils ce Couurent le Corps ne lai[...]
et frileux et toujours la Teste [...]
Isles de Ste Elisabeth, St Geor[...]
et particulierement les femmes [...]
ripes de poissons ou d'oyseaux [...]
arbres de moyenne grosseur q[...]
Sont vert toutte l'année R [...]
qui forme le port galant les q[...]

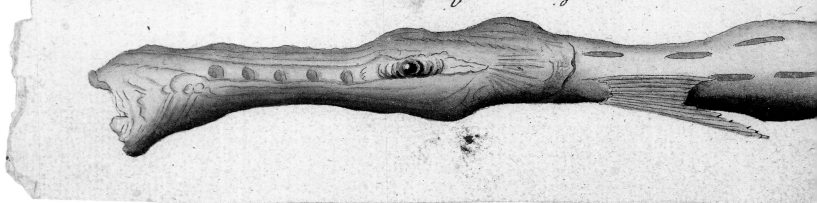

On donne plusieurs noms a ce poisson dont voycy les troix plus com...
dans la Rade & l'Isle de S.t Vincent vne de celle du cap Vert; Il auoit...
...luante comme celle d'une Anguille, Sa Teste a apeu pres la moitié d...
...oute euidée par dedans jusqua l'œil, formée de longues arestes d...
...a chair est courte delicate et d'un fort bon goust.

ninety-five original illustrations inserted between the pages, more than half are
views of towns and coastlines (some of them long panoramas that fold out).
There are plans of bays, islands, canals, towns, natural harbours and ports, as
well as more general maps. In the large-scale plan of the Strait of Magellan (51
x 76 cm), which opens in several sections at the end of the journal, the bays
explored are listed, and a significant amount of space is devoted to the
accounts and reports made during expedition excursions. The plan is also
accompanied by commentary on precautions necessary for navigation, and the
occasional piece of maritime history.

Fish, birds and Patagonians

Numerous drawings of animals, together with comments about them, give a
naturalist's feel to Duplessis' work. The first watercolour shows a flying fish that
'fell into the vessel during the night', and a shark described as a 'dangerous sea
fish'. In general, animals are drawn in their entirety, but without much attention
to detail. An exception to this is a large-scale drawing of the head of a bird 'we call

*'To the men, Monsieur de Beauchesne gave knives and arrow tips that were especially
forged on board. To the women he gave scissors, haberdashery and ribbons
with which they immediately ornamented their heads.'* 7 September 1699

œ, Bicoude, Trompette, ou Grand Gosier, Nous le primes a la Senne

s pieds de long Sancr Escailles la peau mouchetée de Violet et

rps de longüeur, Il est représenté la Gueulle ouverte laquelle est

vne peau par dessus ou lon voit presque le jour au trauers,

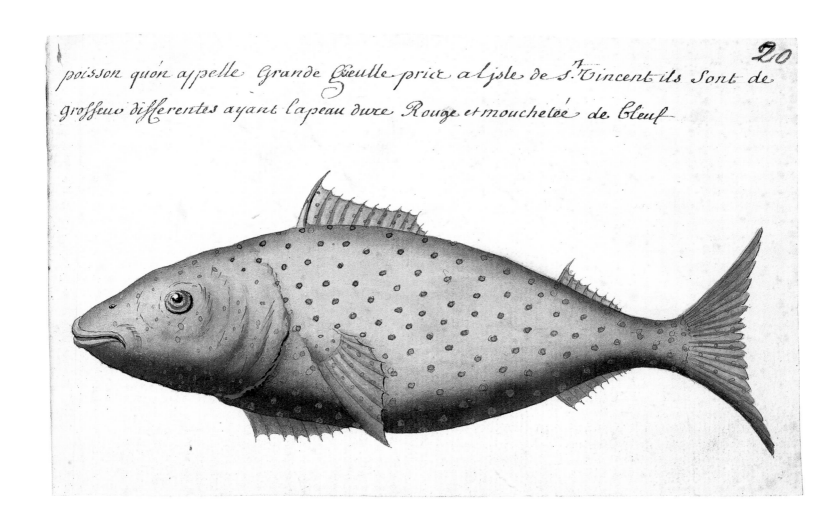

poisson quon appelle Grande Gueulle pric a l'jsle de Sᵗ Vincent ils Sont de

groffeur differentes ayant la peau dure Rouge et mouchetée de Bleuf

maistre & Oyseaux, qu'on trouve dans le Detroit de Magellan delagrosseur

nos pigeon ils vont barbottent le long du Riuage de la mer toujours deux en

ils sont gras tendre et de fort bon goust —

△ **BIRDS IN THE STRAIT**
OF MAGELLAN, 1700
'Birds the size of large
pigeons are to be found
in the Strait of Magellan.
They splash about all along
the shoreline, always
together, and are fleshy,
tender and very tasty.'
Duplessis often drew his
subjects in two different

positions. These birds are
shown first on firm ground,
then floating on the sea.
The sea is painted in a
shade of green he used
on both maps and in
paintings, varying tones
being achieved by using
different thicknesses.
*Service Historique de la
Marine, Vincennes*

a gull…which has an extraordinarily shaped beak'. Precise and detailed descriptions are given of plumages and fur, and groups of birds are sometimes drawn in flight. This was not, however, simply because Duplessis was interested in their anatomy and behaviour: these illustrations were put to a far more direct use. In the captions that accompany the drawings he noted the way in which different species were caught ('we took it with a hook and line' or 'by rifle shot'), the difficulties experienced in capturing them, and, above all, what they were like to eat. Information about the food available at different anchorages was a crucial element of expedition goals. With the exception of 'Peruvian mutton or lamb, the flesh of which is very good to eat', domesticated animals and land mammals are absent from the journal because the men on the *Maurepas* rarely ventured far inland.

The traditions and way of life among the Patagonians – environment, fishing techniques and boats – are also covered in the journal. On these topics the pictures are considerably more detailed. Letters above different individuals refer

'*We saw many birds and, on several occasions, seaweed, but it should not be concluded
from this that we were close to land. Indeed, birds are often blown far
out to sea by the frequent offshore winds.*' 26 January 1701

to explanatory captions, as in the drawing of a family of 'savages from the Strait of Magellan' in which we can see, among other things, their home, clothes and jewellery. Sometimes images are boxed, and a theme is covered from several different angles, as in the drawing of 'a kind of boat that the South Sea Indians call "balse" which they use to navigate the length of the coastline in the way shown in pictures A and B'.

Only the map of Tierra del Fuego from Duplessis' journal was published, and that not until 1764 because Captain de Beauchesne wanted the discoveries and information gathered to be kept secret. It was not until 2003 that this exceptional account was revealed to the public and published in its entirety.

△ **FISHING FOR MUSSELS IN THE STRAIT OF MAGELLAN,** 1700
'Every day throughout the year, the women and girls go diving in the sea along the shoreline for large mussels and other shellfish that make up part of their basic diet.' Fortunately, Duplessis was not offended by their nakedness because the women 'dive with their legs crossed one over the other in so skilful a way that, although they are quite naked, it is impossible to see anything of that which a sense of decency obliges one to hide'.
Service Historique de la Marine, Vincennes

JAMES COOK
Scholars and Artists in Unknown Lands

James Cook's three voyages over twelve years resulted in a huge number of illustrations. Six talented artists with a variety of backgrounds, including science, medicine, graphics and navigation, executed hundreds of watercolours and pencil, ink or pastel drawings, which were collected in expedition portfolios. Although these weren't, strictly speaking, travel diaries, the works themselves were nevertheless completed during Cook's voyages and are part of the ethnographic, naturalistic and landscape study associated with the journal genre. Whatever their specialisms, the artists, all naturalists, produced works of high artistic value. In addition, a whole post-expedition iconography grew up, retracing the different episodes of the voyages. Inspired by Cook's log, many of these post-expedition illustrations are reinterpretations or reworkings of originals done during the expeditions. There is, then, an extensive collection of works covering Cook's discoveries, enabling us to revisit in great detail what is a veritable legend in the history of navigation. The character, exploits and tragic demise of the explorer all combine to create an image of a hero of 'civilising' Europe that still feeds the Western imagination today.

The first circumnavigation

On 26 August 1768 the *Endeavour* left Plymouth under the command of Lieutenant Cook, carrying on board Sydney Parkinson, natural history artist, and Alexander Buchan, a landscape painter. The objective of the voyage was to send a team of eight scientists, led by Joseph Banks (the expedition's young patron), to the South Seas to study the Transit of Venus across the sun, an event predicted for the following summer. Having crossed the Atlantic, the ship put in at Rio despite opposition from the Portuguese authorities. Then it rounded Cape Horn, crossed the Pacific and, in mid-April, anchored in Matavai Bay, where it was given a warm welcome by the Tahitians.

While the scientists were observing the eclipse of one of Jupiter's satellites, Buchan suffered a fatal epileptic fit. He left behind a collection of very precise zoological prints, watercolours and ink drawings of insects, fish and shellfish, as well as portraits of the indigenous people. Parkinson continued to illustrate samples of the flora and fauna, most of which had never been seen before by Europeans.

A WOMAN *of the Island of* TERRA DEL FUEGO.

△ **A WOMAN FROM TIERRA DEL FUEGO, ALEXANDER BUCHAN,** 1769
The figure in this watercolour portrait, set on a plain background without scenery, seems miserable and frightened. This image comes from the collection of drawings made on Captain Cook's first voyage (1768–71). On 16 January 1769 the *Endeavour* dropped anchor, and members of the crew met the Indian inhabitants of Tierra del Fuego. 'They have long hair…their clothing consists of a llama or sea-calf skin, no more no less, worn as it comes taken off the animal's back.'
The British Library, London

◁ **PORTRAIT OF CAPTAIN JAMES COOK, NATHANIEL DANCE HOLLAND,** 1776
In this painting, completed just before his third voyage, Cook is wearing the uniform of ship's captain. His index finger is resting on the map lying unfolded in front of him and there is a questioning but also determined and courageous look on his face. The image suggests both the assurance of a man who has already seen distant lands and the uncertainty that any new departure inevitably brings.
National Maritime Museum, London

△ VIEW OF RIO DE JANEIRO, WITH THE CHURCH OF OUR LADY OF SAFE PASSAGE, SYDNEY PARKINSON, 1768
On Cook's first voyage, the *Endeavour* arrived in the bay of Rio on 14 November 1768. The viceroy of Portugal would not allow the crew to visit the city, but Banks and Parkinson, together with the botanist Daniel Solander, nevertheless succeeded in getting off the ship and secretly touring the outskirts of the city.
The British Library, London

▷ PORTRAIT OF A MAORI DIGNITARY IN NEW ZEALAND, SYDNEY PARKINSON AND S. CHAMBERS, 1772–3
Published in London in 1773, this engraving was made from the original ink-wash drawing completed in 1770 by Parkinson. In the engraving the man's physiognomy is more European than in the original drawing. His face has lost the beard that could previously be seen on his chin, but his jewels, the feathers in his hair, his costume made from foliage and his facial tattoos have all been faithfully reproduced.
The British Library, London

Leaving Tahiti on 13 July 1769, the *Endeavour* began the second part of its mission, known only to a few on board: to discover Terra Australis Incognita (the Great Southern Continent), which some firmly believed existed, but Banks thought 'a phantom continent, a product of our imagination'. Landing in New Zealand on 9 October, the crew was confronted by Maori in dugout canoes, who lay down a challenge to the ship, a scene Parkinson illustrated in an ink wash. Another drawing, a somewhat naive view of Tolaga Bay, has been attributed to Cook, who also kept the ship's log up to date. On their way around New Zealand the scientists collected many different species of animal and plant life. In April they were in Botany Bay and in June in the north of Australia. It's there that Parkinson did the first drawing of the astonishing creature Cook named the kangaroo. The *Endeavour* left Australia and in October reached the island of Java, where it docked in the port of Batavia (present-day Jakarta). Here the crew was struck by an outbreak of dysentery and several men died, including Parkinson. He left an impressive collection of thirteen hundred drawings. The ship pressed on to the Cape of Good Hope, where the sick received medical treatment, and eventually reached London on 12 July 1771, having lost over a third of its original number.

The second circumnavigation

On 11 July 1772 the former coal ships *Resolution* and *Adventure* left England on a voyage round the world. This time Cook, promoted to the rank of commander, wanted to 'sail south, further than any man has yet travelled'. Charged with illustrating the voyage, the painter William Hodges accompanied a team of scientists that included the German naturalist Johann Reinhold

'We met two…other savages who had just feasted on human flesh and one of them gave me the freshly severed bone of a man or woman's forearm.' James Cook on the Maori, January 1770

Plate XVI.

S. Parkinson del.   T. Chambers Sc.

The Head of a Chief of New Zealand, the face curiously tataow'd, or mark'd, according to their Manner.

△ **PORTRAIT OF A NEW CALEDONIAN,**
WILLIAM HODGES, MAY 1773
Although William Hodges,
known for his theatre scenery
and pre-Romantic landscapes,
was commissioned to
illustrate coastal landscapes
and the inland areas of the
territory crossed during
Cook's second voyage, this
didn't stop him from doing
portraits of the indigenous
peoples he met. This pencil
sketch of a New Caledonian
is part of a huge series of
anthropological drawings.
The Natural History Museum,
London

△▷ **A RED HARTEBEEST,**
JOHANN GEORG FORSTER, 1773
This watercolour illustration
of a member of the antelope
family was completed at the
Cape during Cook's second
voyage (1772–5). There
Forster met Anders
Sparrman, a Swedish
naturalist and former pupil
of the eminent Carolus
Linnaeus, whom he was still
helping with research. Among
other things, Sparrman was
studying animals in their

natural habitat and in the
Cape menagerie. He had a
particular interest in seals,
and communicated
extensively with the French
naturalist Georges-Louis
Buffon, who acknowledged
Sparrman's help in his multi-
volume and much-admired
Natural History.
The Natural History Museum,
London

▷ **THE PYGOSCELIS ANTARCTICA**
PENGUIN, JOHANN REINHOLD FORSTER,
DECEMBER 1774 – JANUARY 1775
When Forster did this
watercolour illustration of a
chinstrap penguin on Cook's
second voyage, *Resolution*
was already some way inside
the Antarctic Circle at a
latitude never before
reached by Europeans,
and sailing alongside
icebergs up to a hundred
metres in height. Forster was
strongly affected by this
region. 'Taken overall,'
he wrote, 'the spectacle
resembled…descriptions
of hell given by the poets.'
The Natural History Museum,
London

Forster. The latter, the translator of Louis-Antoine de Bougainville's *Voyage around the World* (1772), took his son Johann Georg along to assist with the natural history research. The ships rounded the Cape, headed past New Zealand and arrived in Tahiti on 16 August 1773. Many watercolours and drawings were produced of fish, birds and trees, some of which included pencil sketches of houses in the background. Apart from illustrating landscapes, Hodges produced pastel portraits, such as his 'Tahitian man with long hair' and 'The King of Otaheite'. Having drawn several Maori, he completed his ethnological series in New Caledonia with portraits of the inhabitants of Amsterdam Island, of Melanesians and Kanaks, some of them entirely in ink or pencil.

In the meantime, the two ships managed to lose each other. *Resolution*, which was heading southwest, travelled into uncharted territory alone. At the end of January it crossed into the Antarctic Circle and became lost in a vastness of ice. Forster wrote: 'As a whole, the spectacle resembled the debris of a world broken into pieces.' One week later Cook decided to head back towards the tropics because continuing to go south would be too much of a risk. Hodges and Forster made the most of capturing the grandiose spectacle of this unknown territory. Hodges was inspired by the landscapes and monumental ice 'sculptures', which he painted under a stormy sky with dramatic light.

The *Resolution* returned to Tahiti, passed the New Hebrides and moored in New Zealand in October 1774. It then returned home via Cape Horn. Even if the artists' collection of drawings was not as methodically executed as that of the first voyage, it nonetheless contains much of interest. The artists were greatly inspired by previously unknown plants and animals, such as the Antarctic beech, the 'tree of fire', penguins, albatrosses, seals and cetaceans.

'In reality, they are far happier than us Europeans, being, as they are, totally ignorant of not only the necessary but also the superfluous commodities we are at such pains to find in Europe.' James Cook on the Australian Aborigines, spring 1770

G. Forster

Aptenodytes antarctica β.2. Forster in Commentar. Gotting. 3. p. 141. tab. 4.
his figure.

Aptenodytes antarctica

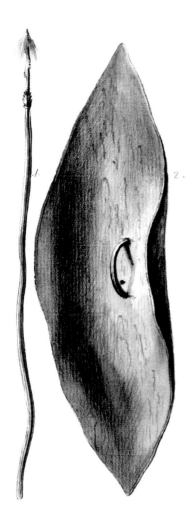

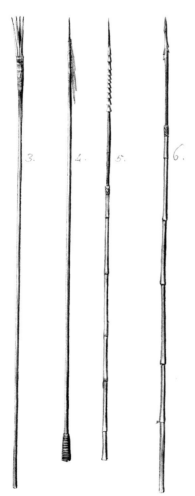

On 29 July 1775 the *Resolution* arrived back in Britain, where Cook expressed his belief that the Great Southern Continent did not exist. Another mystery, however, remained to be solved. Was there a passage around the top of North America that would link the Atlantic and Pacific oceans?

In search of the Northwest Passage

On his third voyage Cook commanded the ships *Resolution* and *Discovery*. Officially, there was no naturalist on the trip, but William Anderson, a surgeon trained by Johann Forster, assumed this role. The painter John Webber was to do landscapes, while William Ellis, the assistant surgeon on board *Discovery*, would do the natural history drawings. The ships rounded the Cape and crossed the Indian Ocean, passing by the Kerguelen Islands, New Zealand and the Friendly Islands (present-day Tonga). When they arrived in Tahiti on 13 August 1777, members of the expedition were invited by the king to witness a human sacrifice. In John Webber's watercolour of this event we can make out a man attached to a length of wood on the ground. The *moraï* (sacred ground) on which the ceremony took place was, Cook informs us, 'probably a burial ground as well as a place of worship and sacrifice'.

At the beginning of December, the expedition discovered the Sandwich Islands, where Webber did a portrait of a masked man. On 6 March 1778 they berthed on the northwest coast of Canada and met the Indians of Nootka, also cannibals. Webber illustrated them inside their homes, which were decorated with sculptures, and showed them preserving fish by smoking it. The ships then made their way up the length of Alaska before crossing the Bering Strait. On 3 August Anderson succumbed to tuberculosis and William Ellis took over his work. Continuing northwards, the expedition encountered the peoples of Siberia, then went further into the pack-ice. Cook did not, however, discover the passage from the Pacific to the Atlantic. *Resolution* started shipping water, so left *Discovery* to return to the Sandwich Islands alone in October. Here, though, relations between the crew and the islanders deteriorated. In February 1779, after a failed attempt to leave, Cook stood up violently against the local people. During this episode he was killed on the strand and probably eaten by his aggressors.

Notwithstanding Cook's tragic death, the numerous drawings and logbooks give a rich account of his three voyages. For Europeans, they were a marvellous window on to the great geographical and human diversity of the tropics.

1 Dart from New Zealand
2 Shield from New Holland
3 Fish Spear from Do
4 Javelin from — Do
5 & 6 Darts from New Guinea

View of the Huts at Tschutschi Noss, Asia.

◁◁ **VARIOUS ARMS, JOHN FREDERICK MILLER,** 1771
The two artists who were part of Cook's first voyage both met with a premature death, and John Miller continued their work. This print shows an arrow from New Zealand, a shield, a harpoon and a javelin from New Holland (present-day Australia), and two arrows from New Guinea.
The British Library, London

◁ **PORTRAIT OF A MAN FROM VAN DIEMEN'S LAND, JOHN WEBBER,** 1784
This engraving was reproduced in 1784 from an original drawing dating from January 1777. Relations were established with the inhabitants of Van Diemen's Land (present-day Tasmania) at the beginning of the third voyage, after the boats had dropped anchor to take on provisions. Cook noted that they were '…entirely naked and wearing no ornament… Most had their hair and beards steeped in a red ointment and some had their faces painted with the same mixture.'
The British Library, London

△ **VIEW OF THE HUTS AT TCHUKTCHIS, WILLIAM ELLIS,** AUGUST 1778
This drawing in watercolour and ink, done during Cook's third voyage, features the Tchuktchis, a Siberian people from the northern Asiatic coast. They lived in huts covered in sea-animal skins during good weather, and in half-buried shelters during the winter. Members of the expedition, who studied them with great interest, found relations with them difficult.
The British Library, London

AUGUSTIN DAVID OSMOND
A Slave Ship's Log

In 1681 a statute was passed in France, making it obligatory for all sea captains to keep a log. The log had to be written up at noon each day after the captain had met with the crew and signalled the course to be set. It had to estimate longitude and latitude, record weather conditions and the prevailing wind, and give an account of the events of the previous day (deaths, accidents, etc.). The directive prompted Augustin David Osmond, first mate aboard the slave ship *La Rosalie du Havre*, to write up the log of a passage to the African coast, beginning on 29 December 1788 and ending on 16 June 1790. The elegance of his handwriting, accompanied by delicate watercolours of fish, boats, coastlines and

astronomical symbols, did not mask the horror of life below decks on the return journey. Some four hundred and eighty-seven men, women and children, inventoried in a neatly drawn table, had been snatched from their land of birth. It is difficult to imagine the horrors they endured when life at sea was hard even for ordinary seamen: poor, sometimes rotten, food; the menace of scurvy; stagnant water; deplorable hygiene. Osmond's account of the slaves was brief, but not in an attempt to make light of the trade he was involved in. It was simply because the slaves, regarded as little more than animals, possessed no identity as far as Europeans were concerned.

▷ **A PAGE FROM** *LA ROSALIE DU HAVRE'S* **LOG,** DAY 33 OF THE PASSAGE, 1788
At the bottom is a watercolour of a shark seen from above and held on a line.
Bibliothèque Armand-Salacrou, Le Havre

▽ *LA ROSALIE DU HAVRE* **LEAVING HER HOME PORT,** 1788
From 1750 onwards, ships became larger, more solid, stable and manoeuvrable, but navigation remained a hit-and-miss affair. It was not until the end of the eighteenth century that a reliable method of calculating a ship's position at sea was finally invented. Before that time, discovered lands were sometimes wrongly marked on maps, and captains would often be unable to find these territories again or even to recognise them when they did. As a result, certain islands were named as many as three times.
Bibliothèque Armand-Salacrou, Le Havre

32.ᵉᵐᵉ Jour

Du 29 au Vendredy 30 Janvier 1789.

Beau temps, la mer venant du Nord, de la
Brume à L'horizon, couru à toutte voille, gouv.
au SSE du Compas, La route de l'Est
NE & NNO petit fraix & Calme, dans
la nuit il a beaucoup Eclairé dans le SE.
au jour il a frichy, La Brume tenant toujours
Jusqua midy que La route Est.ᵉ ma vallu

W.ᵈ Est.ᵉ NO
10 E 30

Petit Vent Varle

Le SSE A.ᵒ Sud Ch.ᵒ 31 Lieux 72.
Latt. Est.ᵉ N 8 29
plus de diff.ᵉ Latt. Obs.ᵉ N 8 29
Longitude Ouest 24 31

33.ᵉᵐᵉ Jour

Du 30 au Samedy 31 Du dit

Depuis cet 24 h.ᵉˢ Le vent ont varié du NO Nord
& NE Joly fraix & Calme, La mer Belle, Le
temps à L'orage & Embrumé, couru a toutte f.ᵉ
Estuinée & royaux Depuis, gouv. au SSE du Compas
Jusqua midy que La route Estimée ma vallu

W.ᵈ Est.ᵉ NO
de 10 E

Le SE 1/4 S Chemin Est.ᵉ de 20 L. 1/3
Latt. Est.ᵉ N 7 37
Longitude Ouest 20 56

Nous avons fait de 2.
à 3. jauges d'eau par h.ᵉ
aujourd'huy, nous ignorons
d'ou ce vent Estre venu
vraye Cause

A midy Le Temps Couvert Je n'ay point eu
hauteur Nous avons eu Connoissance de La
Lame du Sud

Pris un Requin

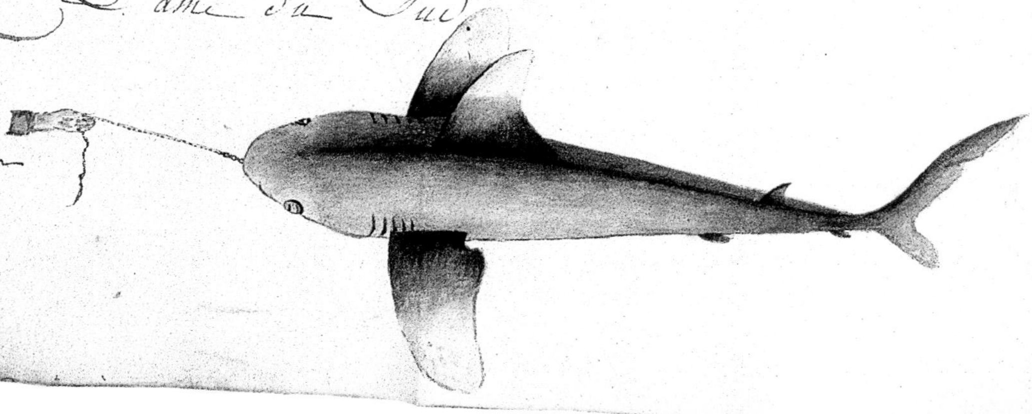

the ship, he leaped into the sea and swam towards her and was f
lowed by one of our men, the same who went over board bef
when we were off New Georgia, they soon got into the canoe
the indians pulled towards the ship and put our man on
board again. these people must have some connection with sh
before as they seemed to take but little notice of us; before I h
done with them I cannot forbear saying, that in conduct, figur
contrivance and ingenuity that they equal if not exceed the Eurp

Period	Winds	Course	Dist:	Lattitude North	Longitude East	Longitude Obs: at 8 D	Thermometer	Bearings Land
Noon	Calm N.E.	S 53 W	44	00 " 15	133 " 7		93	At 6 P. M. th land bore S distant abou 3 leages

moderate breezes and exceeding warm weather and inclinable t
calm. saw some parrots and paroquets flying over the ship, li
wise saw vast numbers of flying fish, the distance some

JOHN WASHINGTON PRICE
On the Minerva from Ireland to Calcutta

John Washington Price was only twenty-one when he went aboard the *Minerva*, a ship transporting two hundred convicts to Australia. For the most part the convicts were Irish, condemned to exile for having participated in the rebellion of 1798. In spite of a brilliant career as a student and his recent marriage, Price was dissatisfied and felt the pull of the high seas. He therefore abandoned his country and obtained the post of ship's surgeon on an adventure that was to take him from the port of Cork to Australia by way of Rio de Janeiro. The voyage then continued to the Solomon Islands, through the Strait of Dampier to Calcutta, where what we know of Price's voyage ends. Price's detailed and documented log is divided into nine chapters, which include twenty-nine magnificent watercolour drawings framed in ink. He ruled off his pages in advance, a margin on the left being reserved for the dates on which he wrote the log. Although punctuation was neglected – he omitted capitals at the beginning of sentences and used commas in place of full stops – he wrote in a steady and elegant hand.

Heading for Rio with the convicts

Price left Dublin for Cork, where he made a point of visiting the convicts on the *Minerva*: 'I went on board to see them, and found them indeed in the most wretched, cruel and pitiable condition I ever saw human beings in, in my life…' The ship departed on 24 August 1799, and in the entry for that day Price remarked, "I sat on the poop viewing my native country gradually vanishing from my sight." Out at sea off the coast of France the *Minerva* sailed south to Madeira, then took a bearing for Rio de Janeiro. During that time Price drew up a full list of passengers (including the convicts), recorded their ages, trades and the ports at which they were taken on board, and made a note each week about the condition of convalescents and of the passengers whose accidental injuries he was treating. During the first few months his observations were confined essentially to medical activities and to changes in weather, but he did slip in a watercolour of a flying fish. He also commented on his relations with Captains Cox and Salkeld, and with the ship's doctors.

◁ **CANOE WITH SAIL NEAR ST DAVID'S ISLAND,** APRIL 1800
We can see six natives of New Guinea in this illustration. One of them is sitting on the outrigger. John Price noted estimations of latitude and longitude in minute detail in the table underneath. When writing up his log, he was principally concerned with navigational information and life on board, but this did not prevent him from producing watercolours and describing the men and landscapes he met en route.
The British Library, London

△ **BATANTA ISLANDER, PULAU,** APRIL 1800
This watercolour portrait is framed in a way reminiscent of the decorative medallions common at the time. Price did another portrait of the same type and in the same shade of imitation turquoise blue. He signed the bottom right of the drawing, which was probably completed during a stopover on the islands of New Guinea.
The British Library, London

'The pleasant scenes every where around soon banished… gloomy ideas…' 20 October 1799

△ **NATIVES FROM THE DELIVERANCE ISLANDS IN A CANOE,** MARCH 1800
Landing on the Deliverance Islands (near the Solomon Islands) en route to Bengal, John Price described the fishermen we can see in this illustration. 'The canoe is now some distance from the shore. The Indians on board seem very hearty, their skin almost the colour of ebony and their curly hair very much like wool.'
The British Library, London

▷ **FLYING FISH, MADEIRA,** SEPTEMBER 1799
This careful reproduction of a flying fish, probably done off the coast of Madeira, was one of Price's first illustrations. He wrote, 'This morning one of [the flying fish] flew in on the forecastle from where I have taken the following drawing. A number of banatas were likewise speared.'
The British Library, London

On 19 October 1799 the *Minerva* anchored in Rio, an opportunity for Price to draw a panoramic view of the bay. He retraced the colonisation of Brazil in his journal. He also gave first-hand descriptions of the architecture of Rio, and painted watercolours of its aqueduct and the surrounding islands. On his wanderings he noted his appreciation of typically exotic sights. 'We…were highly amused with the groupes and squads of slaves, ever[y]where perambulating the streets, they were curiously, richly and fantastically dressed, playing on the different kinds of their native indian musick…' He was astonished at the 'children playing about quite naked, indeed the women were nearly so too from the waist up, which generally affords a sight by no means agreeable to a person lately arrived from Ireland or England'. The ships departed for Sydney on 8 November 1799, and a month later he mentioned the name of a travelling companion, the artist and naturalist John William Lewin, who gave him 'lessons in drawing and natural history'. These had an obvious influence on Price's illustrative work. The *Minerva* arrived in Sydney on 12 January 1800.

Observing natural history in Australia

During a one-month stay in Sydney, Price drew and made a record of the town's different monuments. His observations, for the most part unpublished, form an invaluable account of Australia at the beginning of its colonisation.

1799
Saturday —
September 21st

and for a considerable distance, they frequently fly into the ship, I believe
when pursued by a larger fish, they are in this respect very unfortunate, for
when pursued by large fish, and fly, they are frequently are caught by birds
on the watch for them, and to avoid which if they take to the water, it
is frequently into the mouth of their first pursuer they drop — This morning one of them flew in on the forecastle from which I have taken the
following drawing. a number of Bonattas were likewise speared and
taken — one of which I have taken a drawing of — as appears on the next
page, they are a large handsome fish but sometimes very pernicious to those
who eat of them. — Latt: Observed — 11 — 49. N.

The Flying Fish.

The study of the flora and fauna was one of his principal preoccupations. Moreover, he said, 'a botanist could find nowhere else a better terrain for his research. This country is one immense forest.' He tasted different edible fruits and noted his reaction: 'We did not enjoy at all the taste of the seeds of wild figs.' He collected birds 'of magnificent plumage, in particular parrots', and took certain specimens back to his cabin.

An unfinished journal comes ashore

On the final leg of the journey the *Minerva* sailed to the Solomon Islands by way of Lord Howe Island, where Price drew two different views that show the summit belching smoke in the way characteristic of an active volcano. On 8 March 1800, he landed in New Georgia. From 9 to 15 April 1800, the eighth chapter of his journal, he was in the Strait of Dampier and produced a medal-

lion portrait of an inhabitant of St David's Island. The log stops abruptly for reasons unknown when Price landed in Calcutta. The following pages have, however, been marked out with margins ready to be written on. From the *Minerva*'s log we know that Price was not among the passengers who returned to England from Calcutta. His journal fell into the possession of the Marquis of Wellesley, a well-known collector recorded as being in Calcutta at the same time as Price. Today it is part of the Wellesley collection in the British Library in London.

△ **VIEW OF LORD HOWE ISLAND,** FEBRUARY 1800
Approaching the shores of Lord Howe Island, discovered twelve years earlier by Lieutenant Ball, John Price sketched two views of a smoking peak. 'Going by the quantity of pumice stone and burnt rocks that we found on the island, it did seem to correspond to volcanic activity. Moreover I found much more at higher altitudes.'
The British Library, London

'A great number of birds of magnificent plumage are to be seen in the forests – parrots in particular.' January 1800

of small fish which now begin to run and are
taken in great quantities in the Columbia R.
about 40 miles above us by means of skiming
or scooping nets. on this page I have drawn
the likeness of them as large as life; it
as perfect as I can make it with my
pen and will serve to give a
general idea of the fish. the
rays of the fins are boney but
not sharp tho somewhat pointed.
the small fin on the back
next to the tail has no
rays of bone being a
= branous pellicle.
to the gills have
each. those of the
eight each; those
are 20 and 2
that of the back
the fins are of
is of a bleuish
the the lower
is of a silve=
part. the
behind the
second of
the puple
a silver
and
like

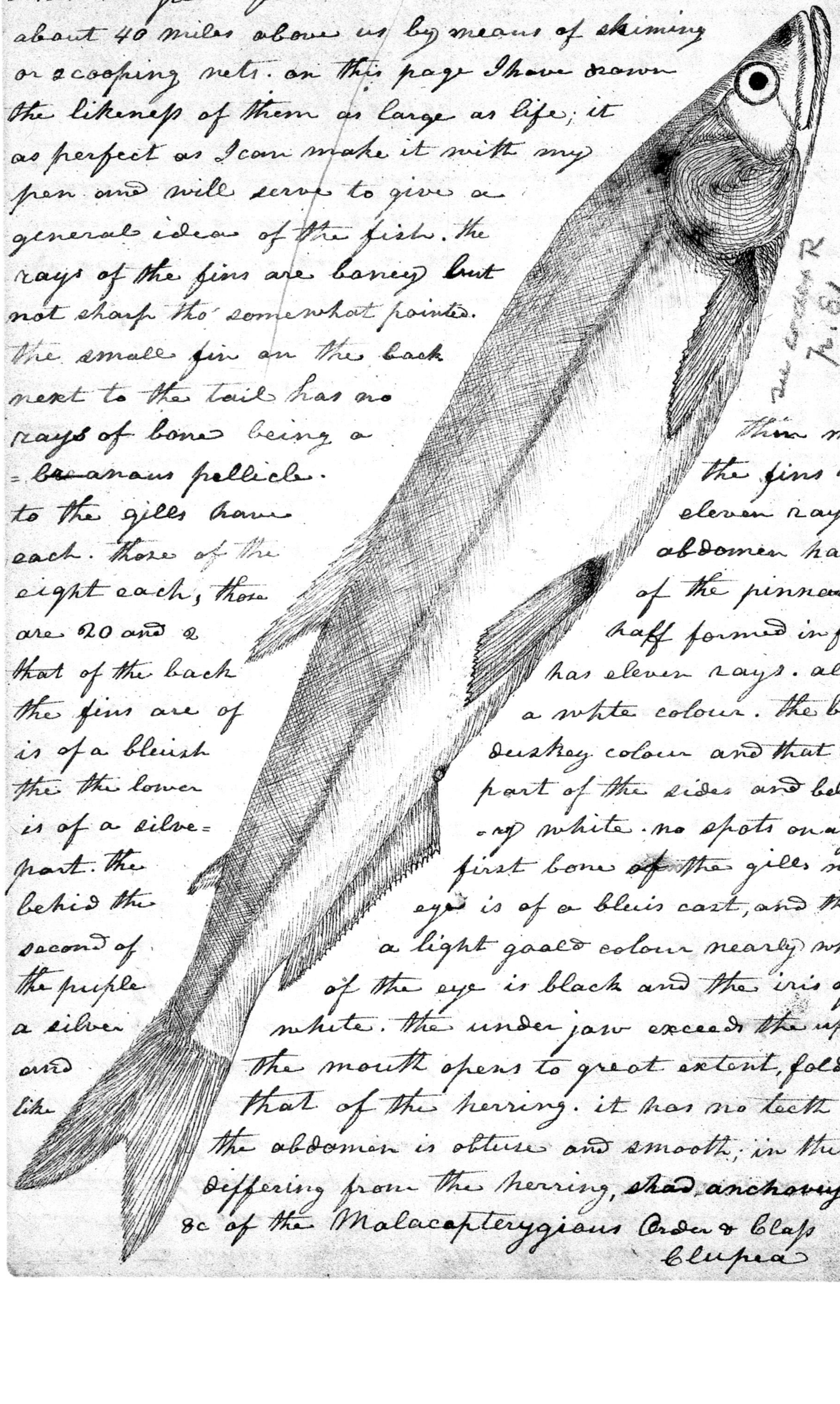

thin mem
the fins next
eleven rays
abdomen have
of the pinnovani
haff formed in front.
has eleven rays. all
a white colour. the back
duskey colour and that of
part of the sides and belley
ong white. no spots on any
first bone of the gills next
eye is of a bleuis cast, and the
a light goald colour nearly white.
of the eye is black and the iris of
white. the under jaw exceeds the uper,
the mouth opens to great extent, folding
that of the herring. it has no teeth.
the abdomen is obtuse and smooth; in this
differing from the herring, shad anchovey
&c of the Malacapterygious Order & Class
Clupea

MERIWETHER LEWIS AND WILLIAM CLARK
An American Epic: The Far West

On 14 May 1804 about forty soldiers and volunteer frontier guards boarded two canoes and a large, flat-keeled boat on the Missouri river at St Louis. Well equipped with arms, munitions, tents, medicines, surgical instruments and provisions, they set off for two years and four months, covering a distance of some 13,000 kilometres across unknown Indian territory to the west of the Mississippi and the Rocky Mountains. They got as far as the Pacific Ocean, then returned to their point of departure on 23 September 1806.

Financed by President Thomas Jefferson, and under preparation since the summer of 1803, this strategically important mission was led by two trust-worthy young men, Meriwether Lewis and William Clark. The first, at that time private secretary to the president, was twenty-nine. The second, the son of Virginian planters, was thirty-three. In a letter addressed to Captain Lewis, dated 20 June 1803, Jefferson set out the mission's objectives, including instructions on what must be logged in the expedition journal. The two men were ordered to write a chronological account illustrated with numerous maps and drawings.

Just as the president ordered

The acquisition of Louisiana from France was what prompted the President of the United States into organising the mission. Its objective was 'to explore the Missouri and its principal tributaries' which 'by its course and its access to the Pacific provides the most direct and practicable link for trans-continental commerce'. Above and beyond any commercial end (considerable profits from the traffic of furs through St Louis rather than around Cape Horn), Lewis and Clark had to devote themselves to three pursuits: geography, study of the indigenous Indian peoples, and observation of the flora and fauna. Before leaving, they were tutored in the principles of botanical and zoological study, and experienced map-makers taught them how to use the compasses, optical equipment, chronometers and sextants necessary for compiling maps.

President Jefferson's instructions were clear. Moving up from the mouth of the Missouri, Lewis and Clark were to note the latitude and longitude of

△ **AN INDIAN CANOE DECORATED WITH SCULPTURES ON THE PROW AND STERN,** 1 FEBRUARY 1806
Speaking of the Indians in his letter to Lewis, President Jefferson specified, 'As much as the conscientious pursuit of the expedition allows, you are to familiarise yourselves with their everyday occupations in the domains of agriculture, fishing and hunting, their methods of war and artistic creation and the materials used therein.'
American Philosophical Society, Philadelphia

◁ **A FISH FROM THE PACIFIC COAST,** 24 FEBRUARY 1806
The men on the mission took only a minimum of provisions with them, relying on hunting and fishing to provide the bulk of their diet. As a result, the animals they studied sometimes found their way on to their plates at mealtimes. A large part of the journey was made on water, but navigating rivers was fraught with difficulties and there were numerous accidents. On 14 October 1805 the mission lost three canoes in the currents. Sometimes steep cliffs on either side of rivers, such as the Columbia, made it impossible to moor.
American Philosophical Society, Philadelphia

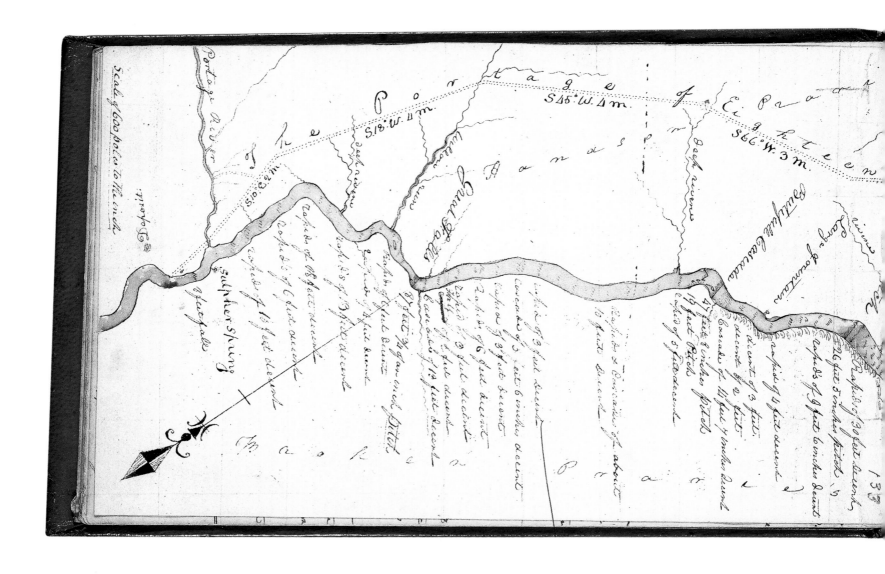

all noteworthy points along the river, its confluences, tributaries, the position of rapids and the main porterage points. They were to pass this information on to the War Department 'so that calculations can be made simultaneously by competent persons'. The first accounts were therefore rough outlines designed simply to break the ground for more thorough inquiries into the nature of the territory. The conservation of these documents was a priority, so a suitable medium was essential. Jefferson instructed them to 'make copies on birch paper, which is less susceptible to damage by moisture than is ordinary paper'. The first part of the work thus completed was dispatched to St Louis in April 1805, accompanied by twelve members of the expedition to ensure its safe arrival. They also took back previously unknown birds and a prairie dog.

'Your observations must be carried out with the utmost precision,
written in a hand, clear and intelligible not only to yourselves but also to others.'

President Jefferson's letter to Lewis, 20 June 1803

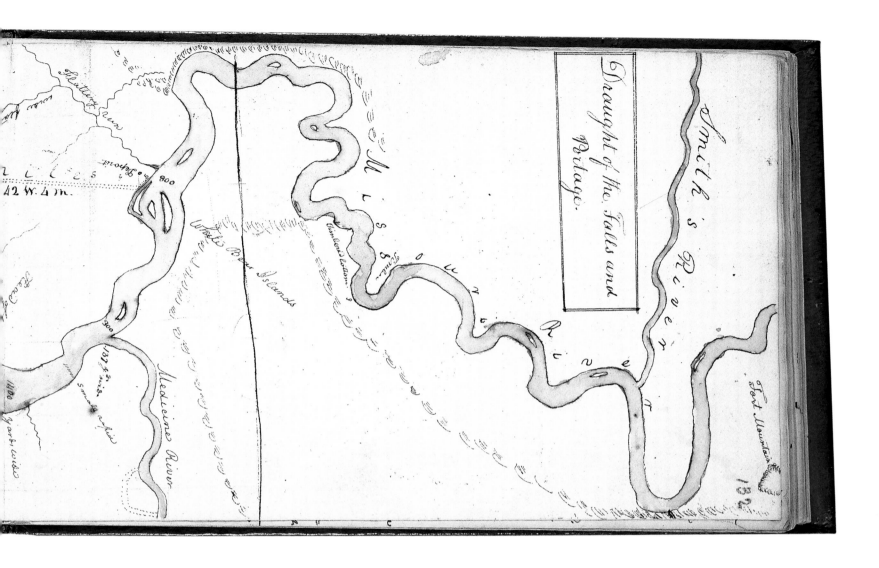

Anthropological and naturalistic study

Acquiring knowledge of the Indians (for the establishment of trade links) constituted the second major objective of the expedition. Lewis and Clark were charged with describing their territories, the relationships between tribes, their activities (types of agriculture, fishing and hunting), their methods of war, their culture (language, art, religion and architecture), their domestic and culinary habits, their sanitary conditions and their physiological characteristics. They were also instructed to investigate 'the products they may have a need of or which they are able to supply us with and in what proportion'. This information was then to be used by 'those who make efforts to civilise them and instruct them in their adaptation'. As the economic benefits of this 'civilising' conquest were already anticipated, Jefferson advised several times on the specific methods the mission should adopt to establish peaceful relations with the Indian tribes.

The mission's final objective was to study natural history in the broadest possible sense. New species of flora and fauna were therefore collected and investigated. Seasonal cycles of flowering and ripening of fruit were noted, and the 'dates on which certain species of bird, reptile or insect appear' were, as far

Drawn for Capt M Lewis
(1806?)
by CWPeale

CWP del!

On his return from the west
coast, Lewis commissioned
several different artists,
including Charles Wilson
Peale, to collaborate in
illustrating the three-
volume account of the
expedition that was
eventually published.
*American Philosophical
Society, Philadelphia*

▷ A MAP OF A WATERCOURSE AND THE
MOROCCAN RED LEATHER COVER TO ONE
OF LEWIS AND CLARK'S JOURNALS, 1806
A strategy for safeguarding
documents from the
expedition was ordered and
put into place by President
Jefferson: 'Copies of these

observations as well as of
your other notes must be
made during rest periods
and then given to your
most trustworthy men
in order to avoid any
accidental losses that
might occur.' The dispatch
of these documents by
courier was to be organised
as frequently as possible
'at convenient intervals'.
On reaching the Pacific
coast, 'if ships under
whatever nation's flag are
to be found in port', two
men were to take passage
carrying copies of the
documents in order to
bring them back safely.
*American Philosophical
Society, Philadelphia*

as possible, identified. Soil was analysed, and geographical features examined for mineral products, particularly metals, limestone, coal, saltpetre, salt marshes and water, as well as any volcanic activity. Climatic variations 'such as that observed on a thermometer', rainfall and the nature of prevailing winds were all noted in the journal.

The expedition was a success. On their return, Lewis and Clark went to Washington to present the fruits of their labour. They had collected twenty-two 'new' species of animal and plant, and recorded information on river systems, geographical features and totally unknown Indian tribes, such as the Nez Percé, who had never before seen the white man). The mission paved the way for a new wave of settlement and enlarged the national consciousness of the size of the continent. Lewis set to work on the publication of the journal, but in September 1809 he committed suicide following a breakdown. Clark completed work on the journal five years later, but only a century later, in 1904–5, did the first edition of what has become a classic in the literature of exploration see the light of day.

'*We are on the point of entering a region at least two thousand miles across on which no civilised man has yet set foot.*' Lewis's journal, April 1805

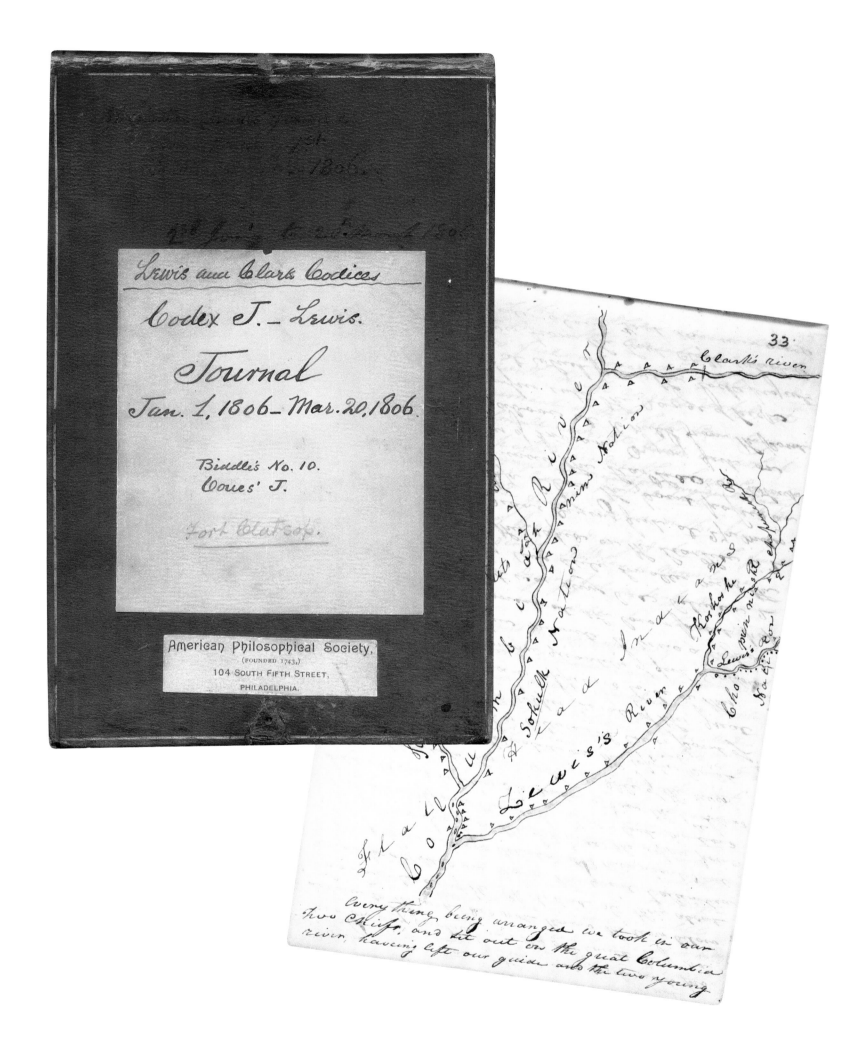

Habitants du Port Dori, Nouvelle Guinée,

JULES LOUIS LE JEUNE
Expedition to the South Seas

On 11 August 1822 La Coquille, a 380-tonne lighter raised to the status of corvette, left the port of Toulon for a scientific expedition to the South Seas. Eighteen-year-old artist Jean Louis Le Jeune was on board. Under the command of Louis Isidore Duperrey, who had previously captained *L'Uranie* on a voyage to the South Seas between 1817 and 1820, *La Coquille*'s mission was to continue the exploration of the Caroline Islands, New Guinea, Easter Island and the Society Islands. One of sixty-five men, mainly experienced scientists, Le Jeune was full of excitement to be heading for the antipodes. His liking for landscapes, portraits and still lifes resulted in excellent illustrations of a happy voyage.

La Coquille set sail for the Americas, making its first landfall in Santa Catarina, Brazil. It then headed for East Falkland, where the mission set up its observation post on the site established by the explorer Louis Antoine de Bougainville in 1765. While there, Le Jeune took the opportunity of studying the site, now lying in ruins. The boat set off again and rounded Cape Horn, making stops in Chile and Peru, where the naturalists pursued their research, before setting a westerly course for Reao in the Tuamotuan archipelago. The islanders refused to allow the mission to land, so *La Coquille* headed to Tahiti. During a stopover there, Le Jeune did many portraits of the Tahitians, sometimes observing his subjects with the aid of a telescope. This allowed him to see without being seen and to produce an objective, detailed and careful record of the costumes, tattoos and attitudes of warriors.

Continuing its journey, *La Coquille* passed Bora Bora, headed northwards to the island of Santa Cruz and moored at the island of Buka. Here the crew met the natives, who had voluminous hair and rings in each nostril, and Le Jeune drew them. After stopovers in New Ireland and New Zealand, the scientists were welcomed with open arms by the inhabitants of Strong Island, who had never seen Europeans before. On reaching the Caroline Islands, Le Jeune executed a number of drawings. Among them was a panoramic view of a village, a woman sitting down, objects used in

Le Capitaine Chinois d'Amboine.

◁ **PAPUANS IN PORT DOREY, NEW GUINEA,** 1825
After visiting the Caroline Islands, *La Coquille* headed towards New Guinea, arriving at the end of July 1825. In this drawing Le Jeune focused on the men's traditional hairstyles. The man sitting down has a wild piglet on his knee.
Service Historique de la Marine, Vincennes

△ **THE CHINESE CAPTAIN IN AMBOINE,** 1823
On 4 October 1823 *La Coquille* dropped anchor at Amboine (now Ambon), capital of the Maluku Islands. The governor organised a reception in honour of the ship's command, but the island's inhabitants were suffering from a cholera epidemic, so the crew had to remain on board in quarantine.
Service Historique de la Marine, Vincennes

Naturels de

60

Hommes

Canons

le Rotumah.

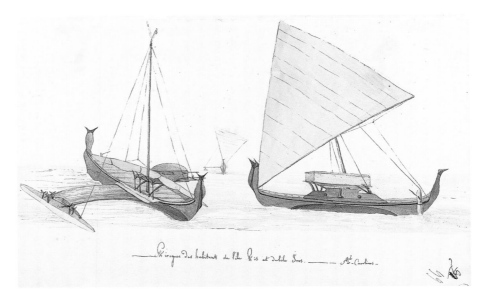

PRECEDING PAGES: INHABITANTS OF ROTUMA, CAROLINE ISLANDS, 1824

△ A COFFEE PLANT AND A PAPAYA TREE ON THE ISLAND OF SANTA CATARINA, BRAZIL, 1822–5

On the outward journey, after a stopover in Tenerife, *La Coquille* crossed the Atlantic and sailed down the coast of Brazil. Le Jeune made the most of this stop to collect information on local plants.
Service Historique de la Marine, Vincennes

△▷ SAILING CANOES ON PIS AND IROS, TWO OF THE CAROLINE ISLANDS, 1822–5

Among other drawings he did on the Caroline Islands, Le Jeune completed this study of a double outrigger canoe used by the Papuans. He also sketched a panoramic view of the village of Lélé, the chieftain's headquarters.
Service Historique de la Marine, Vincennes

▷ SPECIMEN OF A FLOWER ON SANTA CATARINA, BRAZIL, 1822–5

In its hold *La Coquille* brought back some four hundred botanical species previously unknown in Europe. Members of the Academy of Science, including the famous Georges Cuvier and Friedrich von Humboldt, praised the mission for the extent of its botanical work.
Service Historique de la Marine, Vincennes

On 1 May 1824 *La Coquille* arrived on the island of Rotuma, where the artist drew a group of six people. Two of the individuals provide a frame for the others, and we can see the influence of anthropometry (measurement of body parts) in the arrangement of profiles, backs and faces. Louis Duperrey, captain of *La Coquille*, tells us, 'They stain their bodies in yellow and red and wear their hair long, hanging down to their shoulders. Their arms are agreeably tattooed with small, regularly spaced beauty spots and their thighs are covered in thinly spaced lines which give their skin an extremely dark tint.' Right from the first meetings, the exotic nature of the inhabitants brought forth a form of displaced eroticism. This original drawing was used as the model for a later engraving in which female nudity is more blatant.
Service Historique de la Marine, Vincennes

rituals, flutes and fish hooks, all on the same page. The illustrations were accompanied by explanatory texts, such as, 'A sea-fish tooth to which a great deal of superstition is attached is worn by the New Zealanders suspended from their ears. The women use it to scratch their faces during funeral rites.'

La Coquille then set sail for France, heading past New Guinea, and got back to the port of Marseille on 24 March 1825. Over the course of the journey Le Jeune made more than three hundred drawings.

Praise from the Academy of Science

The expedition was an unprecedented success. The Academy of Science paid tribute to the mission's naturalists, who had returned with a large collection of unknown species – some four hundred plants, twelve species of quadrupeds, forty-six birds, and around twenty reptiles and amphibians. Le Jeune received special mention for his forty-three portraits, fifty-seven drawings of costumes, eighty-three landscapes and views, forty small paintings and fifty-nine ethnological drawings showing, among other things, weapons, utensils, sculptures, jewels and religious objects.

Two years after the ship's return the first of seven volumes of *Voyage autour du Monde* (Voyage around the World) appeared. For this survey of *La Coquille*'s voyage, Le Jeune was able to provide illustrations taken from his original work. Strangely, there is no record of any later graphic work by Le Jeune. Maybe he didn't do any. Nonetheless, he completed this first mission – part of an expedition described by the eminent naturalist Georges Cuvier as 'exemplary from a scientific point of view' – with great success.

'[The women] are graceful and well proportioned. Moreover, they shine by the whiteness of their teeth, the vivacity in their eyes.' Louis Duperrey on the women of Strong Island

Ile de St Catherine

$\frac{7}{10}$

n° 348.

n° 340

*I*LLUSTRATED STUDIES:
The JOURNALS *and* SKETCHBOOKS
of TRAVELLING ARTISTS

Colonne triomphale de l'antique Élorine colonie de Syracuse dont on voit les ruines
près de vindicari entre Syracuse & pachino ———— planch. gravé 203.

Monument triomphal appelé l. Cuglia, les lieux

JEAN PIERRE LAURENT HOUEL
The Italy of an Enlightenment Painter

In 1772 Jean Pierre Laurent Houel, a French landscape painter, returned from a voyage to Italy. So impressed was he with what he had seen that he decided to make a second trip to work on a huge panorama, which he intended to publish later in France. Being a man of the Enlightenment, he was as interested in the sciences then developing across Europe as the customs and art of the regions he visited. Houel presented his project in a 'prospectus' that he drew up to advertise the sale of his work by subscription. He planned to include 'perspective drawings, with plans, cross-sections and flat projections of all the scattered monuments that these islands have to offer the curiosity of the traveller'. He also intended to picture the grandeur of the countryside and of 'objects likely to arouse the interest of naturalists, such as lava, basalt and bituminous lakes'.

A handwritten journal of the second voyage still exists today, as do the preparatory notes and the portfolio of drawings and paintings he did while in Italy. Although the format of his drawings (30 x 45 cm on average) does not correspond to the smaller and more easily manageable size of a pocket notebook, Houel's work is important in the contribution it has made to the travel journal as an artistic genre. His illustrations also possess architectural qualities, feature many different aspects of travel and present a new approach in terms of aesthetic and narrative quality.

Houel's island travels

On 16 March 1776 Houel left Paris for Marseille. There he boarded ship for Naples, going on to Palermo and Agrigento in Sicily. He then spent several weeks in Malta and Lipari before returning to Sicily. For Houel, an artist in love with Italy, this voyage was the opportunity for an in-depth study of the country's natural resources, its history and the people who had already conquered his heart. History, he wrote, 'not only informs us of the facts and keeps a country's glory alive, but also restores the monuments and can resuscitate a nation centuries after its disappearance'.

◁ **REMAINS OF THE TRIUMPHAL COLUMN KNOWN AS 'LA GUGLIA'**, 1776–9
Houel did this illustration in Sicily, mixing gouache with pencil and black and brown ink. He used many different materials when executing his drawings, which required a certain amount of logistical organisation, and sometimes commissioned help to carry his equipment.
Musée du Louvre, Paris

△ **INTERIOR OF A CAVE**, 1776–9
During the course of his trip, Houel was attracted by caves and other rock formations, executing this illustration in gouache and watercolour. He also visited the St Paul cave in Malta, where a statue of the saint attributed to the seventeenth-century Italian sculptor Gianlorenzo Bernini can be found.
Musée du Louvre, Paris

Partie des ruines du temple de jupiter olimpien d'agrigente ou l'on voit un chapiteau dont la colonne a 9 pieds 4 pouces de diametre en le triglife dix pieds de haut — pl. on. grav. 228

As he enjoyed royal favour, he gained access to the houses and estates of Malta's nobility. The Grand Master of the Order of Malta was particularly helpful, and provided him with everything he needed in order to draw the island's architecture and works of antiquity. Houel consulted the grand master's library and was impressed with the collection, which inspired several drawings. Moved by the strange megalithic sites on Gozo, he carried out a precise examination of the stones, whose origins were still a complete mystery. The islanders' traditions fascinated him, and his work included precise studies of the hats, scarves and corsets that made up the local women's costume. His rational and pragmatic take on life led him at times to mock certain local beliefs. For example, the religious procession he witnessed on the island of Lipari, asking God to send rain, he described as a 'real charade'.

Exploration of Sicily

In a little less than six months he went right around Sicily, stopping off in towns to soak up 'whatever might be of interest', and taking the time to speak Italian to the Sicilians he met en route. In Selinunte he sat down with them in the shade, later recalling, 'I was finishing a drawing or description so as to make the most even of this pause. My hosts were interested in my work and I

*'For an eye accustomed to the picturesque beauty of nature,
the day was fine, the weather tranquil.'*

told them something of life in France.' By mid-July 1778 he had completed
more than a hundred paintings. In common with most landscape painters of
his time, he usually chose very large views stretching towards the horizon.
These pastoral scenes were an idyllic portrayal of work in the fields, often
showing someone going about everyday activities against a background of
ancient monuments and ruins.

A comprehensive visual survey of Houel's travels in Italy was published in Paris
between 1782 and 1787 under the title *Voyage Pittoresque des Isles de Sicile, de Malte
et de Lipari* (Picturesque Travels in Sicily, Malta and Lipari). It consisted of four
volumes illustrated with two hundred and sixty-four copperplate images – a bulk-
iness that was very much in keeping with the encyclopedic spirit of his time. As
much taken with the geography and customs of the local inhabitants as with the
archaeological remains, this erudite artist opened his contemporaries to a new era
in terms of their relationship with travel. His work was learned and personal, open
towards other civilisations, vivid, nostalgic and sensitive.

△ **THE ROCKS OF THE CYCLOPS**, 1776–9
This gouache and black
pencil drawing illustrates
the small port to the north
of Catania in eastern Sicily.
'These basalt rocks are very
different one from another,'
Houel wrote. 'The one that
has the most regularly
pyramidal form is made up
of prismatic columns.'
The figures are holding an
eel and another type of fish
or shellfish, and they are all
no doubt commenting on
the day's catch.
Musée du Louvre, Paris

midletown le 26 aoust 1816

CHARLES ALEXANDRE LESUEUR
An Artist's Sketchbooks of the Northeast United States

'We have been in Philadelphia since the 20th of May and are setting off for the [Great] Lakes in four or five days at the most,' wrote Charles Alexandre Lesueur to his father in June 1816. An illustrator and naturalist famous for his part in Nicolas Baudin's scientific expedition to the Antarctic Ocean [in 1800–1804], Lesueur was to accompany his sponsor, the American geologist and philanthropist William Maclure. He was not aware that he would remain on American soil until 1837. Two books of drawings resulted from this first tour in 1816, which lasted five months. Lesueur completed another tour, of Philadelphia and its surroundings, in 1819, and a third in Albany in 1822. The two sketchbooks from the summer of 1816 are more the work of a landscape artist than a scientist (although Lesueur did in fact include numerous notes on geological observations), and give a unique snapshot of a country on the brink of expansion and industrial development.

The sketchbooks of 1816

Lesueur and Maclure landed in America on 9 May 1816. In the contract drawn up between them in August 1815 Lesueur agreed 'to complete drawings relating to the natural history of the regions that will be crossed'. He was also to 'organise for the stuffing or the preservation in alcohol…of objects Mr Maclure judges to be worthy of his attention'. The objective was clear. This private excursion was to expand the personal collection of Lesueur's naturalist sponsor and lead to a publication. In his luggage Lesueur packed numerous books by other naturalists and explorers, including the survey carried out by Meriwether Lewis and William Clark (see page 53), as well as maps, engravings and 'objects necessary for the completion of drawings' (the architectural drawings included in the sketchbooks are indeed drawn with instruments). To this equipment he added two quantities of drawing paper, a box of paints, a dozen Conté crayons, six dozen artist's pencils and an assortment of inks. The illustrator was thus well prepared to make the round trip with Maclure across Pennsylvania to Lake Erie, then across New York State via Rochester, the Finger Lakes and Albany into Vermont, and back south following the Connecticut

◁ **MIDDLETOWN, CONNECTICUT,**
26 AUGUST 1816
These ink wash and pencil drawings are taken from Lesueur's second sketchbook, which covers the trip he and Maclure made from Lake Ontario to the Atlantic coast. The artist enjoyed drawing pigs, and there is a certain humour in this pencil sketch of a rear view. The previous month he had included a pig in the middle of countryside scenes. Two sows lying down in a landscape also feature in the first book near the sketches of Niagara Falls.
Musée d'Histoire Naturelle, Le Havre

△ **WEYBRIDGE, VERMONT,**
19 AUGUST 1816
This drawing in pencil and watercolour is the third of a series completed at Weybridge, between Vergennes and Middlebury, near the southern end of Lake Champlain. The series also includes a sketch of a wooden bridge over a torrent in a forest and another of a waterfall. The hugeness and beauty of nature in these sparsely populated areas (no man-made structure can be seen at all here) inspired Lesueur. In one letter he said of a Frenchman who had settled in a heavily wooded area of New York state, 'I feel sorry for anyone who has possessions of this type unless they have strong arms, youth, courage and strength to spare for cultivation and clearing of land… One must do everything oneself in these places.'
Musée d'Histoire Naturelle, Le Havre

△ **LAKE ST GEORGE, NEW YORK,**
8 AUGUST 1816
The handwritten text
on this grey ink wash
and pencil drawing informs
us that the artist sat 'above
Lake St George while
we were fishing'.
The rectangular shapes that
we can see lining the edge
of the lake are piles of
wooden planks. Lesueur
was proud of his talents
as a fisherman, naturalist
and illustrator, and that
he could bring all three
together while on board
a boat.
*Musée d'Histoire Naturelle,
Le Havre*

▷ **THE *NORTH CAROLINA* IS LAUNCHED
FOR THE FIRST TIME, PHILADELPHIA,** 1822
We cannot be sure that
Lesueur drew this superb
pencil sketch from life.
A boat called the *North
Carolina* was launched in
this place two years
previously, so he might
have seen the launching
of a different vessel of the
same name in 1822, or have
made the drawing in 1820
and used the same
sketchbook for later
drawings. In fact, the most
likely scenario is that
Lesueur copied the scene
from another painting or
engraving without quoting
his reference. This kind
of ambiguity is of course
in the very nature of
sketchbook entries.
*Musée d'Histoire Naturelle,
Le Havre*

river to the Atlantic. They then made a final loop north through Cape Cod, Boston and Newburyport before crossing Massachusetts in the direction of New York and arriving back at their starting point, Philadelphia.

During the course of this trip Lesueur completed two books of drawings, but the original of the first book no longer exists. The books contain more than one hundred and twenty pages illustrated mainly in pencil and colour washes. These drawings concentrate on the landscape of the areas visited – countryside, rivers, mountains, lakes, farms, houses, churches, small settlements, barrages and bridges. Several pages are devoted to the Niagara Falls, and to scenes sketched on the Atlantic coast while 'passing by and visiting all the small harbours of the cod fishermen'.

Although Lesueur concentrated on landscapes, the scientific aspect of the trip was not ignored. He made numerous comments on the geological make-up of the soils, such as 'quartz-like pudding stone' or 'compact chalk'. The flora and fauna were also featured. At the end of June, on the banks of Lake Erie, Lesueur described a pike-perch, which he drew in pencil. On the following page the 'head of a catfish' appears. On 6 August, near Lake Saratoga, he even drew up a list of fish to be found there. As far as trees are concerned, the 'chestnut oak' and the 'maple with orangey-red leaves' feature frequently in the pages of the sketchbook. These notes, sometimes found above drawings of the leaves, are not developed further.

'The straightforward nature of the pretty local women is not hidden from strangers passing through.' Charles Lesueur, 8 October 1816

The sketchbooks of 1819 and 1822

As he explained in one of his letters from 1819, Lesueur travelled to Albany, where he went 'to finish the map being drawn up by the commissioners of the American government charged with determining the frontier line between Canada and the United States of America'. More than twenty drawings in pencil and watercolour, in a format of 17.5 x 12 cm, remain from the sketchbook that he put together over this two-month journey. The first, in ink and pencil, was done in April during his descent of the Hudson river. In the next, a group of men can be seen carrying a net towards the riverbank, and boats fishing for American shad are pictured. Further on, under an illustration of a family of colonists making a stop, there are some technical drawings (rare in Lesueur's work) of their coach. Brief notes such as 'scaly, blackish shale' remark on the nature of soils. The only illustration of an animal in this sketchbook is the head of a snake drawn in pencil.

By 1822 Lesueur had been living in Philadelphia for six years, and he produced a sketchbook in a larger format than previously (15.5 x 22 cm) in which he made drawings of the town and its surroundings. Although similar in content to his previous books, this one had mainly pencil drawings. In fact, only five of the thirty-seven pages were in watercolour.

In 1826 the artist settled in New Harmony, Indiana, while continuing as a correspondent member of the Musée National d'Histoire Naturelle in Paris. In 1837 he returned to Le Havre, where he became a museum curator, a post he occupied for only a short time as he died the following year. The collection of drawings he left as a legacy to the town survived the bombings that devastated the museum in 1944. Lesueur, who gave drawing classes while in the United States, had a recognisable style that found many imitators among his students, but he remains little known by the general public.

△ **BOATS ON THE ATLANTIC COAST, BETWEEN THE RIVER CONNECTICUT AND NEW BEDFORD,** AUGUST/SEPTEMBER 1816 The box beside the dinghy in this ink wash and pencil drawing is, Lesueur notes, for 'putting fish into so that it stays alive and fresh'. The sails on the two-masted boat lower down are carefully rolled up.

The drawing that follows this one in the sketchbook also has a maritime theme: it is a panoramic view of a vast bay peopled by fishermen looking for the species of herring that is found all along the American shoreline. *Musée d'Histoire Naturelle, Le Havre*

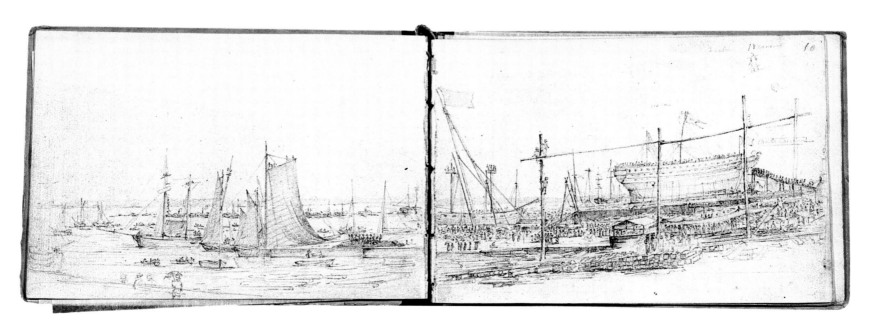

Ville du Caire
1819
Jeune esclave à mon
service
P. C

40c

PASCAL COSTE
An Architect in Egypt

On 6 October 1817 the architect Pascal Coste left Marseille on the corvette *La Bella-Niña*. He was heading for Egypt to oversee the construction of a saltpetre works. In the company of 'a large crew made up of Turks, Greeks, Maltese and Italians', he found the voyage had an exotic flavour. For Coste, then thirty, and a talented artist from a very young age, this departure marked the beginning of an ambitious pictorial project centring on Islamic architecture, ethnology and Egyptian archaeology.

During this visit to the land of the pharaohs, which lasted five years, he developed a real passion for Egyptian civilisation. He returned there in 1823 and stayed another four years. Over the course of these two visits he produced six albums (bound in red shagreen several years later), thus bringing together a collection of fifteen hundred illustrations, including maps, plans, pencil sketches and ink and watercolour drawings. The collection, a precursor of similar projects, was used during architectural restoration work later in the nineteenth century. Above and beyond its usefulness, however, the collection reveals an artist of rare talent.

An eventful itinerary

From the moment he arrived in Alexandria in 1817 Coste set to work on 'several sketches of Egypt's largest town'. 'Pencil in hand,' he wrote, 'I record on paper the impressions I have of every locality I visit.' The methodology was much the same for the series of studies he produced for the building site that occupied him until 1819. The Pasha Muhammad Ali, who came to hold Coste in great esteem, commissioned him to work on the layout of an explosives magazine near the old part of Cairo. The construction of a canal followed, then a pavilion on the edge of the Eastern Harbour of Alexandria, a palace, the enlargement of a garden and the reconstruction of the fort in Abu Qir.

After a visit to Aswan in May 1821, Coste carried out a survey of eight of Cairo's mosques and did a series of drawings showing vertical sections of minarets. Thanks to designing two mosques for the pasha, he was granted permission to enter many other sacred buildings, and seventeen studies of mosques appear in his albums.

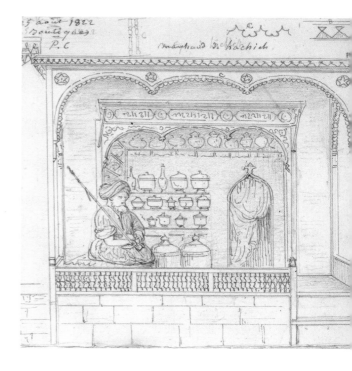

◁ **A YOUNG SLAVE IN MY SERVICE, CAIRO,** 1819
Pascal Coste no doubt got the child to pose for this ink and watercolour drawing. In 1819–20 a plague ravaged the Nile Delta, forcing Coste to put the men constructing his first canal into quarantine. His interpreter, three servants and a young slave, perhaps the one we see in the portrait, came down with the disease and died. *Bibliothèque de l'Alcazar, Marseille*

△ **A HASHISH SELLER'S BOUTIQUE,** 25 AUGUST 1822
On his walks around the streets of Cairo, Pascal Coste often stopped in front of buildings or scenes typical of life in the city in order to capture them on paper. In this pencil and ink drawing the hashish seller appears to be preparing a mixture to put into the pipe that he is holding between his knees. Visitors to Cairo would often take the opportunity of indulging in the pleasures of artificial paradises. *Bibliothèque de l'Alcazar, Marseille*

△ THE HASSAN MOSQUE,
CAIRO, APRIL 1822
Pascal Coste studied this
mosque with a great deal
of care, doing seventy-six
drawings of it. Among
them are various plans of
the building, perspective
and detail drawings, and
studies of decorative
elements. This unfinished
watercolour has a dream-
like quality, with the
mosque seeming to appear
from some kind of cloud.
Coste was perhaps happy
to leave the painting
as it was.
*Bibliothèque de l'Alcazar,
Marseille*

All types of building caught the eye of this indefatigable explorer, who also
enjoyed rendering panoramic views, such as the one he did of the port of
Alexandria in 1819. His sketchbooks include drawings of gates, a citadel
viewed from the top of a minaret, fountains, houses grand and small, even
pigeon lofts. He often labelled the drawings with the name of the construction,
and also noted the materials and colours used.

In October 1822 he returned to France, but yearned to revisit Egypt in order
to complete 'ongoing architectural projects and finish other work begun and
planned'. On his return to Alexandria in October 1823, the pasha promptly
named him chief of works of the Nile Delta. Coste now devoted himself to the
study of palaces, mosques and canals, which offered numerous opportunities
to fill the pages of his sketchbook. In 1827, however, he was the victim of a
scorpion bite and, in a weakened state, returned to France.

'Bad weather forced us to lay up in port… I had time to do a sketch of the harbour.'

Pascal Coste, *Mémoires d'un artiste, 1878*

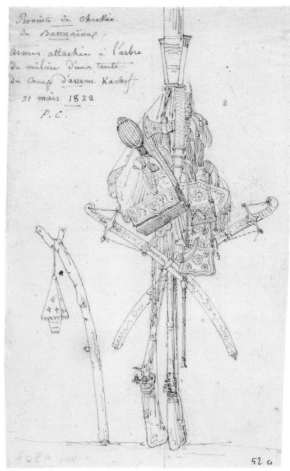

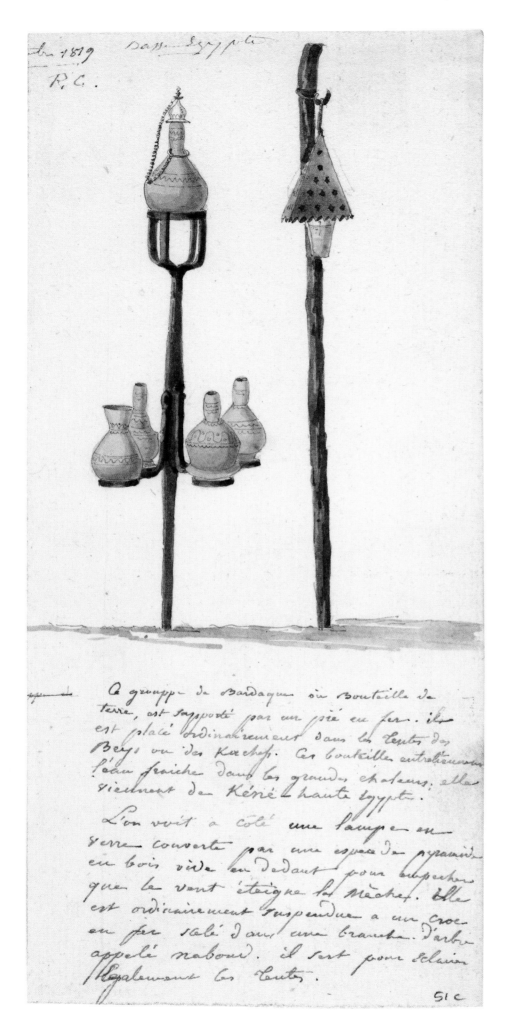

◁ **'BARDAQUES' AND LAMPS
FROM THE NILE DELTA,** 1819
As the handwritten note
on this watercolour tells us,
the word *bardaque* means
'earthenware bottle'.
The iron stand on which
the bardaques are placed
was 'usually put inside the
tents'. These bottles 'keep
water cool during periods
of high temperature'.
We can also see a glass
camping lamp protected
by a wooden pyramidal
lampshade.
*Bibliothèque de l'Alcazar,
Marseille*

△ **ARMS STACKED IN THE MIDDLE OF A
TENT AT THE CAMP OF ASSAM KACHEF,**
31 MARCH 1822
The lamp pictured in the
watercolour illustration left
appears again in this ink
drawing. Coste, who did not
leave out a single detail of
the decorative motifs, had
the eye of an ethnologist.
*Bibliothèque de l'Alcazar,
Marseille*

OVERLEAF: VIEW OF FOUA, 1820
Around this time Pascal
Coste began to wear Arab
dress in order to pass
unobserved by the local
population. He visited
Foua (present-day Fuwna),
a hamlet situated on the
west bank of the Nile, on
two occasions – in October
1819 and in August 1820.
This watercolour showing
the Abu al-Nagah mosque,
based on an ink drawing
Coste completed while in
Foua, provides us with
a few details of daily life.
A child, probably a young
slave, is following a man
and carrying his long pipe,
while a group of people
pray beneath a large tree.
*Bibliothèque de l'Alcazar,
Marseille*

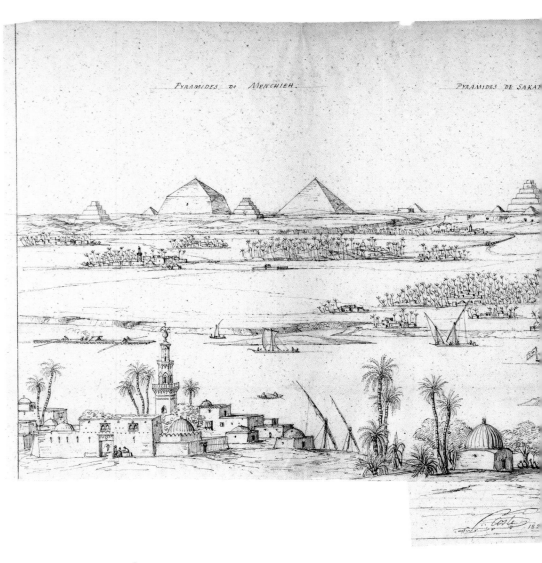

PYRAMIDES DE MENCHIEH.   PYRAMIDES DE SAKA[?]

△▷ **THE WEST BANK OF THE NILE WITH THE MEMPHIS NECROPOLISES AND PYRAMIDS,** 1820
Coste lived near the Memphis site while he was overseeing the construction of a saltpetre works (1818–19). In this splendid panoramic view, probably drawn from a promontory, it is as much the Nile as the pyramids that inspired the artist. Different types of boat are drawn in impeccable detail.
Bibliothèque municipale, Marseille

A memoir of Egypt

Coste was fascinated by ancient Egypt. Ruins, temples, obelisks, hieroglyphs, catacombs, statues, bas-reliefs and mummies were all fodder to his artistic appetite, but he didn't confine himself to antiquity. He made eight rough sketches of traders and prisoners during a visit to a slave market, and these, as well as his sketches of café life, barber shops and steam baths show that he was equally interested in the people and culture of that time. He also paid special attention to local dress, as shown in his drawing of a veiled woman he met in a street in Cairo in 1822, which includes notes about her clothing – 'black silk veil', 'silk striped trousers', 'red belt'.

On his return to France, Coste was feted for his drawings, and he went on to produce a number of publications, notably *Carte de la basse Égypte* (Map of Lower Egypt, 1829), *L'Architecture arabe* (Arab Architecture, 1837) and *Mémoires d'un artiste: notes et souvenirs de voyages, 1817–1877* (Memoirs of an Artist: Travel Notes and Reminiscences, 1878). In 1998 an extensive exhibition paid homage to the vision of this extraordinary traveller's artistic oeuvre.

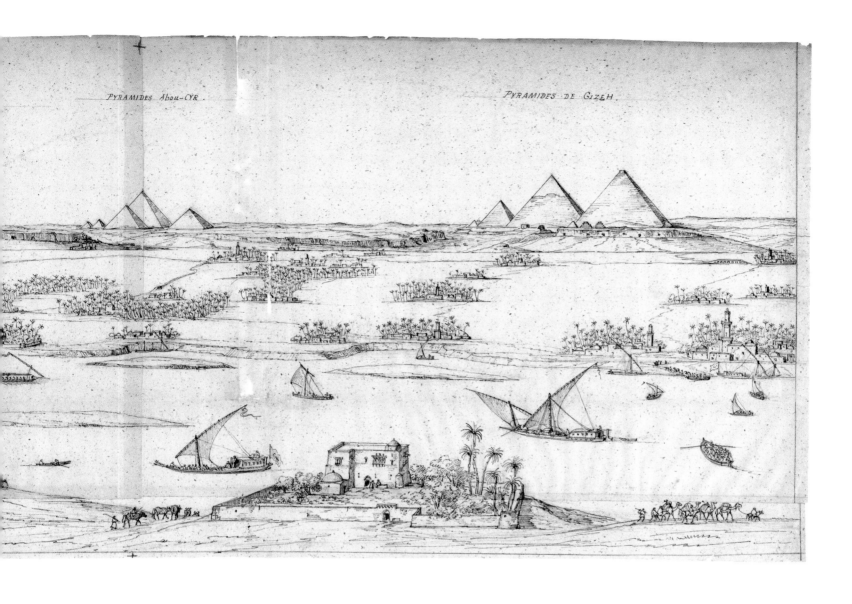

PYRAMIDES Abou-CYR.   PYRAMIDES DE GIZEH.

'The sphinx, cut out of the mass of the rock, is buried in the sand… 31 metres in length, it is of colossal dimensions.' Pascal Coste, *Mémoires d'un artiste*, 1878

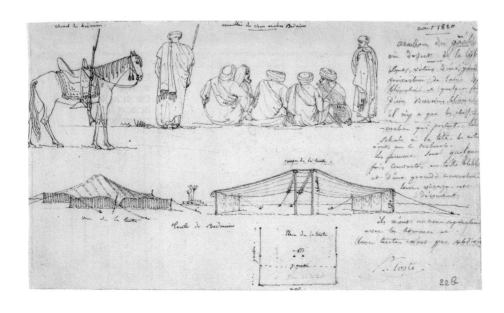

◁ **BEDOUIN TENTS,** AUGUST 1820
The nomadic way of life is just one of the many subjects covered by the artist during his time in Egypt. He devoted a chapter to Bedouin and Arabian camps in his book *L'Architecture arabe* (Arabic Architecture). This pencil and ink drawing is accompanied by a key detailing different aspects of Bedouin dress. *Bibliothèque municipale, Marseille*

WILLIAM TURNER
French Sketchbooks

At the end of August 1826 William Turner left England for France, his sixth visit to that country. After passing through Normandy and Brittany, his love of rivers and waterways took him up the Loire, by boat and stagecoach, and his tour ended in Paris. At this time the fifty-year-old Turner was reaching full artistic maturity. Following in the steps of painters before him, he chose an itinerary that, give or take a stage or two, can be fully traced across the crowded pages of his sketchbooks and in the watercolours that resulted from the tour. The work is rich in poetic imagination and artistic reference. Rather than setting out on unbeaten tracks in search of new discoveries, Turner cast his eye over the towns, ports, monuments and riverside landscapes he saw on his travels with a creative sensitivity that elevates the art of drawing to an almost metaphysical level.

From paper to canvas

Apart from sketchbooks (some of which have been lost), Turner also took various sorts of paper with him. Sheets of white vellum, sometimes folded, as if carried in a pocket, were used for sketches. Blueing paper was for more complete creations, such as a pencil drawing later finished in gouache and ink. Some of the studies on blueing paper (of which there are eighty in all) were completed during the trip itself, but the majority were worked on in the years that followed, often elaborated from drawings in the sketchbooks.

There were also, in fact, some watercolours in the sketchbooks, in some cases without the prerequisite sketch. On the other hand, a series of sketches did not necessarily lead to a painting. The work in the sketchbooks and the studies *in situ* were done, in the first instance, without consideration for critics and the public. Turner then drew on this material for the execution of more complex compositions, whether paintings or engravings. The sketchbook was, then, a place in which he rearranged and creatively reinterpreted his subject matter. Thus, bridges are apt to lose their arches, steeply sloping roofs to flatten and towers to change position.

◁ **BOATS ON THE LOIRE, POSSIBLY NEAR INGRANDES,** 1826–8
On board a steamboat Turner made the sketches that were to result in this painting done later in watercolour, gouache and ink. Studies of the small boats and architectural features in the background can be found in the pages of his sketchbook. The grey sky, heavy with menace, promises a shower like the one that is so cleverly rendered in another of the sketchbook drawings.
The Tate Gallery, London

△ **NANTES: THE FAÇADE OF THE THÉÂTRE GRASLIN, FRONT AND PROFILE; A BARGE IN THE FOREGROUND,** 1826
The Théâtre Graslin interested Turner, who probably lodged in a nearby hotel. Its architect, Mathurin Crucy, constructed numerous buildings in the town at the beginning of the nineteenth century. Other than this study in pencil of the columns of the theatre, the painter also produced some watercolours of the building over the next two years, interpreting and adding to its architectural features as the mood took him.
The Tate Gallery, London

Sketching en route

Whether in Rouen, where he began one of the sketchbooks, in Bayeux, or the towns of Brittany or the Loire valley, the painter's predilection was for architectural masterpieces and views of landscapes and rivers. The architecture of ports, lighthouses, religious monuments, residences and military buildings were all drawn with care, Turner often rendering an overall view rather than a detailed study. For panoramas of towns and buildings, such as the ones he completed on the outskirts of Morlaix (the outstanding success of one of the sketchbooks), Turner took up a position at a distance from his subject.

Even though faces and scenes of local life seem to have been a secondary preoccupation for him, he didn't altogether neglect the human aspect in his work, as can be seen in his drawing of a pardon being handed down at Quimper. Here the costume and trades of the locals were sketched or drawn in colour on blueing paper.

Turner never stayed long in one place, allowing his mode of transport (boat or stagecoach) to determine both the speed of his output and how he viewed the country he was passing through. While crossing Touraine, the castles of Cinq-Mars-la-Pile and Luynes and part of the cathedral at Tours were hastily captured on a single loose sheet. When he did stop for a short time, it was to get a better sense of a town's layout. When travelling past river scenes, he used a technique developed by sea-going artists, reducing the scale of motifs in successive drawings to create the impression of a ship progressively distancing itself from the scene that is pictured. This technique was used at St Florent, and in

△ **SAUMUR: A VIEW FROM THE EAST WITH NOTRE-DAME DES ARDILLIERS IN THE MID-DISTANCE, AND A VIEW FROM THE ILE D'OFFARD,** 1826
The chateau at Saumur holds pride of place in several of the views Turner drew, and many are the artists before him who fell under the charm of the building. He stayed two days in the town, exploring it and its surroundings in the course of his walks. Other than the pencil sketches in the sketchbooks – this one is taken from the volume 'Nantes, Angers and Saumur' – he did seven other colour views.
The Tate Gallery, London

▷ **ORLÉANS: DETAILED STUDY OF THE CATHEDRAL, 1826–8**
This study concentrates on three elements of the cathedral at Orléans: the spire, situated over the crossing of the transept; the southern tower; and, on the right, the western façade. This pencil sketch is taken from a page in the 'Loire, Tours, Orléans and Paris' sketchbook. This small-format (15.2 x 10.1 cm) volume has a mottled cover and forty-four pages of French laid paper, with a bunch-of-grapes watermark.
The Tate Gallery, London

'*Turner was in his element, taking great delight in such beauty and power.*'

Leitch Ritchie, travel writer, on Turner during his French tour, 1833

reverse on the cathedral bell-tower at Angers, which gradually appears out of the distance in one sketch, showing his imminent arrival.

The trip up the Loire inspired over fifty pages in one sketchbook (one hundred and eighty sketches and around twenty colour drawings). Notes on the drawings are sporadic, the words, sometimes in French, thrown down on the page. In Blois, beside a sketch of the Pont Jacques-Gabriel, Turner noted his enthusiasm for the 'splendid effect of the sun rising through the mist'. On arrival in Paris he captured the most famous monuments, such as the Louvre and the Ile de la Cité, in yet another sketchbook, before heading back to London at the end of October. The tour inspired two oil paintings in the three years that followed his return – *The Harbour of Brest: the Quayside, Château and the Banks of the Loire* and *Views of the Loire*. In 1833 he published twenty-one views of the Loire in a collection of engravings, *Wanderings by the Loire*, edited by Leitch Ritchie, a popular travel writer of the time. France, like Italy and Germany, continued to inspire the remarkable works of this gifted English painter.

△ **SAUMUR: ILOT CENSIER FROM THE PONT DES SEPT-VOYES,** 1826–8
In this watercolour on discoloured blueing paper, touched up with gouache and ink, the woman in brightly coloured clothes is turning her head in our direction as if to invite us to cross the bridge. Someone playing a similar role is to be found in the foreground of another of Turner's sketches from this tour, 'Nantes: the northern approach to the Pont Pirmil', which features a medieval bridge. At one time there were six old bridges spanning the river at Saumur.
The Tate Gallery, London

les lumieres qui coulent sur les épaules nues, sur ce retour d'épaule
de femmes mince qui tournent le dos. — Le chant des tons pâles.
et la chair, avec les violets pâles, les bleues, les rouges. les
jaunes d'or, les gris argentins.

(ML)

Longhi maître du 18ème siècle de l'École de Watteau
ou du moins s'il n'a étudié à Paris formé à l'École de
ses gravures et de ses tableaux, ecole de savoir il
et vraiment né de lui même du carnaval de Venise,

EDMOND AND JULES DE GONCOURT
A Journey to Italy

On 8 November 1855 the Goncourt brothers, Edmond and Jules, left Paris to explore Italy. Once in Domodossola, they procured a 'sketchbook of rough paper, bound in white leather and fastened with a thin leather strap such as horse dealers have in Lorraine'. Jules made the first contribution to the volume, which would be filled with notes on the brothers' impressions and reflections during their journey, as well as one hundred and thirty drawings. Sixty of the images are reproductions of paintings by great Italian masters, including Pietro Longhi, Vittore Carpaccio, Andrea del Sarto and Leonardo da Vinci, and twenty-six are watercolour studies by Jules. Some of these were decorated in iron-red pigment or shaded in India ink and pencil. The journal, an initiation into fine art history, was really a sort of workout for its authors' critical and analytical faculties, helping them to develop their own personal aesthetic. The brothers' predilection was not for works of classical antiquity, or for those influenced by them, but they did remain within a framework set out by the art world establishment. To this they brought a sensitive and poetic subjectivity that gives a contemporary touch to the pages of the sketchbook.

Impressions of Italy

'Italy starts here [at Domodossola]. There are houses in love with colour, daubed in tones of sea-green and red. There is false marble and *trompe-l'oeil* colour washed on carved stone.' From here the brothers made for Milan, where they visited a famous collection of medals and coins, the museums and the religious buildings. Then they went to the charterhouse at Pavia, which appears in several of their watercolours. They also did some detailed drawings of bronzes and fragments of decorative borders. After this they visited Brescia and Venice, which marked a new chapter in the sketchbook. Edmond contributed a self-portrait in graphite, showing him huddled up in a gondola, then Jules added descriptions of buildings, and his brother wrote a short piece of fiction. A note above a description of Paolo Veronese's *Apotheosis of Venice* concerns their budget for the trip: '11th December 1855, 1570F left, of which 1500F in the belt.' Leaving Venice in December, they explored Padua, Mantua, Parma, Modena and Bologna, where they were shocked at

◁ **WOMAN IN CARNIVAL COSTUME, JULES GONCOURT, AFTER PIETRO LONGHI,** 1855
While Jules was finishing this watercolour, Edmond wrote, 'Longhi, master of the eighteenth century, part of the Watteau school, or, if he did not study in Paris, certainly schooled in Watteau's engravings and paintings. Curious to know if he really did create himself without French influence, if he really was created out of the Venetian carnival, as the Venetians proudly boast.' *Musée du Louvre, Paris*

△ **THE LEANING TOWERS OF ASINELLI AND GARISENDA, BOLOGNA, JULES GONCOURT,** 31 DECEMBER 1855
Alongside Jules's watercolour Edmond wrote: 'In Bologna titanic metalwork at the exit of boutiques creates arcades in all the streets and makes this sunny town a place of alternate brightness and shade. There are pillars of yellow plaster with the brickwork showing underneath, columns with chipped corners.' *Musée du Louvre, Paris*

△ PUNCHINELLO ANTONIO PETITO,
AN ACTOR FROM THE SAN CARLINO
THEATRE, NAPLES, JULES GONCOURT, 1856
This drawing, made in
black pencil and India ink
enhanced with iron-red
pigment, inspired Jules
to comment on a play:
'The comedy played at San
Carlino with exemplary
naturalness. The scenes
between man and wife were
absolutely right. The troop
of actors carried it off as
if they were in their
own homes.'
Musée du Louvre, Paris

▷ THE PIAZZA DELLE ERBE, VERONA,
JULES GONCOURT, 1855
Edmond's description
of the architecture in this
square is particularly vivid:
'The Maffei Palace is
flooded with light, pagan
hanging statues mounted
on the colonnade.
The column carrying
the lion of Venice casts
a shadow over the luminous
palace, and clothes are hung
out to dry in front of
painted walls. There are
golden stripes where
the sun scars the frescos,
the white statues in
the fountains and
marble illuminated
in blue steam.'
Musée du Louvre, Paris

cafetteria
Giovanni Invernesi

Longhi (le Watteau de Venise) comme

△ **BUSTS OF A WOMAN AND A MAN IN CARNIVAL CLOTHING, JULES GONCOURT, AFTER PIETRO LONGHI,** 1855

It was to the Correr Museum in Venice that the Goncourt brothers hastened in order to admire the work of Longhi. After the museum director showed them some notebooks of studies in his office, Edmond wrote: 'The mask, then, for men and women, is a kind of lace hood that covers the shoulders and allows the pink tones of the skin of the throat to show through from underneath, a strange and striking contrast to the whiteness of the mask...'
Musée du Louvre, Paris

▷ **ITALIANS: WOMEN AT THE POULTRY MARKET AND A HORSEMAN, JULES GONCOURT,** 1855

The Goncourt brothers met the woman shown in this watercolour at Novara. Jules noted: 'A market under very elegant arcature. Yellow and white sheets hung side by side, against which women and green vegetables can be made out. Black is the dominant colour in the women's dress. Charming black hairstyles.' The horseman, drawn from the back, was probably spotted on the road from Novara to Milan.
Musée du Louvre, Paris

the poverty of the inhabitants. Finally, they reached Florence. The handwritten menu of a dinner they had there was inserted among their descriptions of the city. They continued to visit museums, and Edmond copied the originals of masks and faces. In Sienna Jules made brisk notes of what he saw en route: 'Four boxes of matches hanging from door, beggar...' In Rome they took pleasure in describing St Peter's, the Borghese Gardens, the Sistine Chapel and the Jewish ghetto. In Naples, on the last stage of their trip, they did portraits of washerwomen, wine merchants and the inhabitants of the red-light quarter. The Goncourts finished both their Italian tour and the notes in their sketchbook on 6 May 1856 to the swaying of the boat carrying them back to France and the song 'a mother is singing as she cradles her small child on the couch in the on-board lounge'. After the death of his brother in 1870, Edmond reshaped the sketchbook, inscribing the title *Notes sur l'Italie* in gold lettering on the cover. Inside he mounted one hundred and thirty-five pages labelled individually in ink. In 1892 he used the remodelled sketchbook to create a volume published as an introduction to Venice by night. Although *Notes sur l'Italie* was partially published in 1913, it did not appear in unabridged form until 1996, its remarkable workmanship finally available to the general public.

'Carnival masques until two in the morning...music from the showmen in St Mark's square every day.' Jules Goncourt in Venice

Marché à la volaille dans un grand cloître. femmes rangées debout. Venant
à la mains allongées coqs à crêtes rouges. formes noires. qui tiennent de
de fragments de tableaux de Benedette. réunion de têtes voilées de
leurs mouchoirs qui semblent la réunion de tous les maîtres primitifs,
avec leurs traits longs, leurs teints d'ivoire, leur grâce souffreteuse, et
leurs yeux profonds — les peintres, simples copistes — distinction
immense de ces ovales amaigris.

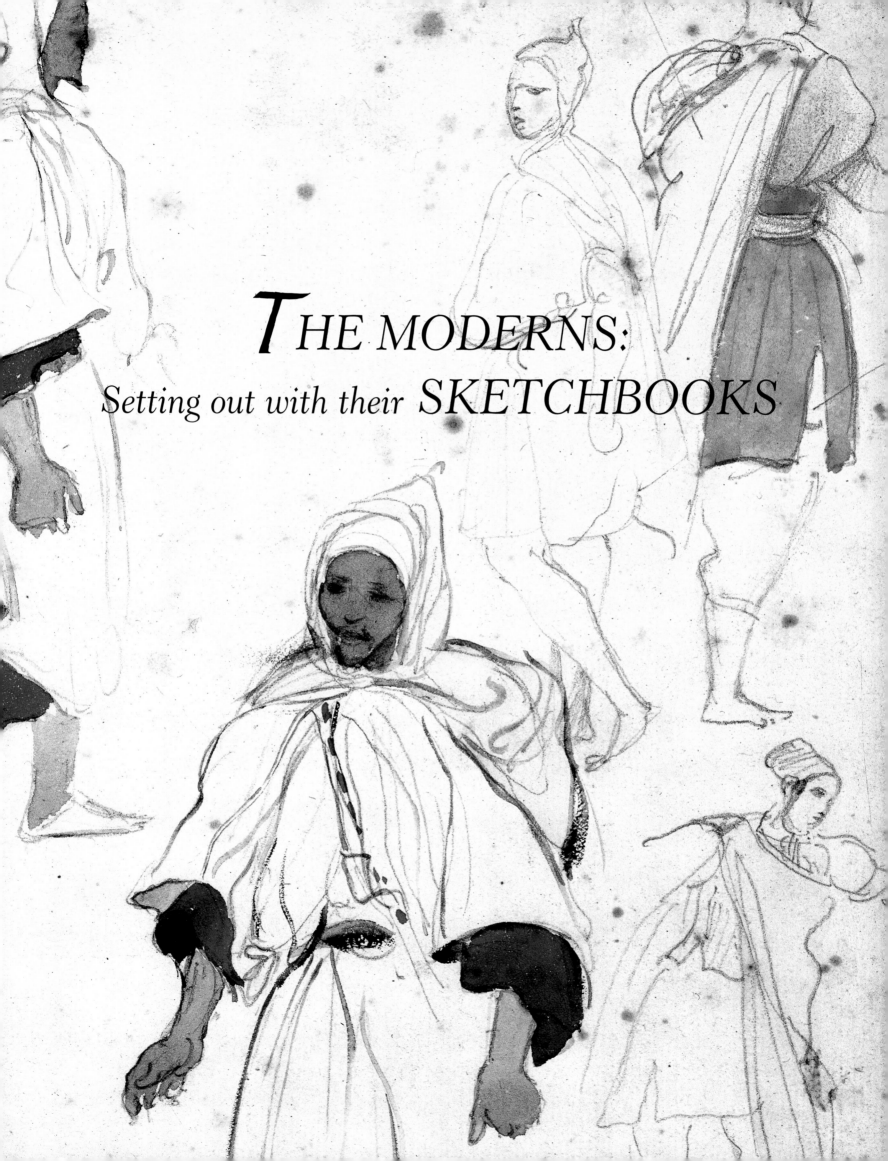

THE MODERNS:
Setting out with their SKETCHBOOKS

EUGÈNE DELACROIX
Moroccan Sketchbooks

In a letter written at the end of 1831 Eugène Delacroix wrote, 'I am in the running for quite a big project. I will probably leave for Morocco next week. Don't laugh too much, it's true.' That this 'big project' would consist largely of filling sketchbooks was no doubt far from his mind. Nevertheless, sketching was the main form his artistic expression took in North Africa. Indeed, he brought back only two small oil paintings from his visit there. Nonetheless, the trip was a moving experience for him, opening up a world of magnificent light and history, and his artistically rich sketchbooks bear the imprint of a truly aesthetic sensibility.

Black thoughts brighten in the Moroccan sun

At three in the morning on 1 January 1832, in the midst of a storm, Delacroix left Paris for the port of Toulon. His mood had been low for months. 'I greatly need distraction from the ennui that is gnawing away at me,' he had written in May 1831. He was to find that distraction in his role as official painter with a delegation to Algeria led by Charles de Mornay. Following the recent colonisation of Algeria by France, King Louis-Philippe was especially keen to keep up good relations with Sultan Moulay Abd al Rahman, the sovereign of Morocco. Delacroix's mission was to illustrate the expedition and the signing of the peace treaty with the sultan, bringing fine art together with diplomacy. Such an expedition was not necessarily a relaxing activity, and could, Delacroix wrote, 'seem quite as bizarre as a voyage to cannibal country'.

On 24 January the delegation landed in Tangiers, and here, on the first pages of an oblong sketchbook, Delacroix drew a panoramic view of the town in pastel. The members of the delegation had to wait a month before receiving authorisation to visit the sultan's court at Meknes, and the timing was not exactly auspicious. The period of Ramadan was starting, and the sultan's brother had just died unexpectedly.

Delacroix made the most of the month's delay, 'allowing life to wash over [him]' and sketching. His sketchbooks are rich in small drawings of street life. The gates to the town and fights on horseback were, he tells us, dashed down on paper 'with a lot of difficulty because of Muslim prejudice against images'.

△ **MOROCCAN JEWESS, SEATED,** 1832
Delacroix was fascinated by the grace of the Jewish women he mixed with and admired in Morocco. He observed these women at the home of the interpreter attached to the French consulate, and during a Jewish wedding that he was invited to.
Musée du Louvre, Paris

◁ **THE JEWISH BRIDE OF TANGIERS,** 1832
With a wonderful finish, this watercolour, traced in graphite on beige paper, was done from notes and sketches made during

the course of Delacroix's journey. One of the sketches shows the bride-to-be wearing a veil over her face, but that does not appear in this version. It was on brief stopovers in Algeria on the way home to France that the painter got several Moorish beauties to pose for him.
Musée du Louvre, Paris

PRECEDING PAGES: **STUDIES OF NORTH AFRICANS IN MEKNES,** 15 MARCH 1832
This drawing was done in graphite and enhanced in watercolour.
Musée du Louvre, Paris

la rue en montant les hommes
blancs sur les murs.

l'homme de
Smith

He got out his sketchbook 'on every street corner' and marvelled at the encounters he had, notably with the Jewish women in the family of the interpreter attached to the French consulate. He referred to them as 'pearls of Eden'. On 21 February he was invited to a Jewish wedding, an occasion he recorded in his sketchbook, making much of light and shade. He also did the sketch on which he later based his wonderful watercolour and graphite picture The Jewish Bride of Tangiers.

Inspiration from past and present

Although continuing to use graphite and brown ink, Delacroix increasingly relied on watercolours as the journey progressed, applying them to the paper in splashes, a technique he used in the sketchbooks of his journey to England. Morocco fascinated and inspired him, and he claimed that 'ready-made opportunities for paintings that would bring fortune and glory to twenty generations of painters' were to be discovered each step of the way. There he found living proof of how he imagined life to have been in antiquity, which led to his idealised accounts of everyday scenes. Inquisitive by nature, and gathering subject matter as he went along, he was interested in every last detail – landscapes and vegetation (he carefully noted the colours of different plants), living conditions and handcrafts, Moorish decor and local dress (he devoted a whole sketchbook of drawings to this). Showing an open-mindedness remarkable for that time, he wrote, 'I have never been able to distinguish clearly the differences between races.' He was, however, sceptical as to how well his drawings would be received elsewhere. 'Far from the country in which they were discovered, they will be like trees pulled out of the ground and transported away from their natural habitat.'

At times Delacroix was forced to work extremely rapidly, and this explains the isolated and fragmentary nature of some of the drawings, and the way in which certain motifs are spread chaotically across the pages. Handwritten comments were often added in order to clarify the drawings. From the beginning of February written comment takes a larger place in the pages of his sketchbooks. Arabic terms, such as *burnous*, *haïk* and *djellaba*, accompany pictures of these traditional garments. The combination of images and text would prove useful in creating future works.

Imprisoned in luxury

On 2 March the delegation left Tangiers for Meknes. Delacroix illustrated the thirteen-day journey in a notebook filled with ink drawings and notes. In the evenings, under the canvas of his tent, he continued work done during the day. He used notes scribbled on sketches while on the move to add a broad palette of colours, sometimes allowing the whiteness of the paper to show

△ DETAIL OF TWO STUDIES OF AN *OUD*, 1832
Eugène Delacroix took great care of his Moroccan sketchbooks. They were to be a great source of creativity right up until his death. It was only on exceptional occasions that he gave away a few drawings and watercolours to those close to him.
Musée du Louvre, Paris

◁ STREETS, WALLS AND BOUTIQUES, WITH PEOPLE, SUCH AS THE MAN FROM SMYRNA, PICTURED STANDING AND SITTING, 1832
Delacroix took seven albums and unused sketchbooks of various formats with him on his trip. Only four of them have survived intact. The three others have disappeared or been found dismembered. This illustration comes from the 'North Africa and Spain' album.
Musée du Louvre, Paris

'I am taken up with work for some of the time, but for the rest I just let life wash over me.' Letter dated 29 February 1832

Eugène Delacroix was still young when he did this oil on canvas self-portrait, showing himself as chivalrous, romantic and sombre. It was probably thanks to his journey to Morocco that he discovered a new palette of colours and became interested in another kind of light.
Musée Eugène-Delacroix, Paris

The pages of Eugène Delacroix's sketchbooks are remarkable for their mixture of detailed drawings and more general views. At the bottom of this image, taken from the Moroccan album, we can see some arcades and two North Africans, one of whom is on a horse. Attitudes and situations were captured in an instant, but the artist took care to write down passing impressions, making hurried comments, as if frightened that something might escape him.
Musée du Louvre, Paris

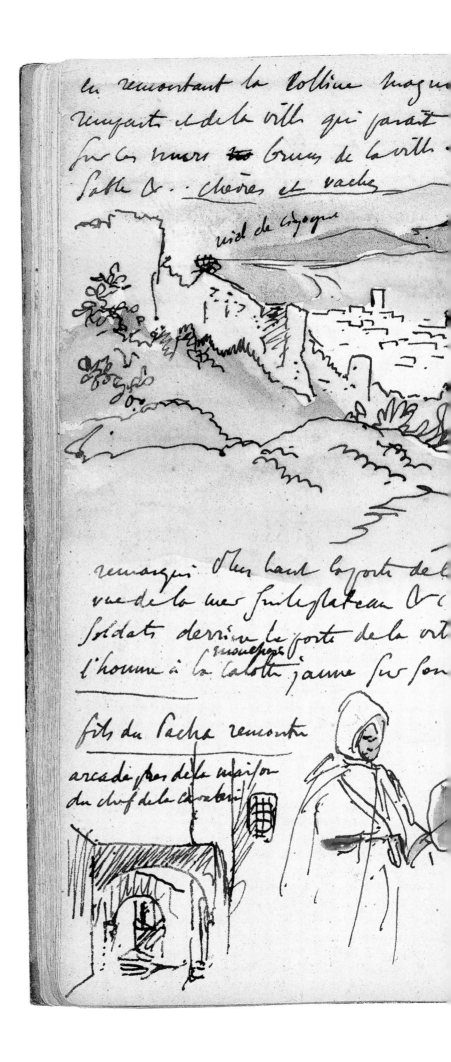

through. Using what might be described as a 'storyboard' technique, like that used in films, he drew a series of pictures that tracked the delegation's arrival in Meknes. A big party was given in their honour, but they had to wait one more week before being welcomed by the sultan himself. The delegates were not granted permission to circulate freely in the town, so they had to stay in their residence unless under escort. The local population was not accustomed to foreigners, and, Delacroix wrote, 'Christian clothing and features are disliked by these people, so much so that we are always escorted by soldiers.' Condemned to remain in his 'prison of marble and faience', Delacroix was not even allowed to sketch the roofs of the town from the terraces of the residence, roofs being reserved as places of privacy and relaxation for women.

Finally, on 22 March, an audience with the sultan was granted. In a little under fifteen days the delegation could retrace its steps to Tangiers. The journey by mule on traditional saddles was a trying one for the Europeans, especially as they now had several ostriches in tow, a gift from the sultan.

Inspiration on the way home

After arriving in Tangiers, Delacroix took several days' leave to visit Andalusia in southern Spain. The sights and people of Cadiz and Seville inspired numerous watercolours in his sketchbooks. On 10 June the delegation set sail for Toulon, stopping at Oran and Algiers en route. It was at Algiers

▽ **CAMP ON THE PLAIN WITH MOUNTAINS IN THE DISTANCE,** 1832
The painter continued working in the evening in one of the camp tents, perhaps the one we can see in this watercolour and graphite drawing. The colour indications he noted in his sketchbooks during the day served as aids in the later elaboration of the drawings.
Musée du Louvre, Paris

'I want to work out how to record the impressions that pass through my mind at every instant.' A reflection on the journey in Morocco

that the painter got the inspiration for his future painting, *Women of Algiers in Their Apartment.* In Morocco men and women could "be persuaded for a few coins into a room in the French consulate" and it was there that Delacroix had discovered Jewish women. In Algeria Moorish women posed for him so that he could do their individual portraits.

The delegation landed back in Toulon on 5 July. As a cholera epidemic was then sweeping across France, Delacroix used the time that had to be spent in quarantine to arrange the work he had done. His sketchbooks were rich in memories and subtle studies of a country that marked him indelibly, that he appreciated and that he had learnt to understand. Many years later he confided to one of his acquaintances, 'The physiognomy of the country will remain in my visual imagination for ever.'

△ NORTH AFRICANS IN TURBANS, HORSEMEN RIDING ON TO THE PLAIN AND THE TOWN WALLS IN THE BACKGROUND, 1832
For Delacroix the double page of a sketchbook was a composition space in which handwritten text, rough sketches, detailed drawings and completed watercolours could coexist in harmony. On this page watercolours are touched up in graphite, and the contrasting images and different scales bring to mind a cinematic montage. We are immediately submerged in the atmosphere of the places pictured. Delacroix really brought the stages of the journey alive.
Musée du Louvre, Paris

VICTOR HUGO
Amorous Escapades to the West of France

Victor Hugo's interest in his country's architectural heritage is evident from the forty-three pencil drawings collected in a pocket sketchbook in 1834. He did them during two successive trips he made to the west of France that summer with his mistress, Juliette Drouet. He also used the sketchbook to keep track of their spending and to note down other thoughts along the way. On the first of the trips, which lasted for five days from 22 to 26 July, the two lovers left Paris behind them and followed the banks of the Seine, turning off at Louviers. They returned to the capital along the river Oise. The second trip, from 9 to 31 August, saw them making a big loop, taking in Brest and heading southwards to Vannes before working their way up the Loire and returning to Paris from the northeast. Showing him to be an artist as well as a writer, Hugo's sketchbook is also a marvellous record of a poetic, passionate and adulterous love affair.

The first trip

From 22 to 26 July 1834, Drouet and Hugo stole a few days of happiness together. The glazed cardboard cover of the sketchbook is decorated with two geometric shapes, one of which, a hexagon, contains the phonetic code g.m.é.a.v.c. (j'ai aimé avec – I loved with). Underneath is a drawing of a woman sitting in profile, perhaps a portrait of Juliette Drouet. On the inside front cover is an itinerary and a list of towns, possibly drawn up in Brest on the second trip. A second series of letters, perhaps slightly harder to decode, appears here: l.n.a.e.t.o.p.y.l.i.r.s.t.l.i.a.v.q.l.i.a.m.e.l.i.a.p.t.l.i.a.v.c.l.i.e.d.c.d.

On reaching Triel, Hugo made various sketches and notes, but these have almost completely disappeared, apart from the gothic initials stamped bottom right in violet ink that appear throughout the sketchbook. A sketch of a burette stall in the grain market is followed by a view of the bridge that spans the Seine 'drawn from the deck of the galliot while departing'. There is then a statement of what money they have spent up till that point, and a drawing of the bridge at Mantes. Stuck above the bridge is a lover's souvenir – a 'piece of wallpaper from the bedroom at Louviers (Hôtel du Mouton), night of 23rd to 24th July'. The following day Hugo drew the knocker of the chapel door at Evreux cathe-

△ **BELL-TOWER AT ST FLORENT,**
AUGUST 1834
On board a 'dirty, smelly and uncomfortable' steamboat Victor Hugo sketched the bell-tower at St Florent, but the landscape was not to his liking. He wrote, 'Near Oudon, Ancenis and St Florent the famous banks of the Loire are flat and featureless with just a few rocks here and there.'
Maison Victor-Hugo, Paris

◁ **CEMETERY AT YÈVRE-LE-CHÂTEL,**
AUGUST 1834
Victor Hugo did this drawing on a folio with a foldable panel, noting the time and place in pencil: '21st August. 4 o'clock'. In a letter to his wife dated the following day, he mentioned the walk around Yèvre: 'I had a lovely day in Pithiviers and its surroundings yesterday. In Yèvre-le-Châtel there is a convent and a castle, in ruins but still standing. Magnificent! I am sketching everything I see, so you'll be able to judge for yourself. I walked the two leagues there in my shoes full of holes.'
Maison Victor-Hugo, Paris

dral and noted down several inscriptions. When they arrived in Pacy, he wrote a little verse about the view he saw while having lunch. The sketchbook is, then, somewhere for all sorts of jottings. He signs off on the last page by copying out a sonnet found in the church of Notre-Dame, unaware that its author is the medieval poet François de Malherbe.

Arriving at Juliette Drouet's apartment on 2 August, Hugo discovered the following note: 'Saturday, midday, 2 August 1834. Adieu for ever – adieu for always. It was you who said so. So adieu then and may you be as happy and admired as I am sad and fallen. Adieu – the word contains my entire life, my joy, my happiness. Adieu. Juliette.' The poet knew that his mistress would have taken refuge at her sister's home in St Renan, so he decided to go there. On 5 August he boarded the mail-boat. At Rennes, at five in the morning and 'in a hurry', he sketched the upper part of a gate and noted underneath that 'An idiotic letter has brought me here, to the Jardin des Plantes!' Three days later he and Juliette were reunited.

The second trip

The day after their reunion the couple arrived in Brest for the second of their summer getaways. Victor was interested in the naval vessels and the prison. 'Full of curiosity and all sorts of other emotions,' he wrote to his wife, and noted that there was 'a convict named Caqueray, who has become prison executioner at a salary of four francs a month. Has his own quarters!' Between Carnac and Auray he sketched the neolithic remains. On one page we find the following reflection on love: 'In order to make it solid and malleable, love must

be mixed with friendship, just as an alloy is mixed with gold.' Throughout the sketchbook the drawings are accompanied by notes on the cost of the trip. At a chateau they visited in Nantes he did two studies of the stonework. Underneath the first can be read the words 'Religions die but not the clergy'. From the top of the cathedral, he drew a rough outline of 'the shape' of the building. In St Florent he decided to sketch the bell-tower of the church. Later the chateau at Chaumont, the detail of a balustrade and the museum at Orléans all caught his attention.

Near Paris he continued to collect drawings of romantic ruins – the Temple at Etampes and the entrance to the tower at Gisors (he made a note of the graffiti on the inside of the tower). On the inside back cover of the sketchbook is a list of dates and names of towns that do not correspond to this trip. A note of money spent reminds us of the sad reality of the couple's situation. In St Germain they went to Moulin-lès-Metz to find somewhere for Juliette to stay, and Hugo returned to Paris on 1 September. From this time until the 1870s all his travelling was done in Juliette's company. In Brest they had vowed never again to part, and on this trip around Brittany their lives 'became joined for ever'.

△ **FROM THE COURTYARD OF THE HÔTEL DE FRANCE IN TOURS,** 17 AUGUST 1834
'Tours is a beautiful town. Old houses, mostly in stone, two beautiful Roman towers, a superb Roman church that serves as a stable for the Hôtel de l'Europe, a gorgeous renaissance fountain, handsome remains of fortifications and, of course, the cathedral, which one can only admire, both for its architecture and its stained glass.' This drawing is taken from the sketchbook relating to the second trip. The book is made up of twenty-two drawings spread over seventy-six pages, some of them on blue-grey vellum. The bundles that Hugo inserted under the cardboard cover of the sketchbook during the first trip consist of sixty-two pages of twenty-one drawings. They are on a mixture of white vellum with gold edging and a white laid paper.
Maison Victor-Hugo, Paris

'I visited Tours today and am here the object of all sorts of persecutions in the name of admiration. I found Lucrèce Borgia *being performed in the midst of a fair, and my arrival at the school met with quite some emotion.'* Letter to his wife, 16 August 1834

JOHAN BARTHOLD JONGKIND
Sketchbooks of a Rambler

Although he did not make journeys to far-off
countries, the Dutch naturalist and writer Johan
Barthold Jongkind went through an enormous
number of sketchbooks. He always carried one so
that he could draw landscapes and everyday scenes
as he came across them. It was Andreas Schelfhout,
his teacher at the Academy of Art in The Hague,
who started him on the sketchbook habit, getting
him to make studies of the surrounding countryside.
Jongkind's sketches, in watercolour, crayon, graphite
and ink wash, came out of direct and intuitive
encounters with nature and urban life. These forms
and compositions, impressions of colour and light,
were sources of inspiration for future works. When
Jongkind moved to Paris to study under the artist
Eugène Isabey, he tramped around the city, and
returned regularly to Belgium and the Netherlands,
sketching all the while. In 1880 his sketchbooks were
stuffed with views of the south of France, including
Marseille, La Ciotat, Sète and Narbonne. Very rare
were the sketchbooks that were not dismantled.
The painter Eugène Boudin, writing in *L'Art* about
Jongkind's sketches, said, 'The more you look at his
watercolours, the more you wonder how they are
done! Indeed, they are done with nothing, and yet
the fluidity and density of the sky and clouds are
translated on to the page with unimaginable precision!'

△ ▷ **BOAT WITH TWO MASTS,**
NYON, 1 OCTOBER 1875
Nyon, a village on the edge
of Lake Geneva, looks out
to Mont Blanc. Jongkind
was always inspired by
the diversity of boats to be
found in the harbours and
canals, at the quays and on
the banks and beaches.
Musée du Louvre, Paris

△▷ **SPANISH DANCERS AT A CAFÉ**
CONCERT ON BOULEVARD
ST MICHEL, NOVEMBER 1878
The writers Emile Zola and
Joris Karl Huysmans were
moved by the modernity of
the eye Jongkind cast over

Paris, by his authenticity and
realism. Scenes like the one
shown in this watercolour,
sketched from the interior
of the café, are quite rare
in Jongkind's oeuvre.
Musée du Louvre, Paris

▷ **BOATS AT SEA AND IN THE NAVAL**
SHIPYARD AT HONFLEUR, 1865
Jongkind stayed in Honfleur
for some time with his
mistress, Joséphine Fesser. St
Siméon farm, where he did a
splendid drawing of apple
trees hanging out over the sea,
was a well-known rendezvous
for artists and painters.
Musée du Louvre, Paris

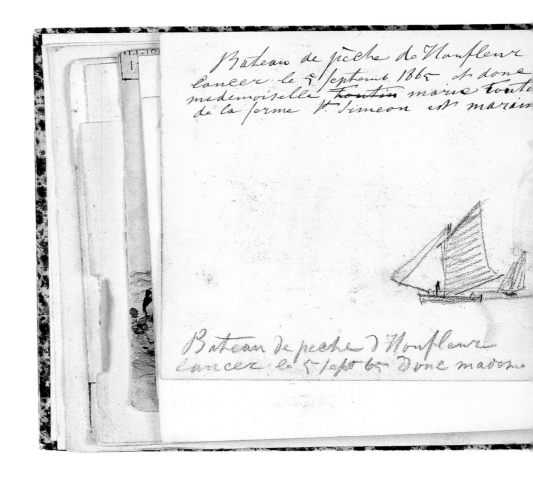

PAUL GAUGUIN
Noa-Noa: The Tahitian Journal

This journal, written entirely on Ingres drawing paper, was folded in quarto and sewn and bound by the author. Always ready to turn his hand to new decorative material, he made use of wood, animal skins, mother-of-pearl, wax and gold in the production of the volume. Flexibly bound and with a flat spine, it opens easily beneath a satiny, tobacco-brown, jointless cover... The text, in pale brown ink in complete harmony with the discoloured paper, is interspersed here and there with watercolours, most of which were done on separate paper, then cut to size and stuck in. There are traces of everything that went to make up the daily life of the artist at this time, wrestling as he was with an existence in the pitiless tropics – magnificent light, great effort and abandon.' This is how the poet-adventurer Victor Segalen described Paul Gauguin's journal *Noa-Noa*, which he was lucky enough to hold in his hands shortly after his arrival in Tahiti. Envoy on board a vessel in the fleet from Papeete, capital of French Polynesia, Segalen did not get the chance to meet Gauguin, who died of poverty and exhaustion on 8 May 1903 at the age of fifty-seven, shortly before Segalen's arrival. From his words, however, it is clear that Segalen greatly admired the work of a man who first explored the Tahitian archipelago more than twenty years earlier.

An awakening of the senses

The author Octave Mirbeau saluted Gauguin's departure in March 1891 with the following comment: 'I hear that Monsieur Paul Gauguin is leaving for Tahiti. His intention is to live there for several years, alone, to build his hut there, to rework with new eyes those things that haunt him. This is the case of a man, fleeing from civilisation, voluntarily trying to lose himself in silence and forgetting.' But the man who wished to escape from 'conventional and deceitful' European civilisation was quickly disappointed. The Westernisation of Tahitian society was already well advanced. After several months, he left Papeete for an isolated village, learnt what he could of the Maori language and was initiated into Maori culture by his companion, a young Tahitian woman named Tehura. 'It is through her that I am finally penetrating mysteries that up till now have remained opaque to me.'

◁ **FARÉ UNDER THE COCONUT TREES,**
NOA-NOA: THE TAHITIAN JOURNAL,
1891–1903
This small format watercolour from the *Noa-Noa* journal shows the traditional Tahitian house in which Gauguin lived for a while. There was friction between the artist and the colonial representatives on the island because he was a fierce critic of their materialistic Western values.
Musée du Louvre, Paris

△ **ILLUSTRATED MANUSCRIPT,** 1891–2
Gauguin's illustrated manuscript *Ancien Culte Mahorie* (Ancient Maori Cult) was the precursor to the *Noa-Noa* journals. He painted geometric shapes and heads in profile on its cover, which was made of Tahitian fibres. These shapes are reminiscent of the bas-reliefs of Central American civilisations.
Musée du Louvre, Paris

△ **POLYNESIAN IDOL,** *NOA-NOA:*
THE TAHITIAN JOURNAL, 1891–1903
Gauguin used a wide variety of graphic techniques in his journals, sometimes combining them to produce different effects. This image of a Polynesian idol is an engraving, which has been touched up slightly in watercolour on the lighter areas in order to soften the contrasts inherent in engravings.
Musée du Louvre, Paris

△▷ **POLYNESIAN GODDESSES,** *NOA-NOA:*
THE TAHITIAN JOURNAL, 1891–1903
This photograph is part of a page on which Gauguin has drawn two Polynesian goddesses facing each other in profile. The composition, in ink and watercolour, is more or less symmetrical.
Musée du Louvre, Paris

▷ **TAHITIAN WOMEN,** *NOA-NOA:*
THE TAHITIAN JOURNAL, 1891–1903
The modernity of Gauguin's artistic practices is clearly shown in these sketches. In defiance of established genres and rules, he experimented with different techniques on the same page. Multiple representations of Tahitian women underline the artist's erotic fascination with them.
Musée du Louvre, Paris

He started working again, and little by little accumulated a collection of 'studies only, or rather documents'. In July 1892 he wrote to his wife, 'I now have a feeling for the sun and its smell and I am painting the Tahitians in a very enigmatic way. They are Maori…and have nothing in common with the orientals of Batignolles.' He threw himself into all kinds of graphic experimentation, applying sheets of paper soaked in ink to sheets of metal or moulded terracotta, creating monotypes that he would then use in his sketchbooks. In his suitcases there was a veritable museum of images he could draw on: photographs of bas-reliefs from the Indonesian temple at Borobudur, reproductions of ancient Egyptian borders, sculpture from the Parthenon – all found their way into the sketchbooks. Gauguin's first voyage was an opportunity to lay the foundation for one of the masterpieces of the sketchbook genre. On his return to France in 1893, he edited a collection of notes that went towards the elaboration of the *Noa-Noa* journal. These notes, although incomplete at this time, were designed to help the public in its approach to the work presented at the Durand-Ruel Gallery in 1893. A sketchbook on Tahiti, he confided to his wife, would 'be very useful in helping to give an understanding of my painting'. It is also the key to the inner journey he was making, which mirrored the outer ground-breaking voyage to Tahiti two years previously.

Fragrant collection
Although the work he put on show brought him no profit, Gauguin persevered with his Tahitian scenes, also doing engravings and sculpture. He formed an association with the symbolist writer Charles Morice to rewrite the collection

'I have set myself to work now that I have a feeling for the sun and its smell. I am painting the Tahitians in a very enigmatic way.' Paul Gauguin

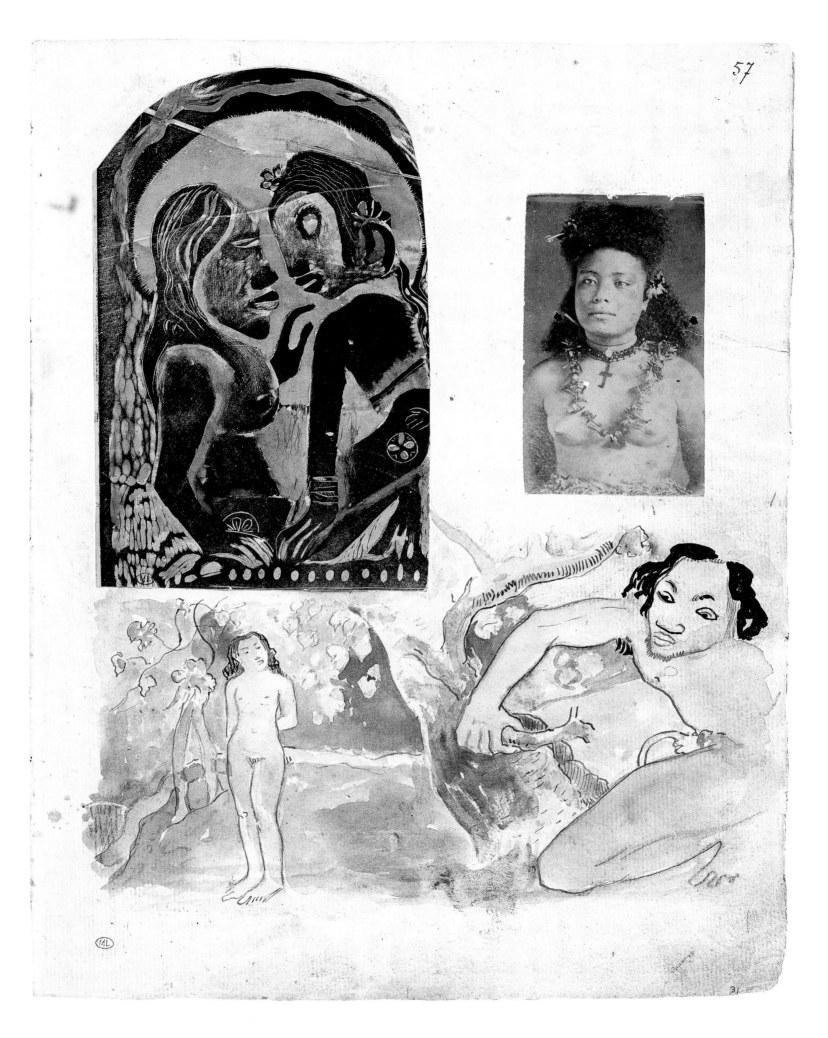

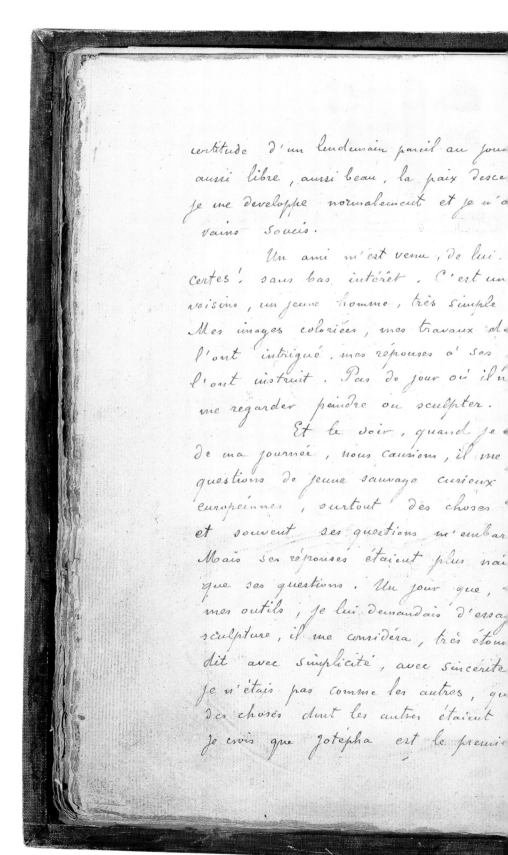

▷ STUDIES OF TAHITIANS, *NOA-NOA: THE TAHITIAN JOURNAL,* 1891–1903

Here we see handwritten text arranged around sketches of a man and woman having sex and a nude curled-up woman. The style is a continuation of the work Gauguin did for his illustrated manuscript *Ancien Culte Mahorie*, which was in fact inspired by Jacques-Antoine Moerenhout's book *Travels to the Islands of the Pacific Ocean*, 1837. In the drafting of his texts, Gauguin borrowed from many other sources without necessarily revealing what they were. The freedom he allowed himself in his working methods influenced generations of artists who followed him. *Musée du Louvre, Paris*

△ STUDIES OF TAHITIAN WOMEN, *NOA-NOA: THE TAHITIAN JOURNAL,* 1891–1903

Gauguin left for the South Seas alone, but was presented with a young woman as a gift during an excursion. He became attached to her and they made a home together in Mataïea. 'So began a truly happy existence,' he wrote. Thanks to the young woman, he was able to fully explore the local culture and religion, and, not least, the sensuality of Tahitian women, which he often depicted in his journal. *Musée du Louvre, Paris*

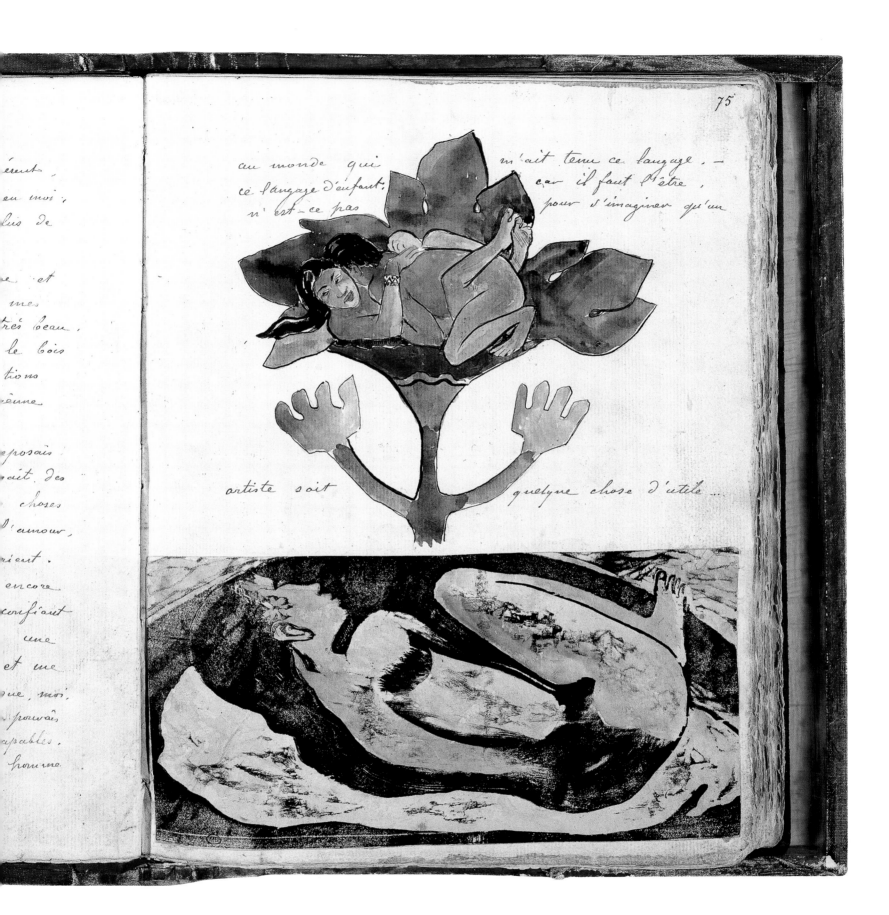

au monde qui   m'ait tenu ce langage, —
ce langage d'enfant.   car il faut l'être,
n'est-ce pas   pour s'imaginer qu'un

artiste soit   quelque chose d'utile ...

Most of the subjects
recorded by Gauguin in his
journal can also be found in
his oil paintings and wood
sculptures.
Musée du Louvre, Paris

▽ TATTOO, *NOA-NOA:*
THE TAHITIAN JOURNAL, 1891–1903
Gauguin often borrowed
from traditional Tahitian art.
Here we see a watercolour
reproduction of a tattoo.
Musée du Louvre, Paris

▷ MAN CARRIED BY AN ANGEL,
NOA-NOA: THE TAHITIAN
JOURNAL, 1891–1903
This 'heavenly' image was
an opportunity for the artist
to pen some lines of poetry.
'Long ago, big cats roared
out in the desert/ Long ago,
an angry sea raised itself in
lofty peaks/ But now, the sea
laps up against the rocks/
Now, the big cats lie asleep.'
Musée du Louvre, Paris

of notes, which now found its title – *Noa-Noa*. (In Maori the word *noa* means 'perfume' or 'odour', and the repetition of the word accentuates the meaning, thus conveying the notion of 'heavily perfumed' or 'strong odour'.) There were two versions of this journal. The first was added to and edited as Morice saw fit. The second was taken back to Tahiti by Gauguin in 1895 and enlarged in scope over the decade that followed. In 1901 the version that Morice had remodelled, and to which he had usurped the rights, was published by La Plume. Printed in facsimile, it contained four hundred and one black and white drawings, six watercolours, cursory notes, silhouettes, studies of faces (from the front or in profile), gestures and animals. It had few landscape drawings and no still lifes. Gauguin, back in Tahiti since summer 1895, voiced his discontent: 'This totally untimely publication of *Noa-Noa* is of no interest to me right now.'

Fortunately, Gauguin had a duplicate of this incomplete version, and continued to work on it, filling it with pictures and comment. It was this second version that was left in a box after the death of the artist and discovered by Victor Segalen. Part of a watercolour was plastered down on to the flat surface of the leather cover. The title and subtitle were written in calligraphy, and Gauguin had made a seal for his initials, to which he had added his signature. Numbered by hand, the book's two hundred and four pages are rich in images designed to blend and correspond with each other in continual experimentation. Gauguin inserted photographs and watercolours into the text, as well as ink washes, studies, wood engravings from different periods (some in watercolour) and decorated pieces from his satirical journal *Sourire* (Smile). He included various monotypes, a reproduction of one of his works by *Le Figaro Illustré*, in which the colours are too strong, prints of sculptured motifs and sketched prints. These incongruous images were arranged according to the artist's moods, the rhythm of his inspiration in the sketchbook owing a great deal to his paintings and sculpture. In the first part of the book, for example, he alternated engravings and watercolours on facing pages, in contrast to the rest of the journal, which was much more influenced by mosaic and collage. He continued working on it until 1901.

'This volume…was sewn and bound by the author. Always ready to turn his hand to new decorative materials, he makes use of wood, animal skins, mother-of-pearl, wax and gold.' Victor Segalen

The variety of genres and techniques, the absence of chronology and the abundance of styles and contrasts produce an unsettling effect. Gauguin's spontaneous creativity made for a real revolution in visual perception. The possibilities offered by new image techniques such as photography and cinema, also influences the project, and it opened the way into an area of fine art in which heterogeneous collage could be freely expressed. Gauguin's loyal friend Georges-Daniel de Monfreid worked for many years to get the Louvre to preserve *Noa-Noa*, finally succeeding in 1929, when the journal found a home in the graphic art section.

bientôt assis dans la brillante demeure d'Odin, nous boirons dans les crânes de mes ennemis. Un homme brave ne redoute point la mort, je ne prononcerai point de paroles d'effroi en entrant dans la salle d'Odin.

Nous nous sommes battus à coups d'épée ... ah! si mes fils savaient les tourments que j'endure, s'ils savaient que des vipères empoisonnées me rongent le sein, qu'ils souhaiteraient avec ardeur de livrer de cruels combats, car la mère que je leur ai donnée leur a laissé un cœur vaillant.

Nous nous sommes battus à coups d'épée ... mais il est temps de finir; Odin m'envoie les déesses pour me conduire dans son palais, je vais aux premières places boire la bière avec les dieux; ma vie s'est écoulée; je mourrai en riant.

———

Jadis au désert les grands fauves ont hurlé
Jadis la mer irritée monta aux cimes élevées
Et maintenant la mer apaisée lèche les rochers
Et maintenant les fauves dégénérés dorment au Désert.

PABLO PICASSO
A Journey to Holland

In the summer of 1905, taking up the invitation of a writer friend named Tom Schilperoort, Pablo Picasso spent six weeks in Schoorl and Schoorldam in the north of Holland. He described his visits to Alkmaar and Hoorn in the sketchbooks he took on the trip, and did a series of landscapes and portraits of the locals. Unaccustomed to the ways of northern Europeans, the Spaniard was impressed with the Dutch way of life, and the observations he recorded in the pages of his sketchbook could almost have been made by a reporter or even an ethnologist. The very objective drawings he did there stand out from the rest of his work. He seems to have put his creative personality aside in order simply to document what he saw.

In the room he rented, which also served as his studio, he completed three large gouache paintings based on sketches he had made of the North Holland Canal. These are *Les Trois Hollandaises* (Three Dutchwomen), *Hollandaise à la coiffe* (Dutchwoman in a Cap – the subject's voluptuous curves also inspired his sculptural work), and *Nu au bonnet* (Nude in a Bonnet). For the nude, he got the postman's daughter to pose for him, causing a scandal in the small village. During this time Picasso was reorientating himself artistically.

He moved from his blue period to his pink period, in which a less negative vision of humanity asserted itself and brought him success.

▷ **DUTCHWOMAN BESIDE A CANAL, SKETCHBOOK NO. 4,** SUMMER 1905
This woman, wearing a traditional hat, is reminiscent of one of the figures in the painting *Les Trois Hollandaises* (The Three Dutchwomen), where the young women are grouped at the edge of a canal as if in conversation. In that painting the roof of a house, pointed like a pyramid, is reflected in the water and replaces the windmill we can see here in the background.
Musée Picasso, Paris

▽ **PROFILE OF A YOUNG DUTCHWOMAN, SKETCHBOOK NO. 4,** SUMMER 1905
Using graphite, printer's ink and gouache, Picasso played with black and white in this image in order to bring out the roundness of the young woman's face. Its shape is accentuated because her hair completely hidden under a hat.
Musée Picasso, Paris

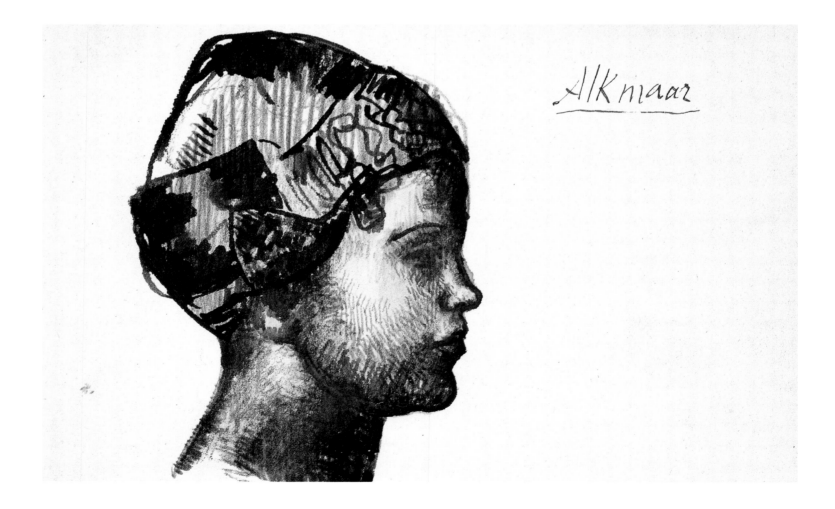

Alkmaar

Edward Hopper

EDWARD HOPPER
An American in Paris

During the early part of his career as a painter, Edward Hopper made three visits to France, and these had a profound impact on his work. When he saw Paris for the first time, in October 1906, he had just completed six years of study at the New York School of Art, where his teacher, Robert Henri, advised students to focus on the great French avant-garde painters of the late nineteenth century. During this first visit, Hopper stayed in Paris until the following August, and assumed the role of discriminating observer, accumulating pencil drawings, charcoal sketches and watercolour portraits in the notebooks that he carried with him wherever he went. Many of these, acutely observed, were later used as studies for oil paintings.

In search of la ville lumière

When he moved into his lodgings at 48 rue de Lille, Hopper, a loner by nature, did not register at any school of art, nor did he meet anyone from the art world. He did, however, visit museums and galleries, and walked the streets of the capital, journal in hand, enchanted by the harmony and gentle way of life. He was captivated by the architectural heritage, the colourful personalities in the streets and the pleasant atmosphere both inside and outside the cafés. The spontaneity of the Parisians and their way of life very quickly imposed itself in his sketches and drawings. In a letter to his mother several weeks after his arrival, Hopper mentioned the constant activity in the streets, the 'pleasure-loving crowd that doesn't care what it does or where it goes so long as it has a good time'.

Having arrived in the city during the winter, he captured its cold mood in his first sketches and paintings. Although the weather prevented him from spending much time drawing outside, he did sketch a series of street scenes in crayon, graphite and charcoal. These included a woman carrying a basket and a loaf of bread, and a man walking along with a businesslike air. In another series, executed in crayon and watercolour, various Parisian stereotypes are pictured in full-length portraits in which we sense the complicity between the painter and his models. In all these images Hopper captures the familiar and

25

◁ AT THE CAFÉ, 1906–7
From his earliest days in Paris, Hopper was in the habit of sitting outside Parisian cafés to study faces. This ink and watercolour drawing of an overweight bourgeois savouring his usual glass of absinthe is from a series of caricature-like portraits. *Whitney Museum of American Art, New York*

△ A PAGE FROM THE SKETCHBOOK OF HOPPER'S SECOND STAY IN PARIS, 1938/42
Solitary women, either lost in their thoughts or, as here, absorbed in a book, are a recurrent theme in Hopper's work. A feeling of sadness and separation emanates from the woman. Isolated among the buildings of the modern city, she is cut off by her own silence. *Whitney Museum of American Art, New York*

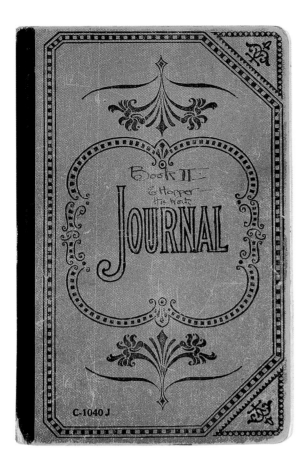

sometimes amusing aspects of his subjects, as in the sketch of a Parisian woman walking down the street and casting a sidelong glance without slowing her pace, or the seemingly relaxed Parisian labourer. Meanwhile, a tramp is pictured with bottle in hand and eyes full of animosity.

During good weather, Hopper set up his easel beside the river and spent hours observing life on the café terrace. He was struck with the fresh colours and light of springtime, and began to feel the influence of the French impressionists. Like them, he drew and painted outside, capturing the smallest changes in light and making notes in his sketchbook on subject matter for future paintings. This new interest in light can be seen in several paintings he completed in 1907, including *Après-midi de juin (June afternoon)* and *Remorqueur du boulevard Saint-Michel (Tugboat on the boulevard Saint-Michel)*.

Paris, an imprint on Hopper's soul

On 21 August 1907 Hopper returned to New York. However, images from his French sojourn continued to find their way on to his canvases. On 18 March 1909 he was back in Paris, and this time stayed for more than four months. The following year his painting *Le Louvre (The Louvre)* was shown at a New York exhibition of independent artists. In May he revisited Paris for a few weeks before heading to Spain. In February 1915 *Soir bleu (Blue evening)*, a depiction of café life (and the largest of his paintings), was put on show in New York.

Although Hopper did not make any more visits to Paris, his creative output was heavily influenced by French culture throughout the next decade. He later confessed that returning from Europe had been very painful for him and that it took him years to get over it.

'Paris is a very graceful and beautiful city, almost too formal and sweet to the taste after the raw disorder of New York.' Hopper to his mother, 30 October 1906

Notre Dame de Paris
23½ × 28
Gift to wife, 10 November 1957

Ile Saint Louis
23½ × 28¾   1909?

Le Pavillon de Flore
1909
Very like Le Sourire et la Seine
but deeper colour — +
no water under boats & left corner
Gift to wife, 10 November 1957

DIARIES *of* SCIENTISTS *and* ADVENTURERS

Eugenia jambos L.

Myrtus Jambos Nov. Gen.
Eugenia Jambos L.
Poma rosa
n.n. n. 130.

Cumana

Eugenia jambos L.
ANNOTATIONS ON AMERICAN MYRTACEAE
Rogers McVaugh, University of Michigan 1965

ALEXANDER VON HUMBOLDT
Journey to South America

"Without rest, I am preparing for a great destination", Humboldt wrote as early as 1793 of his travel plans. Being acquainted with both Johann Georg Forster and his father, Johann Reinhold Forster, who had both sailed once around the world together with James Cook (see pages 37–43), and having been left a substantial inheritance by his mother after her death in 1796, Humboldt was at last, in 1799, able to indulge his yearning for foreign parts. On 5 June 1799, Alexander von Humboldt, then aged 29 years, left the Spanish mainland together with his travel companion Aimé Bonpland, both furnished with the warmest letters of recommendation for the governors of the Spanish colonies. Just under two months later they landed the corvette Pizarro in the Venezuelan port of Cumaná, after a brief stay on the Canary Islands. On board they had what at the time would be considered an ultramodern collection of around 50 different measuring instruments, including sextants, theodolites, inclinometers etc. Humboldt installed himself in the town of Cumaná for a longer stay. He set up his astronomical instruments on the flat roof of the house he rented and conducted his measurements from here. Among others, he was able to observe a Leonid meteorite shower in the night from 11 to 12 October, and to observe an eclipse of the sun. On 18 November Humboldt continued thier journey to Caracas, where they stayed for two and a half months and from where they set off on their legendary Orinoco journey. It was to lead the two travellers over 2700 kilometres into the uncharted basins of the Orinoco and Rio Negro Rivers. Humboldt discovered that the Casiquiare connected the Orinoco with the Rio Negro, thus linking it with the Amazon River.

Their search for the source of the Amazon River led them farther to Lima (Peru). It was the rich diversity of species they encountered in the dense rainforests which kept the men in a never-ending frenzy of enthusiasm.

On 24 November 1800 the friends sailed from Cumanà to Cuba where they arrived on 19 December. From here they continued towards Columbia on 9 March the following year, landing there on 30 March 1801.

Continuing along the Magdalena River they crossed the hostile world of the Andes mountains and, in January 1802, reached Quito, in present-day

◁ **EUGENIA JAMBOS**, C. 1799
Humboldt and Bonpland collected this branch of myrrh in Cumana, Venezuela, and classified it in their herbal. A small tropical tree, it bears white, intensely scented flowers and delicious fruits.
Patrick Lafitte/laboratoire de phanérogamie du Muséum national d'Histoire naturelle, Paris

△ **ALEXANDER VON HUMBOLDT AT THE ORINOCO**, 1806
Immediately after his return from South America, Humboldt charged the

painter Friedrich Georg Weitsch with the creation of several tableaux that were to swerve as an aide-memoir of his journey. This portrait in oil is part of the series of paintings, which gives us an accurate view of the life of the travellers.
akg-images, Berlin

PRECEDING PAGES: TOUCAN,
MARCH 1828
Hercule Florence did this watercolour and pencil drawing at the port of Rio Prêto.
Academy of Science, St Petersburg

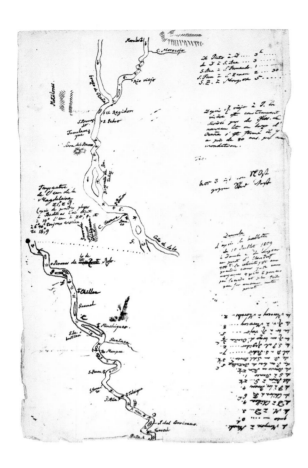

Ecuador. There they ascended – the first Europeans to do so – the twin peaks of the Pichincha Volcano (4,690 and 4,794 metres high). The two adventurers also attempted to scale the Chimborazo (6,310 metres high) which brought them a world record and science a first description of altitude sickness.

In Callao (Peru), on 9 November 1802, Humboldt observed the Transit of Mercury. He also discovered the outstanding properties of guano as a fertiliser, which marked the beginning of its export to Europe. From Peru the travellers sailed across a stormy sea to Mexico. Here, during a one-year stay, they studied and analysed the Aztec calendar. Before the Pizarro's return to Bordeaux on 3 August 1804, Humboldt and his shipmates visited the American President Thomas Jefferson in the USA.

During their entire journey of exploration through Central and South America, Humboldt and Bonpland covered some 9,650 kilometres – partly on foot, partly by horse or in a canoe. What drove the men, in the face of immense physical effort and danger, was their quest for knowledge – it was the only motivation for the expedition as they did not exploit it commercially. Humboldt's private diary notes, his scientific discoveries and documentations from the journey, however, were to revolutionise the world of science.

Adventure story and scientific gem – the travel journals

With few exceptions, the journals Humboldt painstakingly kept of his journey to South America in 1799–1804 survive as nine volumes of original manuscripts, kept in the manuscript department of the Staatsbibliothek Preußischer Kulturbesitz in Berlin. Humboldt used notebooks of different colours, in the octave, quarto and folio formats. Only towards the end of his life, Humboldt had the numerous notebooks bound together as nine pigskin volumes in order to ensure their completeness. The extensive exploitation of his recordings showed up a number of gaps and leaps in their chronology even in those days. Humboldt's travel journals are considered among the most magnificent examples of the 'genre' not only in terms of their sheer quantity but also with respect to their literary and artistic diversity. As is typical of the mindset of a collector, Humboldt noted down everything, without knowing for certain what might prove useful later for his publications. Not only did he describe what he experienced and observed every day, he also combined his instantaneous personal notes with notes from the scientific writings of others and with his own conclusions in the various notebooks. Thus the notebooks contain at the same time adventurous travel reports as well as the most accurate of measuring tables, sketches of plants, animals, landscape descriptions and hand-drawn maps. The passages of the travel journals that he noted down during the course of his journeys were created under varying conditions and at different points in time. The measuring tables, for example, were

'There is something very moving about the moment when you first leave Europe.'

from the *Reisetagebücher*

Pleurothallis elegans (HBK) Lindley

3.

Dendrobium elegans.

n.n. 2122.

Il y a dans l'Orinoco
un poisson Mapurito qui
pue horriblement!

Pristigaster Cuv. II
mais sans p. ventrale
Pl. 10. n 3 mon petit
un Serra Salme
Cuv. II p 165

Palometa

des Abdominaux. Corps. large ovale, comprimé. Bouche petite. dents acutissimi in utraque
maxilla. yeux très grands. Ecailles très petites couleur de nacre de perle. Une grande pinne
dorsale, 2 petites pectorales. et 2 ventrales plus petites encore. Queue fourchue. Les ecailles
forment au bas ventre des épines comme une scie, cette scie ... v.s. qui à ⅔ de corps
où commence une enorme pinne anale. Orinoco! Guarico. ... Rio Apure.
Long 7 po. largeur 5 p.

Long 1 p à 7 po. haut 4 po. base 1 po.

Pri Pimelodes scheilan
nomé clarias au cabinet

Barbanche

cod. loco. des Abdominaux sans ecailles peau de cuir. azul obscur. la tête
aplatie horizontale. Des setae au lieu de dents. 6 barbes, filaments en
forme de rubans de 1 li de large et 6 po de long. Corps allongé trian-
gulaire, comprimé par en haut, plat à la base. Une pinne dorsale et
derrière elle une crête de cuir jusqu'à la queue 3 li de haut. 2 pinnes pectorales, 2 ventrales plus grandes et une petite anale. Queue fourchue. 4 n
Loricaria. 2 babes dans la machoire super. et 4 dans la machoire intérieure.

Le Bagre de la Lagu-
ne de Valence est
le Silurus Bagre.

Caparro

cod loco. à grandes ecailles. argenté verdâtre. bouche sans dents. toutes les
pinnes, l'anale très large, queue fourchue. la pinne dorsale a par devant deux épines, tournées vers la tête! Long 11 po. large 3½ po. Corps
oblonge, comprimé. un Cyprinus?

voisin des Scombers

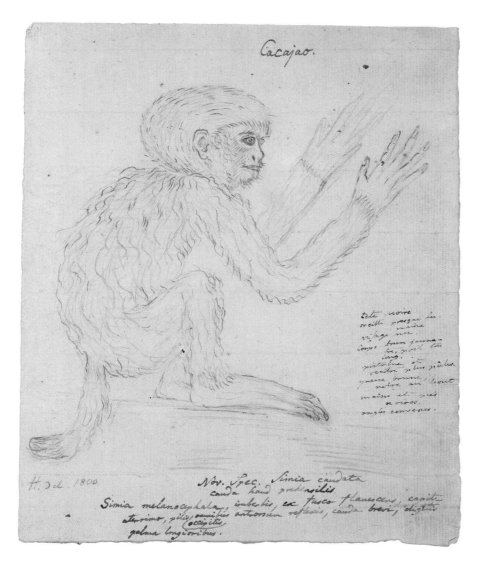

Cacajao.

H. del. 1800

Nov. Spec., Simia caudata
cauda haud prehensilis
Simia melanocephala, imberbis, ex fusco flavescens, capite
aterrimo, pilis omnibus antrorsum reflexis, cauda brevi, digitis
(occipitis)
palma longioribus.

created there and then, while their analysis followed at a later stage of the journey
– when a longer stay afforded the opportunity. Often, Humboldt marked the pages
with marginalia referring to his own previously published works or other publications he had read. Most of the cross-references within the notes, however, are to
passages within the notebooks. After his return from the journey on 4 December
1805, in order to have a better overview, Humboldt created a multi-page, alpha-
betical index for the travel journals. It lists the individual diary notebooks, which
were bound in varying colours, that Humboldt referred to in his marginalia.

Immediately after his return from South America, Humboldt publicised the
diaries he had written in Venezuela in the *Relation historique* (Historical Relation).
They form part of a giant 34-volume publishing project, which he began in
Paris. The final volume of this incomparable travel opus appeared in 1839,
when he was aged 70. However, the larger part of his documents was not made
public until 200 years later, just like his travel journals which were published
in a new edition in Germany only in recent years.

'*We will lose our minds if the miracles do not stop soon.*'

from a letter to his brother Wilhelm

Discoverer and humanist

In 1784, Wilhelm von Humboldt wrote about his brother Alexander, two years his junior, that he was the only one capable of "combining the study of physical nature [...] with that of moral nature, and thus of bringing a true harmony to the universe [...]". In this sense, the travel journals fuse scientific findings with clearly stated moral views into a complete unit. It was Humboldt's humanist view of mankind to honour the dignity of the individual, to respect the cultural autonomy of the indigenous population he visited and to campaign for the abolition of any manifest abuses and injustices that he encountered on the way. "It was impossible for me to ride on the back of human beings…", Humboldt commented in his notes on the common practice at the time of having Indians carry one across the Andes mountains on their backs. He did however not so much criticise specific instances, which served only as an example, but rather he openly formulated a general criticism of society, and in response Humboldt encountered rejection or at the very least open scepticism from his politically influential contemporaries. Humboldt's mindset was strongly marked by the Enlightenment and echoes of the French Revolution, yet the assertion that he was the father of the independence movement in the Spanish colonies seems a gross exaggeration, especially since the entirety of his notes was not made available to the public until long after the onset of the unrest.

'How inhospitable the world has been made by European cruelty.' from the *Reisetagebücher*

L. Nach Torquemada der Trachtwar, ... Mexico ... illsten Giganten, ... den Tultecas (artifices) ... Campeche, Guatemala ... Chichimecas in ... Montezuma II.

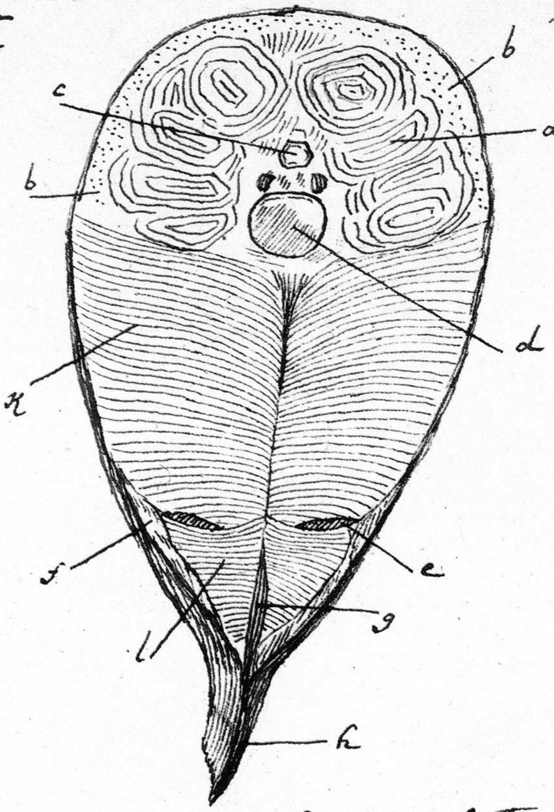

Corps du Gymnotus electricus.

a. huit paquets de muscles dorsaux composé de couches concentriques.
b. graisse.
c. épine dorsale
d. vessie
e. deux petits muscles
f. quatre muscles longitudinalement placés.
g. muscle impair inséré dans la pinne ... trale
h. pinne
i. k. les deux organes électriques, chacun divisé en deux lobes égaux.

voyez p. 197.

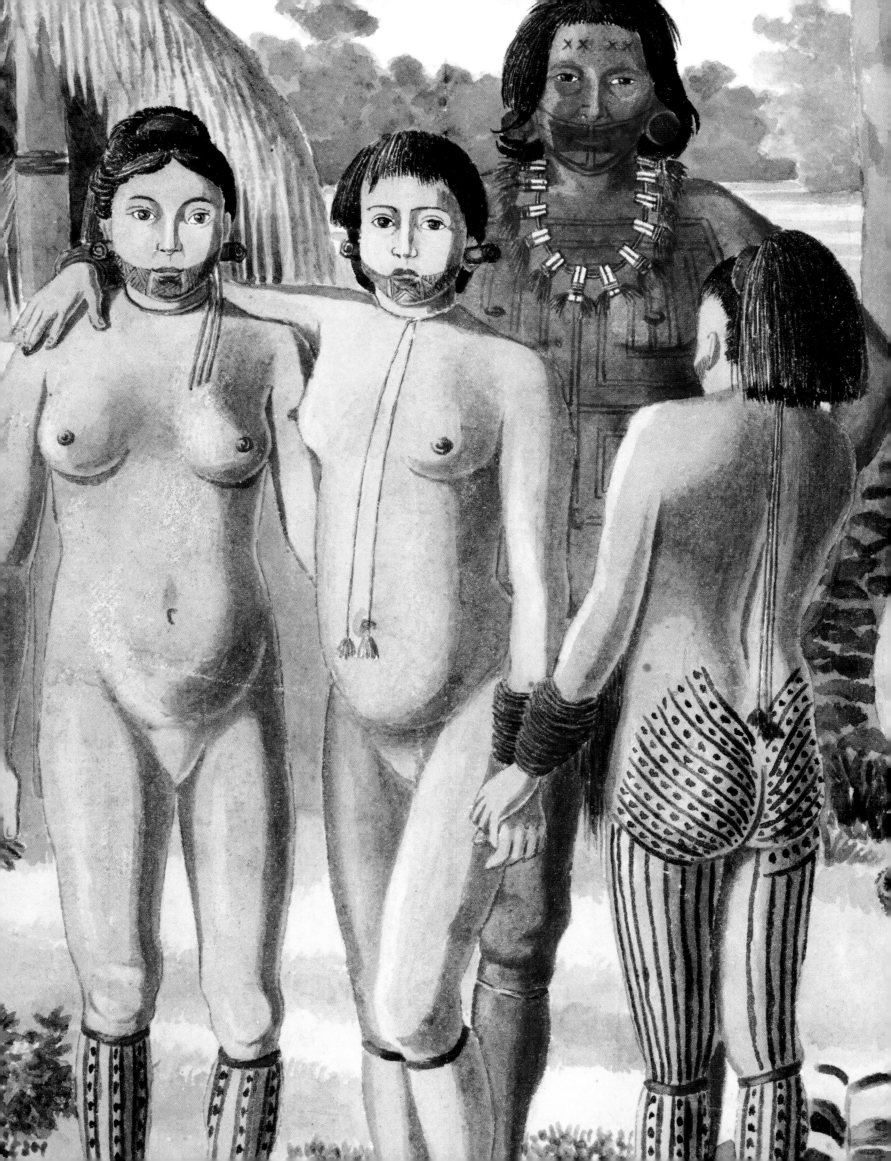

HERCULE FLORENCE
Journey into the Brazilian Interior

On 22 June 1826 an extraordinary procession made its way along the main street of Porto Feliz in southern Brazil and down towards the landing stages on the river Tiete. The Russian consul-general, Heinrich Baron von Langsdorff, was at the head of the procession, marching to the accompaniment of salvos of musket fire. On reaching the banks of the river, silence fell, the men took off their hats and began to pray, and a priest gave them his benediction. A long exploration of the Brazilian jungle was getting under way. Its objective was to explore the flora and fauna, and enrich collections in the Museum of St Petersburg. Six days later, Hercule Florence, the expedition's illustrator, wrote in his journal, 'This is where the wilderness begins, and already there is talk of savages, leopards and puma.'

Malaria and madness

Florence, a young, self-taught artist, began his journal, *Journey into the Brazilian Interior*, at the beginning of September 1825, having set off in advance of his future companions in order to prepare for his part in the coming journey. While waiting in Porto Feliz, he drew landscapes and seascapes as a prologue to the journal, and also did studies of the sky and portraits of the Indians. By June 1826, all the expedition members had arrived and exploration of the jungle could begin, but it was far from straightforward. On the way, they had to navigate hazardous rivers and endure terrible mosquito attacks, and after six months of gruelling difficulty Langsdorff was displaying signs of madness. The mission, forced to a halt, divided into two groups. One party, led by the botanist Ludwig Riedel, continued in a westerly direction, while the other group, which included Florence, made towards Santarém under the command of the astronomer Nester Gavrilovich Rubtsov. During the testing journey through marshy jungle, Langsdorff was carried in a hammock, the victim of hallucinations from which he would suffer to the end of his life in 1852. Meanwhile, Florence, like other members of the group, was 'suffering from sezões [fever], which I have felt coming on for several days'. At Santarém it was decided to go back to Rio, passing through Belém do Pará on the way, where they linked up with Riedel again. The abortive expedition did not achieve its aim of travelling up the Orinoco, nor did it reach Caracas or the eastern provinces of Brazil.

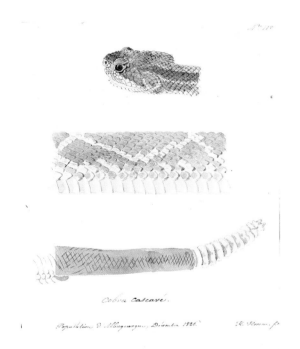

Cobra Cascavel.

◁ **APIACAS INDIANS,** APRIL 1828
Hercule Florence first saw these Indians on 11 April 1828. He wrote: 'In the morning, not long after we started, we caught sight of a canoe in which there were around twenty Indians of this nation.' For this watercolour, he was inspired by the Indians' nude bodies decorated in paint, and by the beauty of their elaborate headdresses, which included 'feathers tastefully arranged in splendid colours'. The three nubile young girls in the foreground were also sketched in pencil and watercolour on another page of the journal. *Academy of Science, St Petersburg*

△ **COBRA, CASCAVEL,** DECEMBER 1826
Florence has delicately rendered the detail of this snake in pencil and watercolour. Despite the artist's identifying label, the creature's tail, skin and head suggest that it is a rattlesnake rather than a cobra. *Academy of Science, St Petersburg*

◁ **CABEXI INDIAN,** SUMMER 1827

As on many other occasions, Florence did this portrait in watercolour, but used pencil for the profile. It was probably drawn on a trip to Vila de Guimarães from Cuiabá, where the mission was based for a year.

The Indians there lived in 'great poverty, and possess virtually nothing. Some are occupied in the search for gold at a mine four leagues away. The gold there is poor but better that that in Cuiabá.' The Indian here is wearing Western dress and lives, it would seem, in a 'civilised' milieu.
Academy of Science, St Petersburg

△ **APIACAS INDIANS IN THEIR HUT,** APRIL 1828

Of the habitat pictured in this watercolour, Florence wrote, 'They have been fishing here for several days and have constructed a large, open cabin covered in straw, where they all live together. There are, however, more than eighty of them, men, women and children, and the hammocks they use for sleeping are suspended one on top of another, making it virtually impossible to walk around the cabin.'
Academy of Science, St Petersburg

▽ **PACÙ PINTADO (MOTTLED PACÙ),** AUGUST 1826

Hercule Florence did this ink and watercolour drawing while sailing on the Rio Pardo and crossing the rapids. Several previously drawn pencil marks can be discerned on the contours of this fish. On 12 August 1826 Florence commented in his journal: 'Pacus and bream are abundant.
The first of these fish, which we had not seen up till now, is a foot in length and almost round; it is so fatty that it is referred to as the "river pig". Its oily skin is not a delicacy, but we do not turn up our noses at it.'
Academy of Science, St Petersburg

△ **BLUE ARARA PARROT**
ON THE SAN LORENZO
RIVER, JANUARY 1827
Parrots, like the one shown
here in ink and watercolour,
were legion in the jungle,
and some specimens were
caught and stuffed during
the course of the expedition.
Florence did numerous
ornithological woodcuts,
including some of nocturnal
birds in full flight. It was
perhaps the incessant noise
of bird cries in the virgin
forest that made him
speculate about the
'language' of animals,
a subject he explored
further in 1831 in a work
entitled *Recherches sur la
voix des animaux*
(Investigations into the
Voices of Animals). Here,
as elsewhere, Florence
attempted in his own way
to get to grips with the
mysteries of creation.
*Academy of Science,
St Petersburg*

△▷ **JACÚ-GUACÙ ON THE SAN
LORENZO RIVER,** JANUARY 1827
This bird was quite
common in the country
Hercule Florence crossed
between Coxim and
Cuiabá, where he arrived
on 30 January 1827. The

expedition had been visiting
the Guató Indians, and its
members were suffering
from mosquito bites: 'It is
a plague sufficient to cause
the depopulation of a whole
country… We are at times
covered from head to foot
in blankets or coats…
They obsess us, get into our
nostrils, eyes and ears, and
when we eat they enter our
mouths with our food.'
*Academy of Science,
St Petersburg*

▷ **PRICKLY QUINCE GARDENIA,**
DIAMENTINO DE MATTO GROSSO,
JANUARY 1828
After the expedition divided
into two groups, Florence
and his companions arrived
in Diamentino on
13 December 1827 for
a three-month halt.
Here Florence made some
botanical drawings, which
are relatively rare in his
journal. In this one, in
watercolour and pencil, we
can make out the abandoned
sketch of a young girl in the
background, looking at us
with large, vacant eyes,
as if she were hiding
behind the vegetation
of the virgin forest.
*Academy of Science,
St Petersburg*

Humanist and poet

Florence's journal is the work of both a talented artist and a humanist, remarkable for its numerous sketches of Indians in tribal groups. The portraits of indigenous people, most often done 'after nature', as he wrote above the drawing of a Camapuã Indian on 12 October 1826, are accompanied by rich descriptions of local life, languages, handicrafts, food, dress, family organisation, the rapport between the sexes and physiological particularities. His account is full of sensitivity and respect, even if he was at times disturbed by what he saw, such as some of the Indians' sexual practices. As a humanist, he also spoke out against slavery, which, he wrote, had 'a hundred faces, all hideous'. Apart from ethnographic drawings and illustrations of different animal species, he did some landscapes, which are more artistic than accurate and informative. A wonderful study of the sky, *Soleil levant ou firmament de tempête* (Rising Sun or Stormy Firmament), which he inserted into his journal in 1832, led him to meditate on colour techniques and nuances of tone. He also did some pioneering studies of light within a series of drawings that traces the expedition's itinerary, attempting to capture a moonlit Amazonian night. Florence strategically positioned a hole in the paper so that the picture could be viewed in the dark by the light of a candle held on the other side, creating a magical scene that prefigured the invention of photography. The inventive curiosity that Florence displayed in this unique journal is evidence of a real passion for imaging techniques. Using these techniques, he was able to create a hugely original document of an expedition that covered enormous distances through a fascinating region. He went on to develop 'polygraphy', a system for the simultaneous reproduction of colours. Although interested in science, he maintained a belief until the end of his life that a power greater than mankind existed as a 'principle of goodness'. He died in Campinas, Brazil, in 1879.

'I have nothing more pressing to do than ride out with my pencil and sketchbook

to take in the views of this picturesque place.'

Marmelo de espinhos
Gardenia
Gr. naturelle

Diamantino de Matto Grosso, 16 Janvier 1828.

Hercule Florence f.

FRANÇOIS-HIPPOLYTE LALAISSE
A Survey of Brittany

Commissioned to do two series of lithographs in the summers of 1843 and 1844 by Charpentier, a publisher from Nantes, François-Hippolyte Lalaisse, a teacher at l'École Polytechnique, left Paris to explore Brittany. His first survey of the region, known in Roman times as Armorica, covers the southern part, from Nantes to St Thégonnec, while the second, carried out the following year, explores the north and east of the region, from Châteaubriant to Plougastel.

Although Lalaisse collected his work in a portfolio rather than a book, his graphic techniques and style of drawings are typical of those used in travel journals. His careful, brightly coloured sketches of Breton life concentrate on regional dress.

An artist in Armorica

Lalaisse was a tireless traveller, unworried that rough terrain often compelled him to journey by foot to see areas that could not be reached by cart, mailboat or stagecoach. Although outsiders who could not speak Breton did not always receive a warm welcome, Lalaisse had numerous friendly encounters with the locals. No doubt he was helped by the fact that he was travelling with a guide and interpreter. In Quimper, as we can see in one of his sketches, he mixed with the crowd outside a courthouse. Elsewhere he met a peasant and spent a day with him, watching him go about his daily activities. One night, a farming family offered him hospitality, and another invited him to a wedding celebration. In Kerlouan and Kerfeunten he made several drawings of superb bridal dresses.

Small public houses were ideal places to get to know the locals and pick up information, and he often found inspiration for his sketchbooks among his eating and drinking companions. Having a particular interest in military uniforms, his eye was always caught first by clothing, and he made numerous drawings of it. From everyday wear to official uniforms, Lalaisse illustrated the detail, variety and richness of regional dress, taking special care with hats and hairstyles.

◁ BANNALEC WOMEN
IN FOUESNANT, 1843–4
This plate in watercolour and pencil shows the façade of a thatched house, no doubt the home of the women pictured. On the clothes of the figure in the middle, who Lalaisse calls 'Woman of Bannalec', the braided fabric is an important feature. The woman pictured from the back is wearing a 'turban that can be seen under the cap'.
Musée National des Arts et des Traditions Populaires, Paris

△ MORBIHAN; PEASANT AND WOMAN IN
COSTUME AT JOSSELIN, 1843–4
Lalaisse got a young woman to pose for this watercolour. She is wearing a shawl over her shoulders, and the volume and folds of her apron are particularly well drawn. The same young woman is also sketched in pencil so that the motif on the back of the shawl and the fixture of the cap can be clearly seen.
Musée National des Arts et des Traditions Populaires, Paris

△ **SARDINE FISHERMEN
AT FAOUËT,** 1843–4
These five drawings and
two sketches, one of which
features an individual
carrying a box of sardines
on his head, were done in
grease pencil on bistre-
stained paper. The darker
patch of paper, around
the group of fishermen,
is probably due to the
application of an oil
or lacquer fixative.
The different postures
of the men allow us to see
their various headgear,
footwear, belt buckles
and long hairstyles.
*Musée National des Arts et des
Traditions Populaires, Paris*

▷ **CLAM FISHERMAN AT
MONT-SAINT-MICHEL,** 1843–4
It is interesting to note that
the artist used watercolours
only on the clothes and
tools in this illustration;
the silhouette of the
fisherman is drawn in
pencil. The wooden batten
structure of the wicker basket
on the man's back is clearly
shown, thus informing us
about the basket-making
techniques traditionally
used in the region. As usual,
Lalaisse noted at the top of
the page where the sketch
was made and the trade
of the man pictured.
*Musée National des Arts et des
Traditions Populaires, Paris*

Details of daily life

Lalaisse alternated between two separate techniques, one spontaneous, the other more considered. Numerous pencil drawings of silhouettes, scenes of local life, markets or village fetes were dashed down on paper in immediate response to encounters along the way. For his full-length watercolour portraits, however, he often paid models to pose for him so that he could take his time, preparing sketches in pencil before starting to paint. The faces in these are often indistinct, the features sometimes rubbed out altogether. The clothing itself, though, is in watercolour, and is shown from the back and front, more rarely in profile. While giving a general impression of the whole outfit, Lalaisse faithfully details volume, folds, braids and other adornments that help to distinguish styles from different areas.

*'We woke Lalaisse. Captivated, he got out his pencils, opened his album and
requested the young girl to pose.'* Anonymous travelling companion

mont - s.t michel

pêcheur d - coque

The artist made a note on this illustration of how the team was guided: the 'bridle…that the driver holds in his hand is always to the right'. This and the other images from Brittany were brought together on one hundred and sixty leaves of paper. At a later date the artist added drawings on different paper from trips to Normandy, Germany, Lorraine and the south of France.
Musée National des Arts et des Traditions Populaires, Paris

▷▷ **STUDY AT MALESTROIT, FROM 'VANNES TO PLOËRMEL',** 1843–4
Two series of lithographs – La Bretagne (Brittany)

from spring 1844, followed by La Galerie Armoricaine, which appeared regularly until 1846 – resulted from this tour. In this pencil and watercolour illustration Lalaisse included children's costume, as well as those of men and women. The lower of the notes at the top of the page tells us 'from Vannes to Ploërmel hair is habitually worn long at the sides'. Different types of pottery, some enamelled, appear among his drawings. To the right of the pottery shown here the artist supplies a caption for the cap: 'white woollen hood for peasant women'.
Musée National des Arts et des Traditions Populaires, Paris

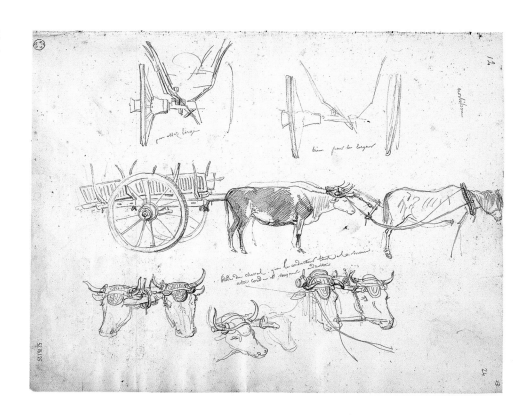

From time to time Lalaisse allowed himself to deviate from the main subject matter of his project, and sketched agricultural tools, fishing equipment, houses, streets, windmills (such as those near Pont Aven), farm animals and teams of bullocks, mules and horses. Handwritten texts accompanying the drawings give helpful information on the use of some of the objects. With landscapes, Lalaisse was able to shake off the restrictions of rendering clothing details and let himself go in more abstract watercolour compositions.

Lalaisse's survey concentrated far more on the aesthetics of traditional dress than it did on any overall social reality. Nevertheless, the portfolio he brought together as a book on his return to Paris is a very complete account of a certain aspect of Breton culture. His work serves as a fine example of the new discipline of ethnography that developed during the second half of the nineteenth century.

'Lalaisse did the drawing while we were drinking the cider that Ledireur kindly ordered for us.' Anonymous travelling companion

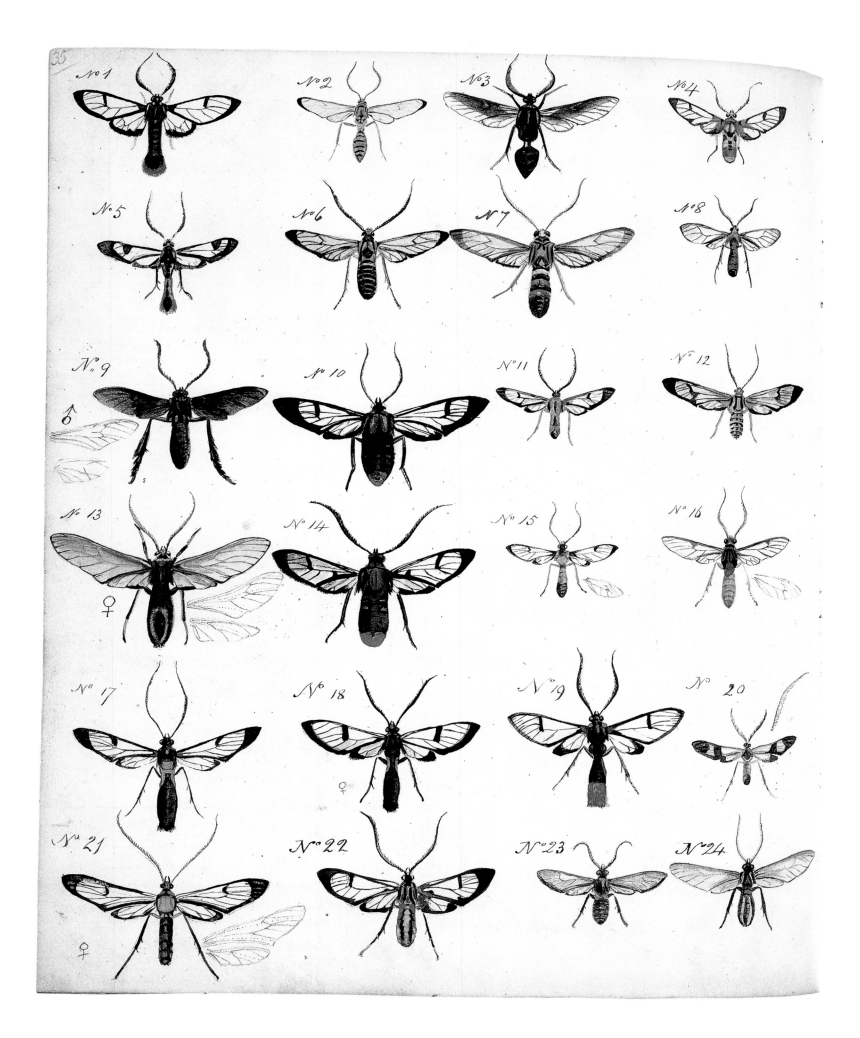

HENRY WALTER BATES
Notebooks of a Naturalist

On 26 April 1848 Henry Walter Bates and his friend Alfred Russel Wallace watched from the deck of their ship as the port of Liverpool disappeared behind them. They were leaving for Pará, the Brazilian town now known as Belém, situated at the mouth of the river Amazon. They landed there one month later. The two men had decided to explore the Amazonian forest in search of animals and insects, which they intended to collect and study. Both men were from modest backgrounds, so had been able to finance the voyage only thanks to pledges from large collectors and museums. (The British Museum had expressed an interest in any new species that Bates and Wallace might discover.)

At first the men explored the area together, getting to know Pará, the banks of the Amazon and the Tocantins river. In 1850 they decided to part company and continue to prospect individually. Wallace returned to England two years later, but Bates stayed in Amazonia for eleven years, during which time he learnt German and Portuguese. He returned to Britain with two thick journals that were stuffed with notes and observations. He also brought back a collection of 14,000 insects, of which one thousand were previously unknown, and some seven hundred fish, reptiles, birds and mammals.

The theory of mimicry

Lonely, starved of intellectual conversation and reduced to re-reading even the advertisements in his few periodicals, Bates concluded that contemplating nature was not enough to 'satisfy the heart and soul'. He seems to have fought the feeling of exile by rigorously devoting himself to his detailed notebooks. These journals, illustrated in pencil and watercolour and annotated in ink, were not merely the place in which he described his study of the jungle environment; they were also where he developed his pioneering scientific hypothesis known as 'Batesian mimicry'.

During his years of prospecting and discovery in Amazonia, Bates noticed that certain insects from different regions and belonging to

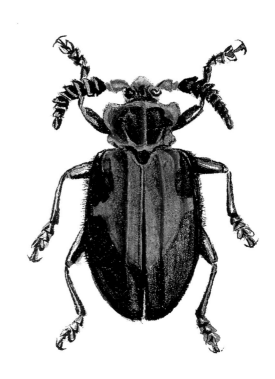

◁ **INSECTS, AMAZONIA NOTEBOOKS, VOL. 1, PAGE 35,** 1848–59
Each specimen illustrated by Bates, in ink and watercolour, was scrupulously numbered. The sex was sometimes indicated with the aid of a symbol (see number 18), and to mitigate colour loss or clarify the membrane of the lower wings, the author sometimes recopied an insect in quill beside the original drawing. *Natural History Museum, London*

△ **CERAMBYCIDE PHYTOPHAGE,** 1848–59
This creature, commonly known as the longhorn beetle, is illustrated in watercolour and easily identified by its imposing antennae. It often lives in the bark of trees, and its larva sometimes takes years to come to maturity. As there are many varieties of this beetle, it is popular among collectors. Alongside the drawings in his journal Bates noted everything concerning the subject's behaviour, movement and morphology. *Natural History Museum, London*

Chrisocerus
to be ~~separate~~. colour, shape
deceptively resemble the elongated
bi... on branches of fallen trees
held close together on the
4 Oct. 55

...d

psis?   ♀ Antennae more
the length of body. In ♂
much longer, but the terminal jt.
.
Prosternum. dilated after
~~sutera~~ & rather advanced
the mesost. being broad &
, there is a narrow slit
~~between~~ ♂ wh. renders
tyloid cav. not closed.
entium as in figure. I
particularly the horny piece
is elongate & narrow in
& its tip furnished with
bristles, exactly as the
in many other Coleoptera
the reverse) no doubt ...
2. 1856

Megaderus Stigma.   The lower lip
is composed of a very broad & short piece
a: of the same horny consistence as
the general integument. its upper edge
is cut out & joined to the membranous
piece b: forming the intermediate
piece between mentum & palpi —
~~c~~ c: is the paraglossæ or ligula
or ligula & paraglossæ united - it is
white cartilaginous & flexible & spring
(as I made quite sure) from the œsophagus
as far down as the base of mentum
it is one piece at its basal half &
soft, membranous or tumid - its upper
half is cleft: & within there is the
usual horny rib on each side running
up each of the lobes.   Now it
appears to me that the ligula
here is reduced & invisible externally
the paraglossæ being in recompense
highly developed.
The roots of lab. palpi are visible
& soft. e.   There is no trace of
the horny solidification of parts.
as in Ctenoscelis No 36 - except
a small dark horny looking plate
at the bottom of the cleft of paraglossa
(d). this latter may be the remains
of the reduced ligula. 5 Oct. 55

♂ Anisocerus Orca, White ...
Allied to Lamia & especially to Ony-
cerus.   The ♂ has fore tarsi ...
its. fringed on sides with long hairs, &
the apical jt. of ant. shorter than
the preced. jts.
The labium is on same type
Megaderus & other Longicorns
but the mentum, altho' horny
softer than the integument & also
coriaceous. The other parts are
narrower & more elongate than
Megaderus.   I see no trace
of rib or keel on the inside of
the ligula-paraglos. 5 Oct. 55
The sp. is frequent at Ega is found
on branches of fallen trees, often
found in cop.
The mandibles have not a tooth
w. apex as in Megaderus, but are
faintly crenulated in the middle of
inner side.

Anisocerus Egaensis
White
very common at Ega - in
depth of forest - on fell...

Chrysoprasis — the large, broad sp. — middle lobe of maxilla, greatly elongated, groove shaped, like the Callichroma & unlike Trachyderes labrum. Ample expanded rounded lobes. 1st jt. of maxpalpi elongate, — mandibles toothed in middle — &c &c.
Ega 25 March 1856

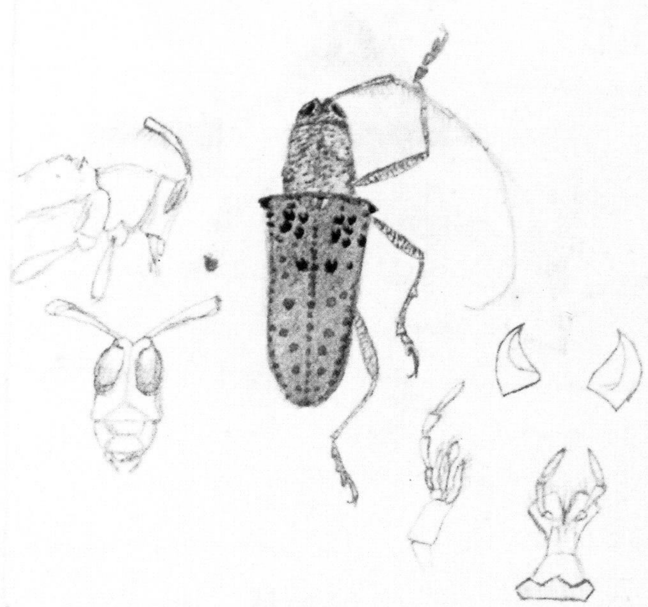

Lamiide Trachysomus. Mandibles broad blades, simply pointed not toothed. — Front-plane elongate, rather narrow, eyes notched slightly, at upper border antenniferous tubercles arising from the notch. —
Ega 27 March 1856

Coremia histipes

Listroptera

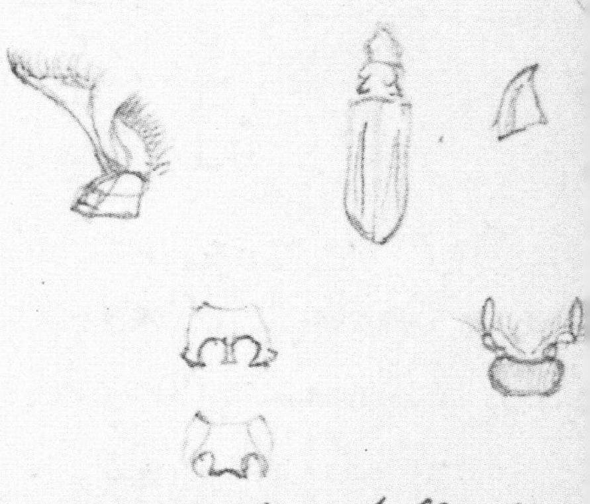

common small. wholly black
½ elytra with black striæ
surface rugose-corroded Ega

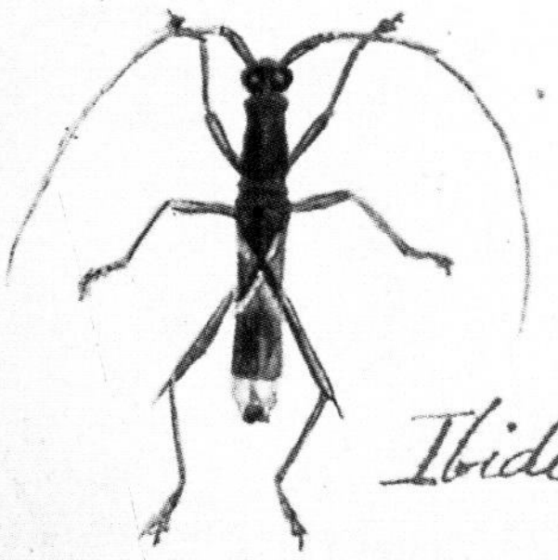

Ibidion with maxillæ
20 June /56

mandibles

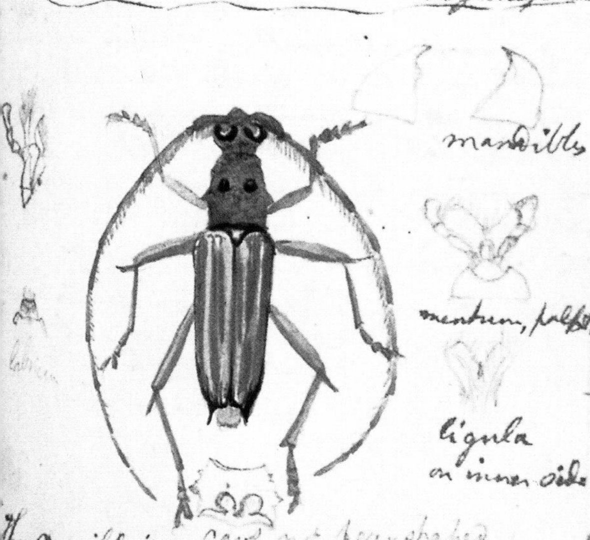

mentum, palps

ligula

Lamiide — nearest Leiopus — the second jt. of labial & the 2d & 3rd of maxipalpi — much enlarged, tip jt. thin & tapering. — the lingua is not cleft like other longicornes, but a single piece, scarce even a sin— on inner side scatture in its upper edge. — The mandibles are suddenly narrowed near the tip, the latter being a narrow very pointed tooth. — there is a semi-spiral fissure — similar to

Cycnoderus basalis

The maxilla are as in Ibidion. palpi small. — labials attached to base front side of ligula; the stipes being very small & I think fixed. The ligula I have no doubt is = paradoxa or

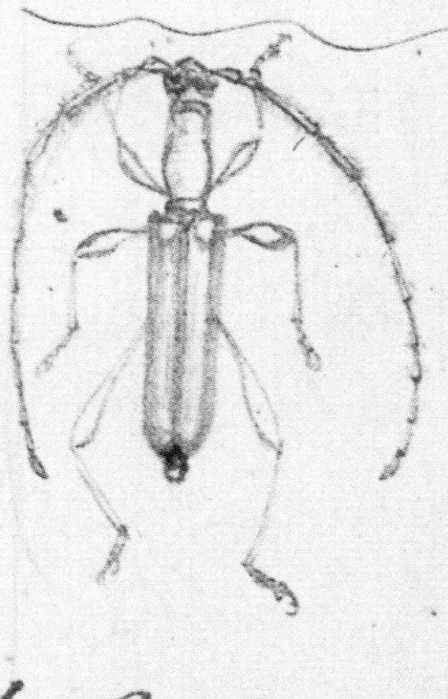

cavæ not pear shaped

parts of the mouth, membranous cartilaginous, semi transparent the mentum & tips of palpi ligula very feebly notched hairs, semi transparent. Ega

PRECEDING PAGES: BEETLES, 1848–59
Bates devoted his afternoons to the study of insects, and beetles were the largest category. In warm countries their shell is decorated with elegant designs in stunning colours. On this page, alongside the ink and watercolour illustrations, are pencil drawings showing the contours of the wings, legs, heads and antennae (fringed or not). Excellent though these are, the importance of Bates's handwritten comments is self-evident.
Natural History Museum, London

△ **PORTRAIT OF HENRY WALTER BATES,** C. 1865
Bates discovered his passion for entomology at a very young age. He published his first article in the journal Zoologist at the age of eighteen. His theory of visual mimicry made him a scientist of great renown.
Natural History Museum, London

▷ **BEETLES,** 1848–59
In concentrating on insects, Bates chose to study a world almost infinite in its complexity and variety.
Natural History Museum, London

distinct groups or types nevertheless displayed confusing similarities. While it was known by both scientists and predators that particular markings are a sign of toxicity, Bates noticed was that several species of harmless butterfly had acquired toxic markings in order to deter their predators. He became interested in how these phenomena of identification, resemblance and morphology worked, and came to the conclusion that they were part of the vast theory that relates to adaptation and natural selection.

'That shady spot was suddenly filled with birds as if by magic. None however had been visible when I entered the thicket.'

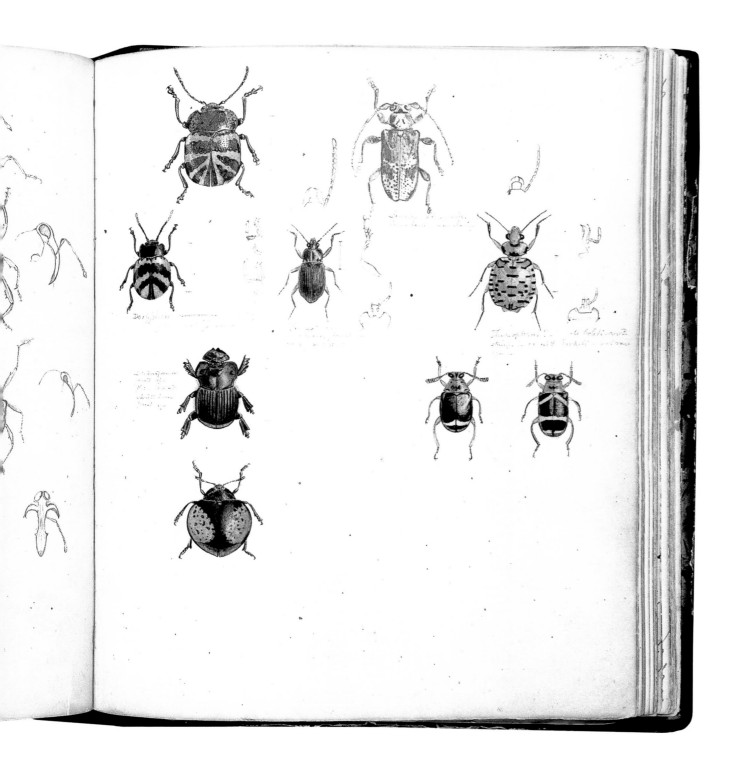

In a paper Bates delivered to the Linnean Society on 21 November 1861 he developed his reasoning and proposed an interpretation. Two years later, to great acclaim, he published *The Naturalist on the River Amazon*, in which he gave an account of his years prospecting in South America. The naturalist Charles Darwin, to whom Bates was philosophically very close, called it 'the best natural history travel book ever published'. Over the next few years Bates was involved in writing many different scientific publications. In 1864, filling a post left vacant by his friend Wallace, he became assistant secretary of the Royal Geographical Society, with responsibility for the publication of its journal, a post he held until his death. His notebooks, impressive in their precision, display a desire for scientific exactitude and great skill in capturing the splendid colours and forms of the tropical rainforest creatures.

妙法院住職
權少教正多喜寂順

TAKI - grand prêtre
u la secte Tenday

Félix Régamey

FÉLIX RÉGAMEY
Japanese Sketchbooks

It was a mutual fascination with Japan that brought together two men of very different backgrounds and resulted in a journal of great beauty. Félix Régamey, a renowned French artist pursuing a brilliant career at the Art Institute of Chicago, was approached by Émile Guimet to accompany him to Japan, the French Ministry of Public Education having commissioned him to carry out a huge study of the religions there. In anticipation of their trip, the two men visited the Universal Exhibition in Philadelphia, where they viewed several masterpieces of Japanese art. Setting off soon afterwards, they made a journey of twenty-three days across Alaska, and eventually arrived at the port of Yokohama in Japan on 26 August 1876. On their arrival, the two Frenchmen were greeted by high-ranking civil servants, who facilitated their work and obtained permission for them to visit various temples. Over the next two months they travelled widely, visiting Tokyo, Ise, Kyoto, Osaka and Kobe, and Régamey began a rich graphic study that came to influence the whole of his oeuvre.

To the heart of Japanese arts and traditions

Félix Régamey was fascinated by the refinement of traditional Japan. The 'beautiful girl dressed like a princess, singing to the child she carries on her back' whom he mentions in his journal was also, perhaps, the girl who appears in a full-length portrait he executed. He was seduced by the street life and the characters he observed while exploring working-class neighbourhoods. He sketched with great energy and at an amazing rate, drawing passers-by, men plying their trades, tattoo artists and rickshaw-runners. On one occasion, he and Guimet got lost and went to a theatre show together. Régamey was enchanted by the countryside and the behaviour and customs of the Japanese. He was able to go about his business without any difficulty. In an article for *La Revue bleue* in 1890, he wrote, 'In this flower garden full of joy, light and life, where everyone, from the top to the bottom of the social ladder, has a more or less developed sense of the beauty of nature, an artist has nothing to fear. He can sketch and draw as much as he likes without arousing the slightest suspicion; neither the camera nor the artist's easel is an object of disgust.'

◁ **PORTRAIT OF TAKI JAKUJUN,** 1876
While Guimet was in conversation with representatives of various religions, Régamey preferred to stroll in the grounds of shrines and temples in search of subjects to draw. This full-length portrait of Taki Jakujun, head monk at the temple of Myohoin, was probably conceived during one of these visits.
Musée des Arts Asiatiques Guimet, Paris

△ **PORTRAIT OF SEKIEHI DE SEKI,** 1876
The technique Régamey uses here was influenced by Japanese art. The heavy ink lines on the model's clothes reinforce the watercolours, and were probably done with a quill, or maybe even bamboo if Régamey's fascination for the aesthetic of Japanese artists is anything to go by.
Musée des Arts Asiatiques Guimet, Paris

Régamey wanted to improve the image of Japanese civilisation in the eyes of his countrymen, and drew numerous parallels with Greek and Roman antiquity. He noted the unfortunate consequences of increasing modernity on Japanese society, the strong Western (particularly American) presence, and regretted the growing industrialisation that was imposing a homogeneity in output. Up till then, protected by geographical isolation, Japanese craftsmen had used techniques dating back several thousand years. Régamey was dismayed at the way most of his contemporaries welcomed unconditionally what they saw as the miracles of material progress. Underlining the romantic and poetic past of Japan, he wrote, 'The old Japan is collapsing. Civilisation, it is said, is advancing by leaps and bounds, and paraffin lamps, opera hats and umbrellas are all the rage.'

Pencils, paintings and religion

As they had been commissioned to do, Guimet and Régamey led an extensive examination of the shrines and temples, the cemeteries and the sacred and spiritual sites that marked their route through the country, and gained detailed information on the changing religious landscape. To their great interest, Japan was undergoing an important transformation at the time of their study. Buddhism and Shintoism had long existed side by side, but now Shintoism was named the state religion and Buddhism was relegated to the sidelines.

Alongside the major religions, they observed the workings of religious cults, and the richness and variety of decors, sculpture and artistic representation. They attended sacred dances and ceremonies of offerings, which Régamey recorded in his sketchbooks. During official visits they spent time with leaders of different sects, these meetings lasting anything from a few hours to several days. Guimet examined the theological ideas of all the different forms of worship and entered into comparative studies – of Buddhism and Christianity, for example – while Régamey sketched his associate questioning groups of monks or addressing assemblies accompanied by his two interpreters. While Guimet was occupied in a private interview one day, Régamey made the most of an unexpected walk to do a drawing of monks going about their everyday tasks.

The two Frenchmen were enormously stimulated by their discoveries, and as the trip progressed, their curiosity increased. After the official part of the visit was over, they spent their time hunting for objects of interest, such as religious artefacts, and met many artists and craftsmen. Guimet made numerous acquisitions, and even commissioned several new works, notably from the painter Kawanabe Kyôsai, who, at least in part, owes his fame to the two Frenchmen. Régamey entered into a friendly competition with Kyôsai, as they exchanged drawings and did portraits of each another.

△ STUDY OF THE SHINTO
PRIEST SABACHE, 1876
Both Émile Guimet
and Félix Régamey were
sensitive to Japanese
spirituality and history,
and developed an empathy
with them. In oriental
metaphysical beliefs
they found a vision
and profundity that
were missing from
Western society.
*Musée des Arts Asiatiques
Guimet, Paris*

▷ A MAN BEING TATTOOED, 1876
On his return to the West,
Régamey was tireless in
promoting the Japanese
interest in art. 'One can
say without hyperbole that

in Japan everyone is an
artist,' he wrote in 1890.
Art is everywhere, he could
have added. Tattooing took
place in public, and
Régamey, who admired
the tattooists, learnt how
to do it himself.
*Musée des Arts Asiatiques
Guimet, Paris*

OVERLEAF: SHINTO CEREMONY
IN KYOTO, 1876
During the course of their
trip, Régamey and Guimet
had privileged access
to numerous religious
ceremonies, such as this
dance ritual in a Shinto
temple.
*Musée des Arts Asiatiques
Guimet, Paris*

'Arrival in Kambara at nine, bed without dinner. Sick. Haven't sketched today, too tired.' Félix Régamey's journal

△ **GROOM,** 1876
Interested in working-class traditions, Régamey did a series of drawings depicting street trades. Among them is this in pencil and ink sketch enhanced in watercolour.
Musée des Arts Asiatiques Guimet, Paris

△▷ **STUDY FOR PORTRAITS OF BUDDHIST MONKS,** 1876
When he accompanied Guimet to meetings with Buddhist monks, Régamey did sketches of them in his notebook. These 'veritable councils' – as many as thirty faces can be counted in some drawings – involved interminable debates on Buddhism and

Shintoism. Many different sects were consulted, including Shin-shu, Zen and Hokke. The monks we see here were almost certainly from Kennin-ji.
Musée des Arts Asiatiques Guimet, Paris

▷ **ÉMILE GUIMET AND FÉLIX RÉGAMEY WITH THEIR INTERPRETERS,** 1876
In this group portrait Régamey (right) is wearing clogs. Guimet (left) is wearing the traditional *ghetta*. They are accompanied by their interpreters and their cook. It is not clear if they are admiring a work of art or studying a map of the country.
Musée des Arts Asiatiques Guimet, Paris

From sketchbook to published work

The Japanese experience was a very fruitful one for Félix Régamey. His journal, its terse notes at times reminiscent of the haikus of Japanese poetry, was used two years later in the publication *Promenades Japonaises* (Japanese Walks). Émile Guimet supplied the accompanying text for this work, justifying the necessity of a second volume with the following remarks: 'And Régamey still has so many sketches packed away in boxes! It can't be helped. He did too many drawings. Never before has a book been seen in which there are so many illustrations, headings, initials, printer's vignettes and inserted engravings.' The second volume did indeed appear in 1880, and became in its turn a resounding success. Régamey's time in Japan went on to inspire much more work. He completed several paintings for the Universal Exhibition of 1878, and between 1879 and 1883 he adapted a Japanese novel for *Le Monde Illustré*. In 1890 he praised the virtues of Japanese art in the respected periodical *La Revue bleue*, affirming in passing its superiority over Chinese art. He continued his promotion of Japan and all things Japanese one year later in *Le Japon Pratique* (The Japanese Experience), thus encouraging the taste for Japanese aesthetics that was then so fashionable in the West.

In 1899 he made another journey to Japan, charged this time with investigating the teaching of fine art. As before, he returned full of zeal for Japanese culture, and participated in numerous conferences about it across France, before becoming organiser of the Franco-Japanese Society in Paris in 1900. His infatuation, which began during the tour of 1876 and is so obvious in his drawings of that time, continued until the end of his life. Its impact on Western culture, though clearly considerable, is still being evaluated today.

'What to choose among all the beauty we encounter?' Félix Régamey's journal

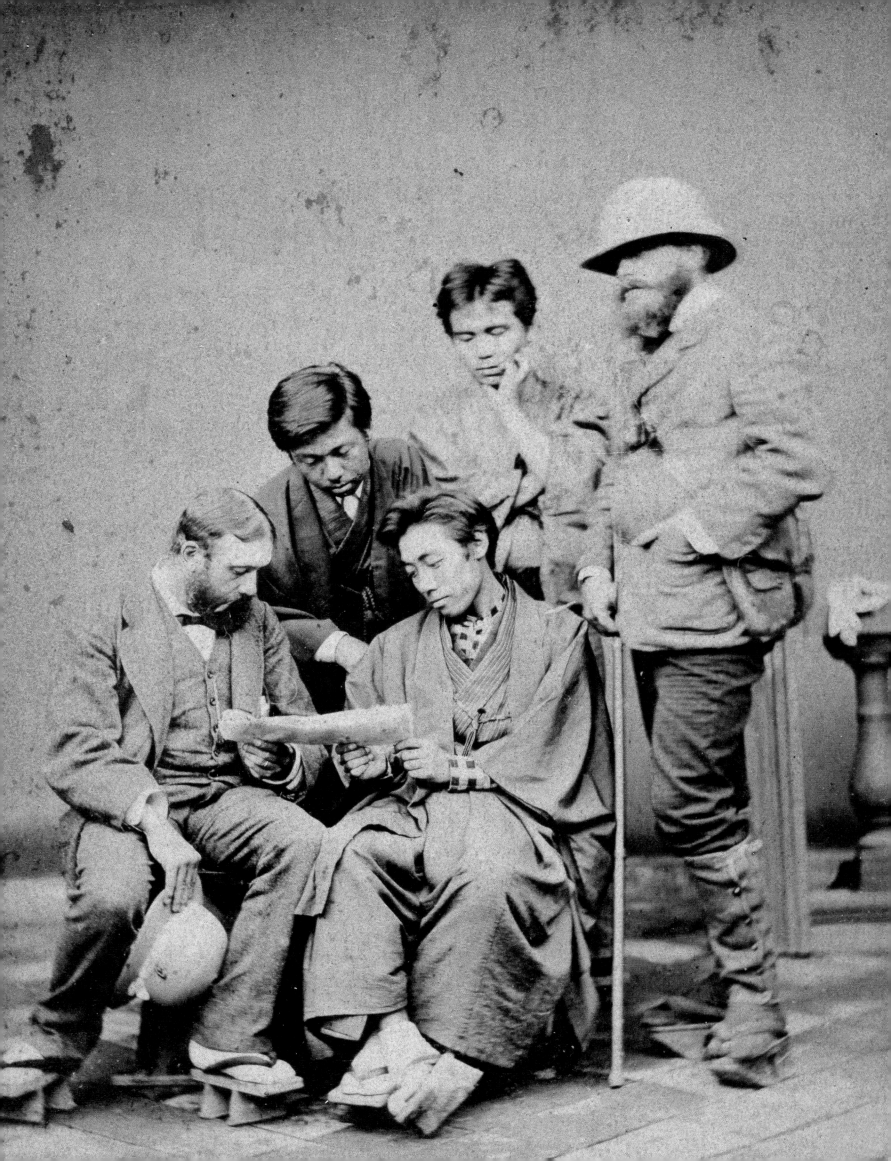

à construire un fortin sur son territoire

Cette singulière proposition, a été re-
nouvelée le 11 janvier dernier, à la suite de
nouvelles exigences du Tha-Luong.

J'ajouterai qu'à plusieurs reprises, et en
différents endroits, les indigènes m'ont engagé
à les débarrasser des Siamois, m'offrant même
de m'aider à les enlever et à détruire le poste de Cam-
Mon.

Types Indigènes - Lou-Thais

Avant mon arrivée le garde principal
Chenet, avait chargé le Quan-huyen de recueillir
des renseignements sur les refuges habituels des chefs
rebelles dans la montagne.

Il nous amena bientôt, deux hommes qui
fournirent en effet des indications utiles, et grâce à
eux, je pus dresser un itinéraire approximatif d'une
nouvelle route de la montagne arrivant à Chö-Rö.

Je n'en parlerai pas ici, car j'en ai fait un
croquis plus exact à mon retour en Annam.

Je veux observer seulement quel progrès nos
postes du Laos, pourraient faire faire à la paci-
fication des provinces du Nghé-An et du Ha-
Tinh, si troublées par les lettrés mutins comme
l'a dit le Quan-Huyen dans sa déclaration.

Prenant à revers toutes les routes de l'Annam
au Laos, ils rendraient intenables aux rebelles
la chaîne de partage des eaux qui leur sert
maintenant de refuge assuré, lorsqu'ils sont
serrés de trop près dans la plaine annamite, et
d'où ils débouchent pour piller impunément,

quand..

J'en ai fait l'objet d'une note spéciale (Note B)

Lou-Thai · Pou-Eun · Annamite
Femmes du Quan Huyen du Cam-Mon

Le 17 au soir les Siamois arrivè-
rent à Nong-Ma, avec 6 éléphants et un
grand nombre de coolies; je remarquerai à

ce....

ce propos qu'ils ne se soucient nullement d'é-
pargner des corvées aux indigènes, mais que tout
au contraire ils ne voyagent jamais sans une suite
nombreuse d'éléphants et de porteurs, malgré la
médiocrité de leur bagage.

Sans doute, leur vanité de barbares à
demi-frottés de civilisation européenne y trouve
son compte, mais leur influence ne peut qu'en
profiter, auprès des habitants d'un pays, où
l'on est toujours pris pour ce qu'on paraît.

De grand matin le 18, les Siamois se
mettaient en route, je fis partir l'escorte qui
prit la tête de la colonne, et je les suivis à
petite distance. Vers 8 heures, ils s'arrêtèrent
pour déjeuner et je les dépassai.

Je m'aperçus alors qu'ils s'étaient
fait accompagner d'une petite escorte, (huit
à 10 hommes armés de fusils) la moitié de
l'effectif du poste de Cam-Mon.

Je ne pouvais admettre l'entrée sur
le territoire annamite d'une troupe siamoise
en armes; j'en fis l'observation au Tha-Luong en

ajoutant...

HENRI RIVIÈRE
Log of a March through Indochina

Captain Henri Rivière's handwritten log is part of a series of documents collected by the Pavie Mission, the body devoted to French exploration of Indochina between 1879 and 1895. The mission's collection includes several hundred reports, but Rivière's journal stands out because of the photographs that accompany the text. One of the main tasks of the Pavie Mission's topographers was to make maps of the areas they trekked across – a total of more than 300,000 kilometres. During the course of their treks, the officers studied many different aspects of the country, including the lie of the land, means of access, climatic conditions, natural resources and methods of economic exchange, as well as the local people, cultural practices and traditions.

Expedition to Cam-Mon

Rivière's log, in a 32 x 22-cm format, was written in brown ink in a careful rounded hand, and runs from 5 January to 12 March 1891. It has a greenish-brown canvas cover on which a printed label bears the author's name and the words 'Mission Pavie' in gold lettering. The text is illustrated with thirty photographs, all printed on albumin paper and developed in a darkroom using a wet collodion bromide mixture on glass plates. The chapters of the journal, dated in a margin on the left-hand side of each page, correspond to the different stages of the mission. Two letters included at the beginning serve as a prologue to the account tion. In the first, dated December 1890 and addressed to 'Monsieur le consul Pavie', Rivière explains the objective of the expedition. The second, also addressed to Pavie, is the covering letter included in the package returning the log at the end of the expedition. The one hundred and thirty-seven pages of the account begins on 10 January in Hanoi. The expedition, which was heading for Vink and Cam-Mon, was under instructions to establish a trading outpost in Houtène, and to accompany the Siamese (Thai) topographers charged with drawing up a map of the region of Nong-Ma.

In Vink, Rivière noted the economic importance of the port and the products traded there, which included cardamom, hardwoods and rattan. From there, the expedition travelled up the Mekong river in sampans (light, flat-bottomed boats) to Ha-Trai. In January, while halted at Nong-Ma, Rivière did the first portrait of the Nguoi-Phu-Tuong people, which he pasted into his journal. He also described the conflicts that were disrupting life in the region. 'The local inhabitants,' he

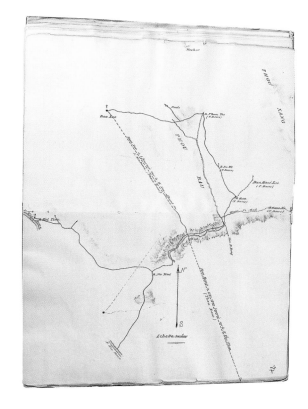

◁△ **INDIGENOUS TYPES, LOU-THAIS,** 1891
In order to document ethnic groups, Rivière was provided with a camera and a case of instruments for measuring the human body. The late nineteenth century saw an enthusiasm for this approach to categorising different racial types. As a rule, the 'strange peoples' were pictured from the front, back and in profile. These photos illustrate the prevailing Western attitude to the body and the racist evolutionary thought of the time.
Ministry of Foreign Affairs, Paris

◁▽ **WOMEN FROM QUAN-HUYEN, CAM-MON, POU-THAI, POU-EUN AND ANNAMITE,** FEBRUARY 1891
Rivière came across many obstacles in the pursuit of his work: 'The indigenous people seem to find it repugnant to be measured, and I was forced to stop after measuring just four of them.'
Ministry of Foreign Affairs, Paris

△ **MAP OF A WATERCOURSE IN THE REGION OF PHOU BAU AU,** 1891
On their way up the river, which we can see here on the map (scale 1:50 000), Rivière was confronted by a number of dangerous incidents: 'I was woken…by the coolies who were shouting to frighten away a tiger attracted by the presence of my horse.'
Ministry of Foreign Affairs, Paris

Ban-Keng-Tiec. Maison Pou-Thai

Caiman des rives du Mékong

△ **HOUSE IN THE VILLAGE OF POU-THAIS, BAN-KENG-TIEC (LEFT); CAIMAN ON THE BANKS OF THE MEKONG (RIGHT),** 1891
In the village of Pou-Thais Rivière had to wait three days to obtain boats for the journey to Houtène. The *chan-ban* (local leader) did not want to supply him with the boats for fear that the 'Siamese mandarin' would 'take the rattan' to him (whip him). On leaving the village, Rivière gave his horse to the *chan-ban* to look after, and reported him 'very moved by such a responsibility'. As he tells us in his journal, Rivière arrived in Houtène without incident on 30 January: 'Near the Mekong I killed a caiman, the photo of which I have included here to document the occasion.'
Ministry of Foreign Affairs, Paris

▷ **IN A RAPID AT THE KENG-NON,** 1891
Describing the scene in this photograph, Rivière wrote: 'Returning to the river, I once again took charge of my boats and continued up the Keng-Tiec. The weather was fine and I was able to take several photographs, including one of a boat in a rapid, which gives an idea of the difficulties of navigation during the dry season.'
Ministry of Foreign Affairs, Paris

wrote, 'have suffered cruelly at the hands of their Siamese Mandarin neighbours.' The four photographs that follow are from the area of Na-Huong. The first two, entitled 'Indigenous Types, Lou-Thai', show a man crouching down, the third pictures a pagoda and the last the entrance to a bronze works in the jungle.

The long second chapter is concerned with the different stages of the journey to Nong-Ma in Houtène. Rivière describes the progress of the mission and its relations with the chiefs of the cantons visited, punctuating the text with photos of houses and the caiman that he killed on the banks of the Mekong. On arrival in Houtène, Rivière went for walks in the Muong district, where he visited 'pagodas, boutiques and even some private houses' and took photos that he inserted into the pages of his journal. On several occasions he drew attention to the fact that the Siamese were resistant to the mission's plans for establishing a trading outpost.

In February, after travelling through Pha-Muang, Rivière arrived in Cam-Mon. The last part of the journal reports on the principality of Kham-Keûte, of which Rivière made a detailed map. It ends with a photograph of a textile maker at work and a technical drawing of a mill. The covering letter sent to Pavie reveals that Rivière had fallen ill during the journey and that he was soon to return home to Calvados. Readapting to life in the Normandy countryside must have been difficult.

'I made the most of the good weather to take a photograph which, in spite of its shortcomings, does show a view of the forest that entirely covers the Tram-Mua plateau.'

Notre
Iphi

LOUIS-GABRIEL VIAUX
Logs of the Iphigénie's Naval Campaigns

Seen here for the first time in public, Louis-Gabriel Viaux's personal log consists of two big tomes, the first with five hundred and eighty-eight pages, the second with four hundred and thirty-four. He compiled them during his two years on board the *Iphigénie*, which he boarded in 1898, aged thirty-six. This young lieutenant and naval instructor was a former pupil of the painter Fernand Cormon (1854–1924), and also taught drawing himself. He made the most of the dead time on board ship to fill the pages of his notebooks with drawings, photographs and watercolours telling the story of the last of this training vessel's naval campaigns. Two separate voyages were made in 1898 and 1899, each voyage following almost exactly the same itinerary. Leaving from Brest, the ship crossed the North Sea, headed south down the Portuguese coast and the coast of West Africa to what is now Sierra Leone, then crossed the Atlantic to the West Indies. On the way back it stopped off in the Azores before returning to its home port.

From words to images

The first of Viaux's journals begins on 12 October 1898 during the preparation of the *Iphigénie* in Brest. The last sailing ship still in commission in the navy fleet, she was soon to begin her penultimate voyage before being retired from service in 1901. 'Everybody is impressed with how handsome the *Iphigénie* looks,' wrote Viaux.

The first seventy pages of the journal contain no elaborate illustrations. Written in lilac-coloured ink in an elegant hand, they are concerned with changes in weather, other boats encountered and manoeuvres executed along the way. There are also occasional comments on the morale of the crew, notes of compass readings and nautical calculations. Then suddenly, on page seventy-two, within the section that describes the passage from Vigo to Lisbon, two Portuguese fiscal stamps appear, accompanied by a caption in black ink that was probably added later. These stamps are glued on to the page and serve as a kind of illustration.

◁ THE *IPHIGÉNIE*, FROM THE ALBUM *'IPHIGÉNIE'S NAVAL CAMPAIGN'*, 1896-7
The *Iphigénie*, seen here in a photograph on albumin paper, was the last sailing ship in the navy fleet, and one of the last large boats to be constructed in wood. She carried a great deal of weight in sail and steel-fibre rigging, and was retired from service in 1901.
Service Historique de la Marine, Vincennes

△ WOMAN IN DAKAR, 1898
This ink and watercolour drawing was completed in December 1898, but is glued into the journal under the entry for 3 May 1899, by which time Viaux was back in Brest. This random placement is typical of the journal as a whole.
Service Historique de la Marine, Vincennes

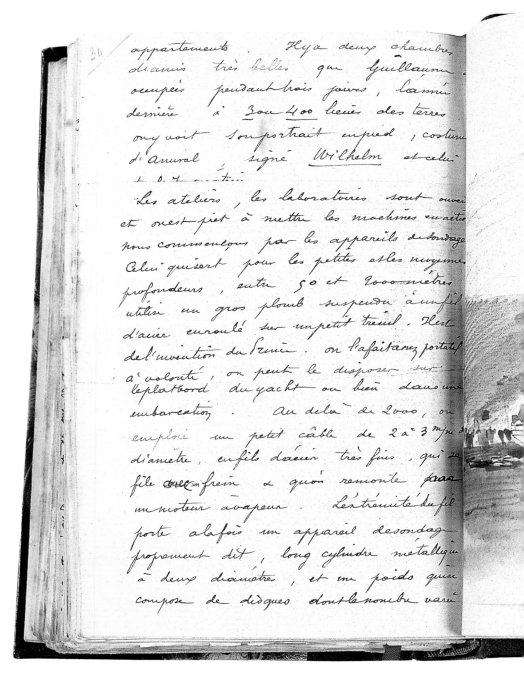

△ SHARK IN GUADELOUPE,
27 FEBRUARY 1900
Viaux made this ink and
watercolour drawing a shark
being caught, and later
wrote, '3.20 metres in
length, 1.50 metres around
the girth, 200 kilograms.
These are the statistics
of the villainous beast we
caught earlier during lunch.

She and another spent all
morning circling the ship,
approaching very close in
spite of the noise.' It is
interesting to note that
Viaux sometimes does
a drawing and a photo
of the same subject
(see shark photo overleaf).
*Service Historique
de la Marine, Vincennes*

In the following chapter, which marks the arrival of the *Iphigénie* in
Lisbon at the end of October 1898, Viaux begins the artistic work that is
such a feature of the journal from this point onwards. His first drawing,
an ink and coloured pencil illustration of a boat powered by both steam
and sail, was completed as part of the section describing the Portuguese
capital and its principal monuments. The range of colours used here, and
the relationship between text and image, set the pattern for the rest of the
work. Viaux uses a dab of yellow for the chimney, grey and violet for the

*'I am going to prepare myself for going to sea – stow my books
and pots of plants.'* November 1898

La Hohenzollern

6 juillet Bergen 1899.

hull and orange for certain sails. He numbers the largest of the sails and explains them in a key describing the type of rigging used ('No. 5, staysail of the large topgallant…').

Little by little, illustrations overwhelm the written account. From page 100 onwards there is virtually one illustration per page, either glued in by the artist or drawn directly on to the paper. The reverse of these pages is left unused in order to preserve the clarity of the images. Pasted alongside the drawings are dried flowers, leaves and pieces of paper to cover handwriting errors. On page 113 the first photographs appear, taken in the Portuguese countryside during an excursion to La Caldera.

On reaching Senegal, Viaux was enchanted by his stay in Dakar. After giving an account of his walks and a description of the region's economy (he

△ **THE HOHENZOLLERN,** 6 JULY 1899
On 5 July 1899 in Bergen, Viaux spotted a yacht belonging to Kaiser Wilhelm II. 'The Hohenzollern raises the French flag on the foremast and the Norwegian on the mizzen, then does the opposite, and at the command of the officer of the watch the crew shout hurrah; the Kaiser appears to the sound of bugles and drums…'
Service Historique de la Marine, Vincennes

was now writing in black ink), he charts the ship's southward passage along the African coast before it sets a bearing for the West Indies. At this point a folded map, showing the route followed from Brest to Freetown, is inserted into the journal. Ports of call now follow rapidly, one after the other, and Viaux alternates between black and violet ink for his sketches and text. Pastels were used for the first time in a view of the sea at high tide, and a multicoloured landscape in Martinique was drawn entirely in colour pencil on the back of an envelope and then stuck on to a page.

Randomness and chance, inherent in any journey by sail, influence the techniques and composition of the work, as do memory, second thoughts and opportunity. A portrait of a woman in Dakar, for example, appears out of sequence at the end of the volume, after the *Iphigénie* arrived back in France. The last entry in the first journal is on 3 July 1899 in Bergen.

The Iphigénie's last long-haul voyage

On the second voyage to the West Indies, which began on 10 October 1899, Viaux used a notebook with much finer, more transparent paper. He had spent the summer on land, but did not write about his leave, proof that it was the long-haul voyage that really interested him. The second trip was identical to the previous one apart from a few minor changes. On this voyage the *Iphigénie* stopped off at Porto Santo and the port of Santa Cruz de Tenerife. Then, in December, she docked in Dakar again.

Changes in Viaux's mood can be detected by the state of his handwriting. He doesn't seem to be in the best of form at the beginning of January 1900. Several scratchings out appear in quick succession, and the handwriting becomes hesitant as the ship arrives in Fort-de-France, Martinique, on the 14th. The enthusiasm and regularity of entries that characterise the notebooks up to this point disappear until the long section without illustrations between pages 137 and 235. Viaux does not start sketching again until 22 February, when the boat arrives at the Iles des Saintes (also known as Les Saintes, this group of small islands lies just off the coast of Guadeloupe). Plants and watercolours reappear and the journal again fills up with images over the next one hundred pages. During the stopover in the Azores at the beginning of April, however, Viaux's entries dry up for good. He chooses to end this second journal by inserting a thick, thirty-nine-page tourist brochure with a flexible blue cover, which reads, 'Valley of Orotoma, Tenerife, the most perfect climate in the world…'

△ SHARK IN MARTINIQUE, 1900
During a stopover in Fort-de-France, Viaux took this albumin photograph of the capture of a shark.
Service Historique de la Marine, Vincennes

▽ LOUIS GABRIEL VIAUX'S JOURNAL OPEN ON THE DATE 22 NOVEMBER 1898
Bottom left, the albumin photo shows officers of the ship. The numbers above the officers' heads refer to a key that details their names and ranks. At the top of the right-hand page we can see a mini-herbarium about which Viaux wrote: 'This comes from a species known as the Bougainvillea. Not a very scientific name, but the flower is pretty.'
Service Historique de la Marine, Vincennes

yacht . · Les premiers jardins de la ville . Partie sud du port franc 413

What sort of journal?

Viaux chose to use notebooks of the same dimensions (21.7 x 14 cm), which were easy to slip into a large pocket. Each volume relates a voyage of a year, and, apart from a few gaps, consists of long daily entries. The journals fall somewhere between a traditional ship's log and a personal diary, although they contain no intimate thoughts. There is a natural reserve in the writing, but Viaux gradually becomes more adventurous in his artwork, happy to risk a diversity of techniques and themes. A preference for quill and ink and watercolours gives way to collages of traced designs, printed articles and even musical scores. He mixes inks of different colours and uses them alongside menus, plants, photographs (in ferrotype and albumin), pastels and colour pencils. Some of these techniques are used for views of shorelines, detailed architectural drawings, maps, still lifes, illustrations of boats and group portraits.

Although Viaux showed an old-fashioned classicism and exaggerated attention to detail, he also made liberal (and talented) use of many modern techniques. His watercolours show a particularly fine touch, and his mastery of volume and economy of brushstroke denote him as an

△ **THE FREE PORT OF COPENHAGEN,** 1898–9
On arrival in Copenhagen, Viaux made this watercolour and ink drawing and wrote, 'We are going with them from the fort at Trekroner to the free port created in 1894. We will enter an 800-metre-long channel, where we will be taken to a small red buoy at which we must moor.' *Service Historique de la Marine, Vincennes*

'We are not yet at the mooring. The winds failed at the last moment and we had to beat to windward once again.' 8 a.m. on 16 November 1898

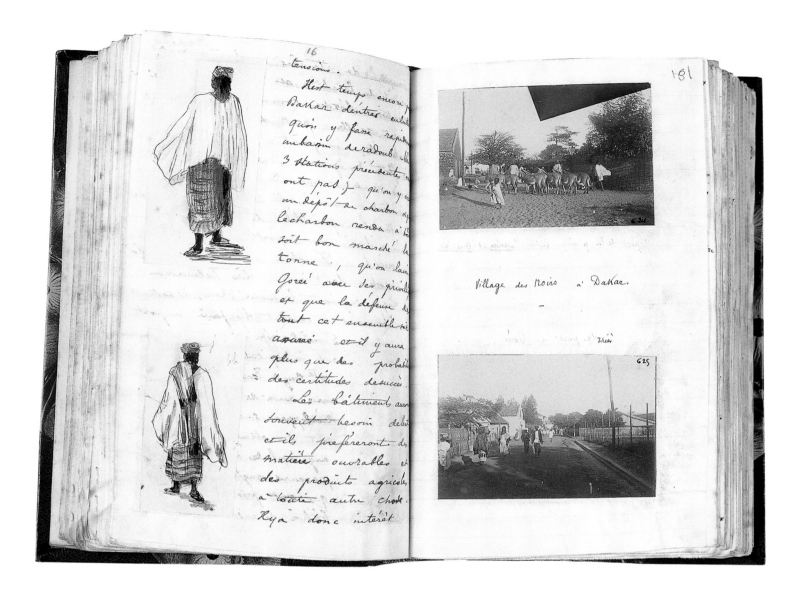

economic and commercial
activity in Senegal and
the Sudan seems to us to
be at a critical turning
point.'
Service Historique
de la Marine, Vincennes

exceptional artist. The modernity, rigour, diversity and abundance of his artistic compositions are remarkable, imbuing the journals with richness and originality.

Around 1925, not long after his retirement, Louis-Gabriel Viaux bound each volume of his journal with a half-leather cover – a mark of his attachment to a work that held so many memories of his first long naval campaigns. An article dated February 1929, inserted into the first volume next to a traced drawing on page 164, shows how the journal continued to aid the memory of the author long after the *Iphigénie*'s last voyage. We can imagine the old sailor sitting at home, taking his journal down off the bookshelf from time to time, poring over the past and wondering, perhaps, what might have been.

'At sea the main occupation consists in observing the stars and calculating one's direction. Not a night passes without a long conversation with Sirius, the most beautiful star in the southern hemisphere.' 25 December 1898

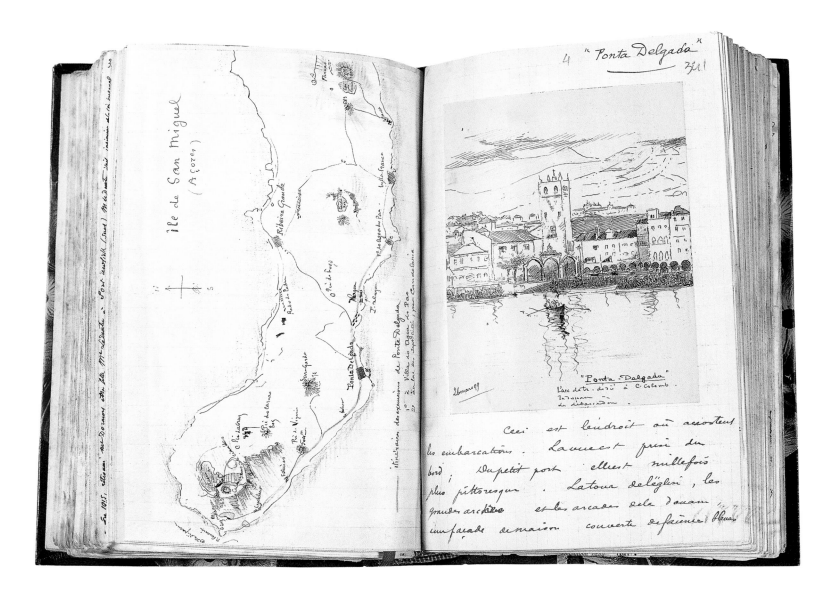

△ **LOUIS GABRIEL VIAUX'S JOURNAL, SAN MIGUEL IN THE AZORES,** 26 MARCH 1899

The ink and colour pencil map on the left shows in red the routes of the excursions led by Viaux to the north of the island. The ink drawing on the right shows Ponta Delgada, with its landing stage and triumphal arch dedicated to Christopher Columbus.
Service Historique de la Marine, Vincennes

▷ **CARMEN IN CADIZ,** 7 APRIL 1899

As Viaux notes in his journal: 'One evening, at the instigation of the consul…we went to see the señoritas Aurora and Carmen [popular dancers]. While…we dined on fried sardines, these professionals gave us a frenzied show of their remarkable talents.' On the page following this photo is the music for 'La Seguidilla', a Spanish dance.
Service Historique de la Marine, Vincennes

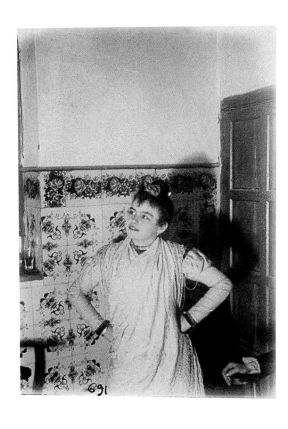

ÉDOUARD MÉRITE

Sketchbooks of Animals in the Far North

In the collections at the National Museum of Natural History in Paris there are three books of Arctic sketches by Edouard Mérite. These drawings were done on two expeditions led by Philippe, the Duke of Orléans, on the thirty-five-metre three-masted vessel the *Belgica*, which had proved itself in the pack-ice in the past. Mérite was commissioned to paint the fauna of the regions visited, finding many of his subjects among the numerous animals killed by the duke. He produced a sketchbook of beautiful drawings, which are presented here to the public for the first time.

Two North Pole sketchbooks

The first expedition, in 1905, carried out oceanographic and hydro-graphical analysis to study winds, temperatures, plankton and meteorological phenomena. Mérite had the opportunity of observing an as yet undiscovered natural world, namely the 'French territory' that the mission laid claim to at a latitude beyond 76° north.

The second expedition, in 1909, visited Franz Josef Land in order to get 'an overall vision of the pack-ice and the Arctic territories in the European sector'. By the time the mission reached the pack-ice, the duke had already bagged an impressive number of animals – around forty hooded seals, one walrus and ten bears. This was the last of his polar expeditions. 'Hunting on the pack-ice was no longer of any interest to him because he now possessed all the animals and had a complete Arctic collection,' explained Dr Récamier, his faithful travelling companion.

Mérite brought back three sketchbooks from these two expeditions, two of which are small (11 x 18 cm) and numbered, with round edges and sheets of paper that can be detached at the top. Somebody, not the author, has written 'Pôle Nord' on the covers, which are bound in leather with cloth spines. There are around sixty pencil drawings and fifteen watercolours in each sketchbook. With the exception of the odd landscape, the illustrations are all of birds (snow buntings, petrels, herring gulls, black-legged kittiwakes) and polar mammals (dogs, wolves, bears, walruses, seals). Drawn in their habitats and

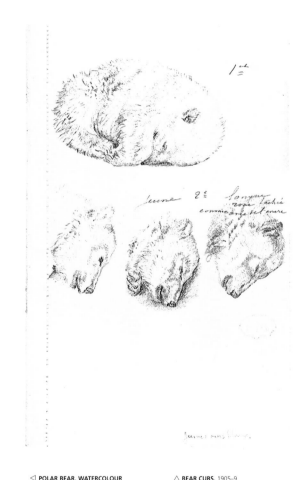

◁ POLAR BEAR, WATERCOLOUR
AFTER R. FRIESE, 1905–9
During both polar expeditions the Duke of Orléans killed numerous bears and brought back their hides, which he had stuffed and displayed in the collections at his museum. The bears were not frightened by the arrival of the *Belgica*, so they were very easy to kill with a shot from a telescopic gun.
National Museum of Natural History, Paris

△ BEAR CUBS, 1905–9
On one occasion, wrote the Duke of Orléans, after a hunting party returned with some bears at 2.30 in the morning, 'Mérite, with typical application [and] in spite of the cold, set himself down in front of the two models, hung side by side, and worked for the rest of the night.' This pencil drawing was the result.
National Museum of Natural History, Paris

△ **HUSKY**, 1905–9
Mérite often used only
the right-hand side of
the sketchbook because
of the transparency of the
paper. He drew with great
attention to detail, showing
the layerings of colour in
the plumage and fur
of the animals, even
when working in pencil.
*National Museum
of Natural History, Paris*

△▷ **GUILLEMOT CHICKS IN TROÏL**, 1905–9
To keep his shipmates
healthy, the Duke of Orléans
made sure they had plenty
of fresh meat to eat.
This is what he had to say
about the guillemots: 'We
boil them, then roast them
in the oven with a little
butter, making for
an excellent dish when
seasoned with an Arctic
appetite. Mérite captured
them here in pencil
and watercolour.
*National Museum
of Natural History, Paris*

△▷▷ **NORTHERN FULMARS
IN FULL FLIGHT**, 1905–9
During both expeditions
Mérite made stereotype
plates, a technique that
certainly had an impact on
his pencil and watercolour
drawings. The studies divide
the movement of the birds
in flight into parts and are
similar to the time-lapse
photography.
*National Museum
of Natural History, Paris*

▷ **BIRD IN FLIGHT AND
ON THE GROUND**, 1905–9
On Jan Mayen Island, during
the voyage of 1909, the Duke
of Orléans wrote, 'Landing
on the beach, we found the
sea covered in thousands of
petrels, which did not move
at all when we approached,
so busy were they in stuffing
themselves. They swim in
the surf in tight lines, facing
towards the land.' Mérite
drew this example in pencil
and watercolour.
*National Museum
of Natural History, Paris*

magnificently detailed, all the animals are named in pencil at the bottom of each page. A shadow of very light watercolour is visible behind certain silhouettes. These two sketchbooks are probably from the 1909 voyage, which resembled a big hunting party rather than a scientific expedition.

The third sketchbook is larger (19.5 x 13 cm) and only forty-three pages are used. The drawings include studies of tern chicks and guillemots, and the head of a large dead raven is drawn alongside. There are twenty-four watercolours and three polar landscapes, one of which is just a rough sketch. While the other two sketchbooks contain no writing apart from identifying labels, the third book contains some handwritten notes on the final page. In all three sketchbooks the artist includes his 'trademark' at the bottom of each page: his initials in capitals surrounded by a jagged oval outline.

When the ship returned to France after the first expedition a volume of scientific observations was published in Brussels. Another work illustrated with Mérite's drawings, À *travers la banquise, du Spitzberg au cap Philippe, mai–août 1905* (Across the Pack-Ice from Spitzberg to Cape Philippe, May–August 1905) came out in 1907. The remarkable precision of Mérite's work was recognised in 1924 when he was made master of animal drawing at the National Museum of Natural History in Paris.

'I can still see…Mérite, fingers blue from the cold, drawing on the bridge in spite of the frost.' Dr Récamier in *L'Ame de l'Exilé* (The Soul of the Exile), 1927

Au moment de me coucher, j'entends de gens, crier ... répété
plusieurs fois le faut. Tout le monde se précipite ... c'est Ricuit qui
dans la fameulle en attrapé un échil de neige, il va jour devant lui
et sur le faut s'est jeté sur lui à plat ventre, le couvrant de sa
blague, en attendant du secours pour le dégager.

Température

M.	−0.9	
m.	+4	
8 m.	−3	
12	−1	
4 s.	−1	
8	−2	

Rafales furieuses ; chane neige énorme . Temps tourm...
Baromètre 713 à midi.

LOUIS GAIN

A Journal of Charcot's Second Expedition to the Antarctic

The Pourquoi-Pas? left the port of Le Havre on 15 August 1908 to cries of 'Bon voyage!' from a crowd of more than 20,000 curious spectators. Led by Jean-Baptiste Charcot, the expedition was sponsored by several eminent institutions (including the National Museum of Natural History and the Institute of Oceanography), and its research programme had been approved by the Academy of Sciences. The crew consisted mainly of Breton sailors, most of whom had sailed on Charcot's first expedition (1903–5) on the *Français*, which had gone down at Buenos Aires to the great despair of her captain. Its team of eight scientists included Louis Gain, a young zoologist and botanist.

Over the two years of the second expedition Louis Gain kept a daily journal. This sometimes messily written account, addressed partly to friends and family back home, is accompanied by drawings in graphite, colour pencils, ink and watercolour. In addition, Gain compiled two albums of photographs, which complement the journal and record important moments on this voyage of scientific discovery.

In search of the cold

The *Pourquoi-Pas?* was very modern for its time, and Charcot dug into his own personal fortune to help finance its construction in St Malo. The result was something to be proud of – a spacious, high-performance, 40-metre, three-masted vessel in solid oak, which could maintain a speed of 8 knots without difficulty. With laboratories (one of which was devoted to photography) and a library specially fitted out for the expedition, it provided an ideal working environment for Gain and the rest of the scientific team.

Just after her departure, the *Pourquoi-Pas?* took refuge in Guernsey to avoid a storm, then stopped off in Madeira and the Cape Verde islands, Rio de Janeiro, Buenos Aires and Punta Arenas. On 18 December 1908 she went down the Beagle Channel, and four days later met her first iceberg. The discovery of these immense, far-off landscapes was both a thrilling and disorientating experience for the young Louis Gain. Before

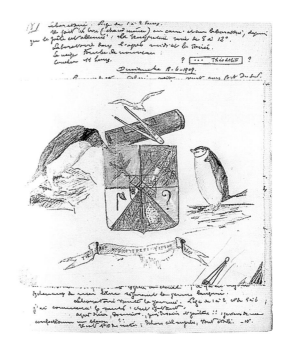

◁ **DRAWING OF AN ICEBERG**, 1908–10
On 22 December 1908 the expedition had an exciting encounter, which is captured here in ink and colour pencil. Charcot noted, 'We are in the Boyd Strait and have met our first glacier. It is, moreover, completely isolated and we have diverted our course a little to get alongside it.' By all accounts from those present, the light and colour from the icebergs, the water and the sky – electric blue, soft reds, purple, all shades of green and kremnitz white – offered a fabulous spectacle. *Private collection*

△ **LOUIS GAIN'S COAT OF ARMS**, 1909
To pass the time, Louis Gain designed a coat of arms for himself in graphite and colour pencil. Topped by a compass and a seagull in full flight, it is framed by two separate drawings of penguins. Other sketches here indicate the work of a naturalist – a starfish, the shoot of a young plant, a plankton net and the question mark from the name of his ship. *Private collection*

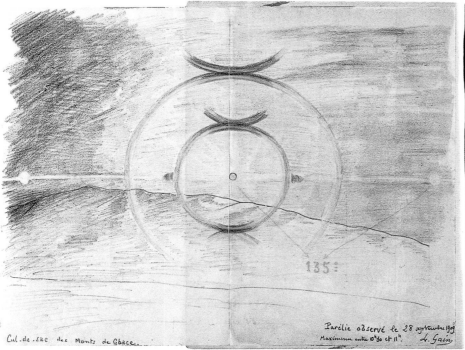

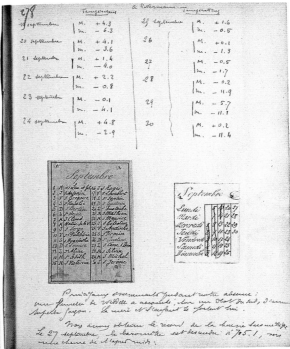

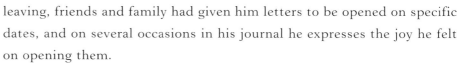

△ A PARHELION, 28 SEPTEMBER 1909,
BETWEEN 10.30 AND 11 A.M.
This colour pencil drawing
of a bright spot on the solar
halo, complete with rainbow
effect, is accompanied by a
comment from the author,
bottom left: 'Cul-de-sac,
mountains of ice.' The
parhelion is a phenomenon
of optical refraction, which
multiplies the sun's image
at the same time as its halo.
Louis Gain captured this
moment while out on the
glacier, and Charcot later
wrote in his log: 'The
meteorological observations

taken down with such care
by Gain will be
of great use.'
Private collection

▽ PORTRAIT OF JEAN-BAPTISTE CHARCOT
ON THE *POURQUOI-PAS?* AT THE PORT
OF LE HAVRE, LOUIS GAIN, 1908–10
Here we see Gain's sister in
conversation with the leader
of the future expedition.
Private collection

leaving, friends and family had given him letters to be opened on specific
dates, and on several occasions in his journal he expresses the joy he felt
on opening them.

Landing at Deception Island, he made his first observations of polar fauna
and flora, particularly seaweed, the subject of his future doctoral thesis.
Alongside these notes he also made frequent comments on the weather conditions. The ship passed down the Peltier Channel and arrived in Port
Circumcision on Petermann Island, where the scientists headed off on foot or
on board tenders to pursue their various investigations. These included glacio-
logical studies, which aimed to measure the size of icebergs and sound their
depths. A little later, in Adelaide Island (also known as Terre Adelaide), they
carried out an examination of some hills, and Gain, a passionate naturalist,
covered a distance of sixty kilometres with one team. He made many sketches
and views of the coastline, and attached celluloid rings of different colours
around the feet of cormorants and penguins in order to study their migrations.

On 13 January 1909, after a visit to Victor Hugo Island, the *Pourquoi-Pas?*
made another stopover in Adelaide Island, where a hydrographic station was
installed, and from where she made several more surveying journeys. She
continued advancing in the ice channels, but with difficulty. As Charcot wrote,
'the ice becomes so compact and presses so tight that we can no longer move
forward', but Gain continued to study the fauna (seagulls and Arctic gulls).

Dragging nets provided a rich harvest of fish, which was sometimes served
to the crew, but they didn't always appreciate the catch, taking a particular
dislike to 'Antarctic prawns'. Unable to find anywhere better, the *Pourquoi-
Pas?* spent the nine-month winter at Port Circumcision, where it survived
swells that threatened to break it from its moorings and throw it against the

'*Although the penguins are a subject of study for Gain, they are a perpetual nuisance for the rest of us.*' Charcot's log, 16 February 1909

quay. While waiting for the weather to improve, Gain found a colony of penguins near by, which provided him with an ideal subject for study.

Meanwhile, scientific facilities were installed here at Port Circumcision – one cabin for the study of atmospheric electricity, another to house a seismograph, a third for a meridian lens and a fourth for a meteorological shelter. A system of cameras taking constant exposures was also set up.

As on most expeditions, people turned their hand to different tasks as and when required, so Gain's work was not confined to his own domain. Among other things, he sank a series of markers into the ice in order to measure the advance of a glacier, and gave lessons in different disciplines to members of the crew. Inquisitive and hard-working, Gain also had a great sense of humour. He participated in a 'musical society' every Sunday, and for Mardi Gras (Shrove Tuesday) celebrations he dressed in tropical costume. He seems to have been an agreeable and effective member of the expedition, often volunteering for various responsibilities, and carefully tending the hyacinths and cress he grew under the skylight in the officers' mess. He reports with great

△ PETERMANN ISLAND, 1909
In this photograph we can see the path down the trench that led to the expedition's cabins, where various scientific installations were set up. Everyone had to lend a hand with these because conditions were very difficult; Charcot had chosen his men with an eye to their physical aptitudes as much as their intellectual ones. Beside the sailor we can see Kiki, the expedition's mascot.
Private collection

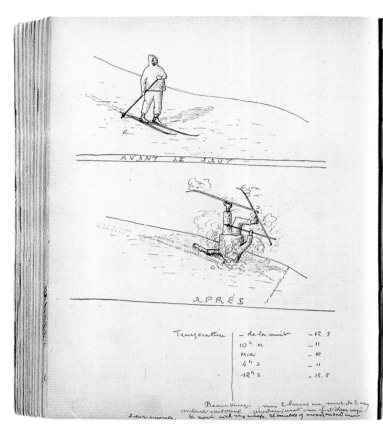

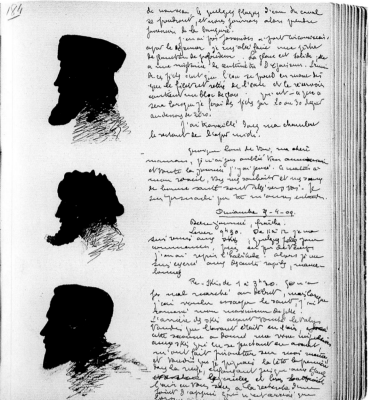

△ **SELF-PORTRAIT AND SKETCHES OF SHIPMATES**, APRIL 1909

Alongside his humorous self-portrait in ink Gain wrote, 'Got up at 9.30. From 11 to 12, I had another go at skiing. I fell flat on my face several times, but got the hang of it pretty quickly. Then I tried out some fast downhill slopes.' A little further on, in a moving letter addressed to his mother, he writes, 'Although far from you, dear mother, I haven't forgotten your birthday and have been thinking about you all day. On waking this morning, I directed all my best wishes for your good health towards you.' In the margin he amused himself by making silhouette drawings of his companions.
Private collection

▷ **THE POURQUOI-PAS?**, 1908–10

This striking photograph of the ship was taken by Gain from the top of a mast. Captain Charcot had to dig into his own personal fortune to complete the financing of this superb vessel, built in the shipyard at St Malo. He never left the ship again, going down with her at sea off the reefs of Iceland on 16 September 1936. The only survivor told how at the last moment Charcot asked that his mascot, a seagull, be set free.
Private collection

enthusiasm in his diary about life and leisure on board – games of dominos, concerts or pieces of theatre – but also mentions that some of the seamen did not always take his scientific work seriously. On one occasion they made an omelette with the eggs he had gathered to study.

An emotional return

Although birds were scarce during the winter, Gain did make studies of the Antarctic petrel and a colony of cormorants. He also observed different species of seal found on the pack-ice. After wintering for nine months, the expedition returned to Deception, and then, on 6 November, Gain and two companions boarded the whaler Almirante Uribe in order to study the two species of cetacean that inhabit the Antarctic waters. On Christmas Day the expedition set down at Bridgeman Island for a short visit – the first anyone had made there. They spent New Year in Admiralty Bay.

By the time the expedition came to an end, it had covered more than 1200 kilometres of coastline and had trebled the mapped areas of the Antarctic Peninsula. The Pourquoi-Pas? reached Punta Arenas in Chile on 11 February 1910, and finally made it back to Le Havre on 4 June. They then travelled up the Seine as far as Rouen, Captain Charcot noting that 'shouts of welcome came from all the villages, all the houses decked in flags'.

'In Gain, moreover, I have the most charming of companions…
This hard worker, intelligent and vigorous, has also shown that he has a big heart.'
Charcot's log, 19 October 1909

masques galoa.

masculin ♂

♀ feminin

mbouanda
(apono)

Les boches avaient commencé à copier des masques, pour les revendre aux noirs

FERNAND GRÉBERT
The Albums of a Missionary in Gabon

The sea is a dirty blue as far as the eye can see. Porpoises are racing alongside the boat.' Dated 25 April 1913, this is the first entry in Pastor Fernand Grébert's album. Beside his comments he drew a few cross-hatched sketches of the Pauillac harbour pontoons and the shadow of the town disappearing on the horizon. Part of a mission led by the Paris Society of Evangelical Missionaries, Grébert had just left Bordeaux on the *Afrique* and was heading for the French Congo (now Gabon). His album (which he initially started doing in order to have 'some documents to show my family') consists of two volumes, and its three hundred and seven pages are filled with fifteen hundred drawings in India ink, ink wash, watercolour and colour pencil. On the flyleaf the carefully written title, *Afrique-Equitoriale française – Ogooué* [French Equatorial Africa – Ogooué], is framed on either side with Grébert's stylised initials. This is followed by an *in memoriam*, a dedication to his family, three dates and his signature. Grébert stayed in the Ogooué valley until 1931. While there, he devoted himself to this considerable illustrated work, which he finished in 1932 after returning to Europe.

In Fang territory

Grébert's long stay in Africa was interrupted by five return trips to Europe, often for health reasons. For a period of seven years, between 1917 and 1923, there were no additions to the album at all. At the bottom of page 182 is the word fin (the end), but on the next page, dated 1924, the author continues as if this hiatus had never occurred. Arriving on African soil, Grébert went to the Samkita mission and learnt Fang before travelling to the outpost on Talagouga, an island situated in the middle of the Ogooué river, which became the subject of a detailed map. Grébert's work was not confined to saving souls. Apart from giving the Sunday sermon and making various evangelical tours (unique opportunities for exploration and discovery of subject matter for his drawings), his days were filled with teaching, administration, animal husbandry, gardening and medical work. Most of the drawings in his well-preserved album were probably elaborated later from sketches that he made in situ. As a rule, several different subjects appear on the same page, and drawings are framed in an ink outline. This study, mostly

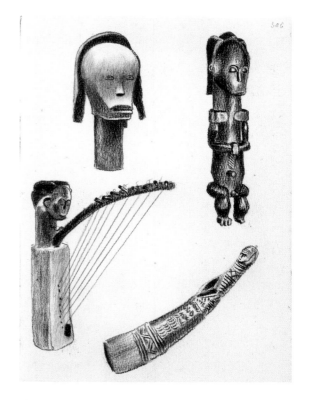

◁ **GALOA MASKS,** 1914–17
This ink and watercolour drawing is taken from Grébert's first volume. *Mbouanda* is the Galoa name for the *okuyi* (white mask) worn by the Bapounou dancers (here called Apono), who come from the south of Gabon. The words noted at the bottom of the page give an indication of when the drawing was made: 'The Boches had started to copy the masks and sell them back to the blacks.' (Boche is a pejorative term for the Germans that gained currency during the French-German War 1870-71.)
Musée Ethnographique de Genève

△ **FANG SCULPTURES AND MUSICAL INSTRUMENTS,** C. 1930
This black pencil drawing is one of the last in Grébert's second volume. In 1922 the Paris Society of Evangelical Missionaries published the work *Grébert au Gabon* (Grébert in the Gabon), illustrated with drawings taken from his album. In 1940 six copies of *La Monographie Ethnographique des Tribus Fang-Bantou de la Forêt du Gabon* (Ethnographic Monograph on the Fang-Bantou tribes in the Forest of Gabon) were published, typed and coloured by the author himself.
Musée Ethnographique de Genève

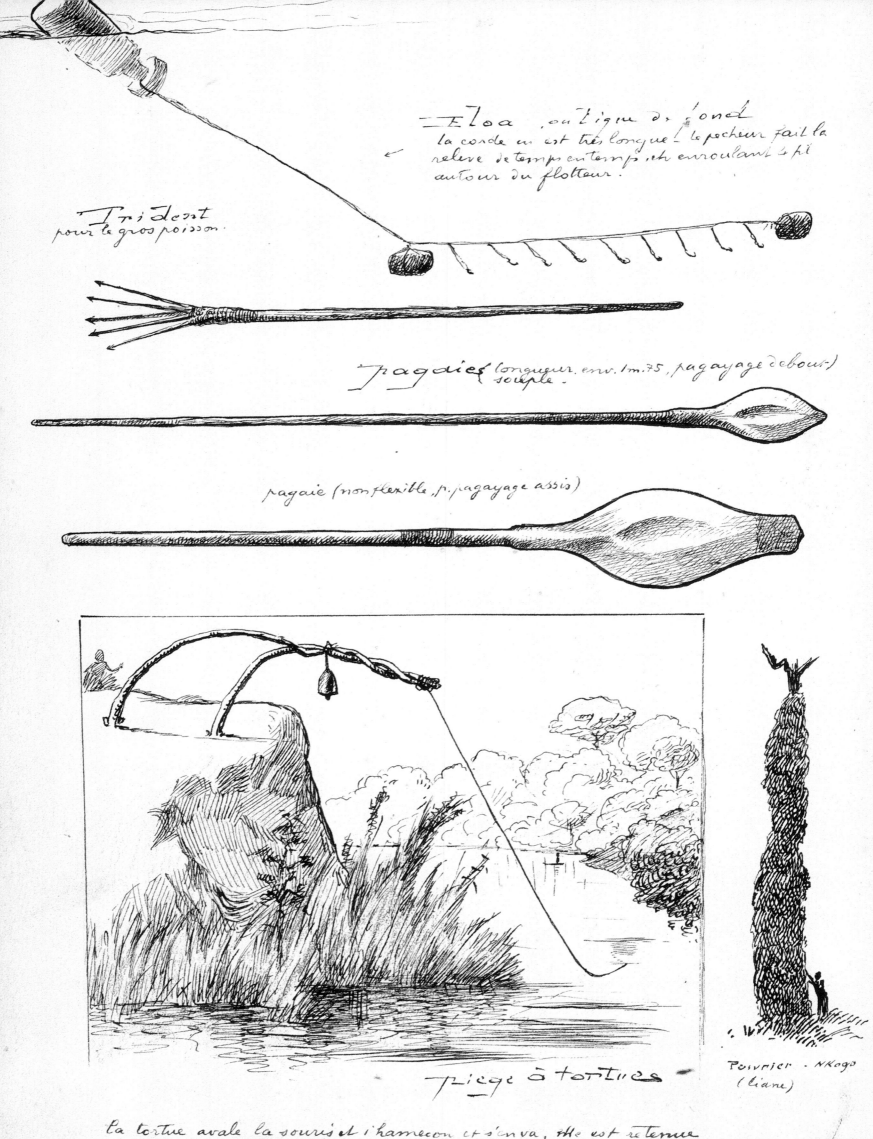

Eloa, ou ligne de fond
la corde en est très longue - le pêcheur fait la
relève de temps en temps en enroulant le fil
autour du flotteur.

Trident
pour le gros poisson.

pagaie (longueur. env. 1m.75, pagayage debout)
souple.

pagaie (non flexible, p. pagayage assis)

Piège à tortues

Poivrier - Nkogo
(liane)

la tortue avale la souris et l'hameçon et s'en va, elle est retenue
par la flexibilité des branches du piège. La clochette avertit le pêcheur

La pêche.
Plante pour la lèpre
Plante rouillée.

Lambaréné. Le 1ᵉʳ dispensaire du docᵗ Schweitzer.
Les malades sont d'une désobeissance desesperante, enlevent leurs panse

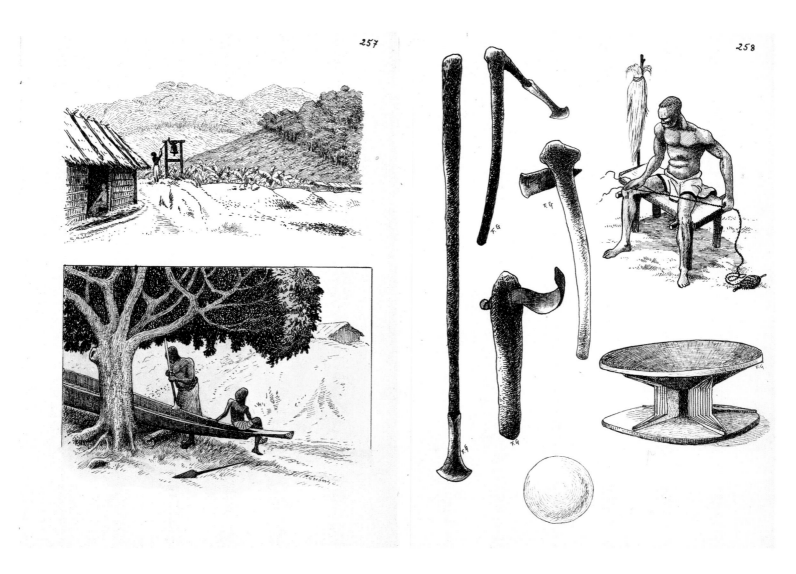

OVERLEAF: PAGES FROM
THE FIRST VOLUME, 1913–17
The right-hand page (ink and watercolour) shows a fishing village, a "plant for leprosy" and Dr Albert Schweitzer's first clinic at Lambaréné. Dr Schweitzer, the great German humanitarian, theologian and physician, welcomed Grébert to the region on his arrival in 1913. The left-hand page (ink and colour pencil) shows, from top to bottom, a ground line, a spear, two paddles, a turtle trap and a pepper plant, with a human figure at its base to reveal the scale of the plant.
Musée Ethnographique de Genève

△ PAGES TAKEN FROM
THE SECOND VOLUME, 1917–1931.
The church at Alembé (top left); a canoe being hollowed out under a mango tree in Alarmekōra (bottom left). The tools used in making the canoe are a Fang adze, a long-handled gouge, a curved plane and a hatchet. On the stool, made from a single piece of wood, a man is twining the threads to make string, a process Grébert describes in his notes.
Musée Ethnographique de Genève

▷ THE BANKS OF THE OGOOUÉ
(SHALLOW WATER), 1913–17
On this page of ink and watercolour illustrations taken from the first volume we read, 'The Pahouins have black skin, but not dark, some of them light-coloured. Walking sticks: 1 Galoan (yellow wood); 2, 6, 7, 8, 9 Pahouin; 3, 5 Galoan (ebony); 4 Eshira.'
Musée Ethnographique de Genève

ethnological in nature (covering food, hunting techniques, music, dance, religion, habitat), also deals with the flora, fauna and geography of the region.

During the course of his discoveries, Grébert used the album to construct a sort of pedagogical kaleidoscope. The detailed drawings and decorative arrangements give an element of subjectivity to what is primarily a work of objective illustrations. The table of contents says a lot about the author's desire to present an exhaustive account: '991 engravings with material on ten subjects representing 46 different types of document on the Fangs or Pahouins, a disappearing indigenous culture'. Grébert knew he was witnessing the end of an 'authentic' culture. We are, of course, only too aware of the devastating role played by missionaries in the destruction of traditional civilisations. The role of this artist/missionary/ethnologist was, then, paradoxical and ambiguous. Grébert's work as an illustrator and informer was infused with a desire to conserve a memory of a world that was disappearing, but his album is blind to its own indirect accommodation of that human tragedy. It now represents a first-class source of documentation as numerous objects from Gabonese civilisations of that time have long since disappeared.

'The man takes a stimulant that gives him the strength, agility and cruelty of a leopard, the skin of which he wears so that the animal can be blamed for the crime.'

Bords de l'Ogowé (eaux basses) les Pahouins ont la peau noire, mais peu foncée; quelques-uns sont claires.

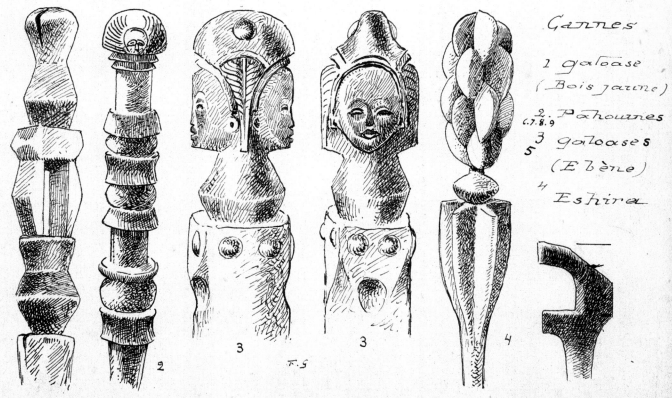

Cannes

1 gaīoase
(Bois jaune)

2. Pahouines
(6.7.8.9)

3 gaīoases
5 (Ebène)

4 Eshira

THÉODORE MONOD
Notebooks from the Sahara

A trained ichthyologist (fish expert) and an outstanding thinker and defender of human rights, Théodore Monod began to observe and write about the world at a very young age. At seven he was already absorbed in 'notebooks and paper'. In 1934 he began to keep notebooks on a regular basis. A methodology gradually developed around these 'collections of pickings', including technical sketches and diagrams, and stayed with him until the end of his life.

The inventory includes twenty modest-looking classroom notebooks, a hundred or so pages in each, filled with writing and drawings that record 20,000 subjects or objects examined. Each is labelled with a name and reference number, plus the place and date where they were observed. The books feature flora, fauna, geology, ethnology and the study of languages (particularly Tifinar Touareg), as well as prehistoric art and buildings.

Monod, who said, 'I am not ashamed to call myself a naturalist, even if it sounds a bit eighteenth century,' participated in an encyclopedic tradition in which both collection techniques and scientific expertise were vital. His notebooks were not created to be shown, but served as a personal aide-memoire, and were part of a whole assortment of scientific tools. Often of his own fabrication, these tools, used in the Sahara, included his 'pain in the arse' herbarium for the conservation of plants, his 'sausage dog' bag for the harvest of minerals, various containers for animals, and a 'camera lucida' with which 'you can draw what you see in detail, be it a cliff face, a rock or a panoramic view'.

Not long before his death Monod declared, 'My motto is "one continent for each incarnation". I've spent this life in Africa, where I allowed myself to try out many different things. At the beginning I was a zoologist, but while crossing the dunes I managed to pick up a bit of everything… The desert led me at times to become a botanist, a geologist, an ethnologist and an archaeologist.' The practice of assiduously keeping a journal was, no doubt, of considerable help.

△ **PORTRAIT OF THÉODORE MONOD IN THE MOUNTAINS OF TIBESTI, MAURITANIAN DESERT,** C. 1950
During his military service in Algeria, Monod became initiated in the camel driver's trade: 'What's more, I'm learning quickly – harnessing, encampments, riding – I'm getting the hang of it all, and I must because gone is the time when my dromedary would appear, already saddled, in front of my door. I have to do everything, learn a thousand little things, all the tricks of the trade, forget nothing. My camel and I now form a single unit, a microcosm that must get on by itself.'
Private collection

▷△ **SKETCH OF ETHNOLOGICAL FINDINGS,** C. 1950
The technical drawings that accompany the descriptive texts were included to keep a record of construction techniques and decorative symbols. In one of his books, *Tais-toi et marche* (Shut Up and Walk), which is presented in the form of a travel journal and tells the story of one of his journeys across Mauritania, Théodore Monod shares his spiritual and philosophical reflections. 'The desert,' he says, 'is one of those landscapes capable of posing certain questions within us.'
Private collection

▷▽ **PAGES FROM THÉODORE MONOD'S NOTEBOOKS,** C. 1950
The notebooks recorded those cultural traditions of which Théodore Monod was such a great defender. 'I would go further: these profound differences, which are to do with much more than just the colour of our epidermis and which separate me from that Asian or that black man, should, far from being publicly concealed as if they were in some way shameful, be proclaimed from the rooftops.'
Private collection

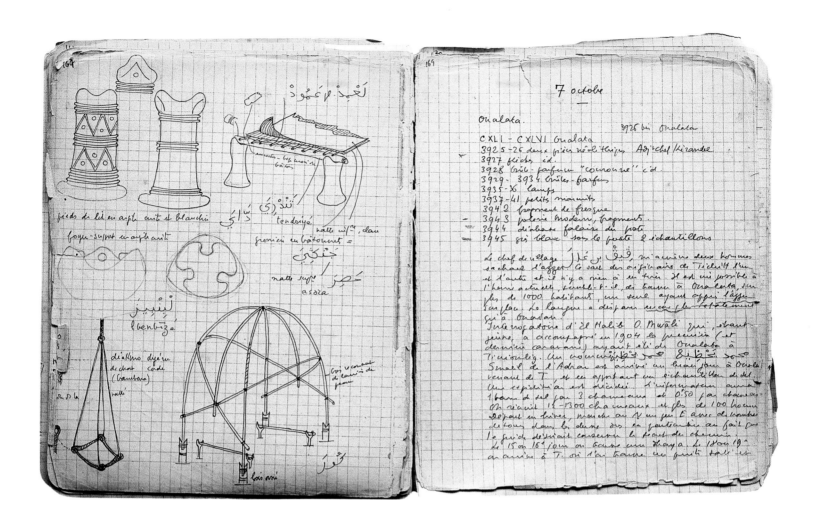

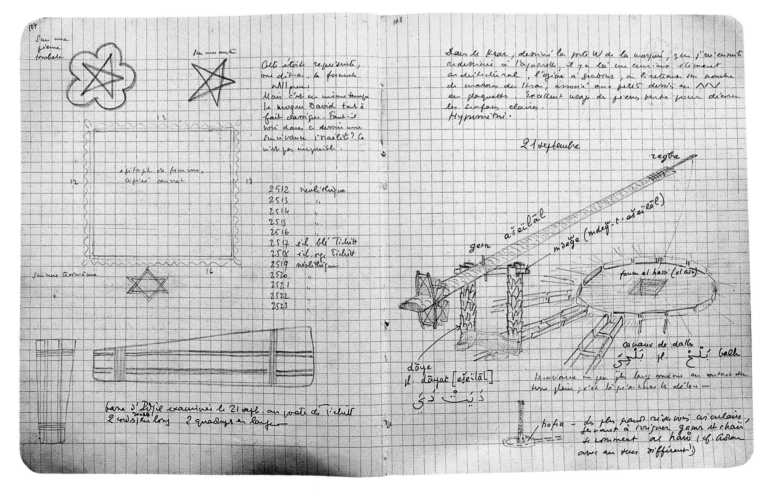

Kiffiak
(mei)
A.R.

JEAN MALAURIE
Journals of an Extinct Inuit Culture

On 17 April 1963 Jean Malaurie left on a ten-day trip across the pack-ice of the central Canadian Arctic. He was accompanied by a hunter, a Netsilingiut interpreter and a member of the Royal Canadian Mounted Police. Covering close to three hundred kilometres, the party travelled southwards from Gjoa Haven towards Back River, a totally isolated region. Once there Malaurie's mission was to conduct a survey for the Canadian government to evaluate the situation of twenty-seven Utkuhikhalingmiut Inuits (seven families) living under difficult conditions. His inventory of their resources and situation would determine the level of government assistance they might require, or the necessity of moving them closer to an outpost. Jean Malaurie greatly exceeded his remit, harvesting a considerable amount of information in a very short time. He took along several different pieces of recording equipment to help him in his work – a tape recorder, a camera and his indispensable green hardback notebooks, his constant travelling companions since his first polar expedition with Paul-Emile Victor in 1948.

Ethnological drawings and maps

Malaurie used two identical notebooks for the fieldwork. In one, a logbook, he described all the events that took place each day. The other, more ethnological, was for personal notes and drawings, some of which were contributed by the subjects of his study. With their help he made an analysis of important historical events. Tattoos, clothing, objects and techniques relating to hunting and fishing were the main topics. On the first evening of the visit he drew a plan of his igloo, showing the space allotted to men, belongings and dogs. Kiggiark, one of his hosts, drew a cross-section of the interior of another igloo, showing the hole that was dug through the ice for fishing in the river.

Many drawings were executed by the Inuit themselves, and the notebook became a medium for spontaneous communication, passing from hand to hand. The maps Malaurie asked them to draw, and their year-round itineraries and activities, provided precious information on the organisation of hunts. Drawings, such as those showing the build-up of different layers of snow under the pack-ice, allowed him to study the nature of the relief. Geography

◁△ **A WOMAN'S WINTER COAT MADE FROM CARIBOU HIDE,** 1963
This blue pencil drawing from the ethnological notebook was done at Black River by Kiggiark, one of the subjects of Jean Malaurie's report. At bottom left is a sketch of an apron, part of the costume that protects the crotch. There are indications as to colour in the drawing on the right. The large hood is designed to accommodate a young child, who can thus benefit from the mother's body heat. Men's clothing, as can be seen in other sketches in the notebook, is of a different design altogether.
Author's collection

◁▽ **MARRIAGE TATTOO (LEFT); TATTOED BODY (RIGHT),** 1963
Malaurie shared an igloo with Inoukshook, who drew the design of a tattoo applied in soot to his mother's body before her marriage. The other drawing, in graphite and colour pencil, shows a body tattooed in the 1910s by the mother of one of the Utkuhikhalingmiut.
Author's collection

△ **NOME, ALASKA, OCTOBER 1997**
Early one morning, on the shores of the Bering Sea, Jean Malaurie began this pastel drawing of the spectacular colours at dawn. He described them as 'Brahmsian', by which he meant romantic and uplifting.
Author's collection

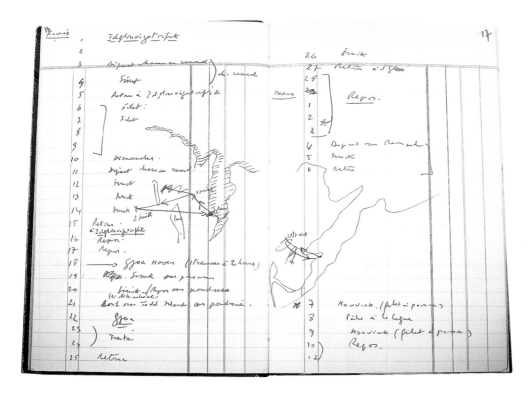

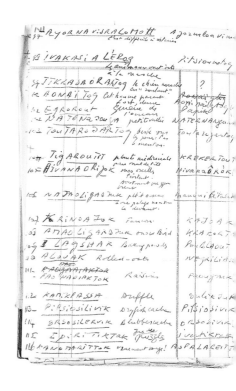

△ **GEOGRAPHICAL SKETCHES,** APRIL 1963
These rapidly drawn sketches by Malaurie include a chronology of activities for each head of family – hunting, fishing, rest in the family igloo – for every day of the year, locality included.
Author's collection

△▷ **LIST OF COMMON ABORIGINAL WORDS AND EXPRESSIONS,** MAY 1963
Jean Malaurie compiled a small dictionary in preparation for a return mission planned for the winter of 1963–4. While reading Knud Rasmussen's report line by line to his Inuit companions, Malaurie carefully noted their comments.
Author's collection

△▷▷ **CROSS-SECTION OF AN IGLOO,** APRIL 1963
This red pencil drawing was done by Kiggiark, one of Malaurie's companions, and alongside is a description of

the sheltered fishing system employed during the winter months. A person near the entryway shows the scale of the igloo. Malaurie remarks that during his stay there was no lack of food, but that the area was prone to sudden shortages, which could lead to disaster.
Author's collection

▷ **POLAR LANDSCAPE,** C. 1990
Malaurie began a series of polar landscapes in pastel on glossy paper at the beginning of the 1990s. Thinking he must be on a solitary 'shamanic' quest, the Inuit who saw him at work asked him to show them what he was doing. That a white man might appreciate the beauty of their land filled them with pride. Since then, Malaurie has been painting this world of ice from memory 'in complex moiré colours'.
Author's collection

determined the living conditions and cultural practices of this people, but nature gave the orders. Malaurie indicated the name, age and position in the sleeping hierarchy of each contributor.

River of no return

It was in cooperation with the subjects of his study that the chapter 'Inuit Spartans' appeared in Malaurie's book *Hummocks*. A surprising collection of photos, *L'Appel du Nord* (The Call of the North) was elaborated using a similar methodology. Malaurie's personal and scientific work thus became part of the history of Arctic discovery, and a corollary to Knud Rasmussen's excellent account of a previous six-day encounter in the same region. (Rasmussen's study had been a constant source of reference for Malaurie while in the field.)

The survey of the Utkuhikhalingmiut signalled a spiritual and intellectual break in Malaurie's life. During this time he was confronted with the metaphysical tension, anxiety and great moral destitution of a people recently converted to Christianity, who blamed the disappearance of animals to hunt on their conversion. Blessed are the poor! Malaurie witnessed abject poverty, and heard one Akritoq endlessly muttering evangelical language, as if to conjure up a reversal of his fate and persuade himself of the power of the words he was repeating. From this time onwards Malaurie was convinced of how much true man, 'hypersensitive' and 'inextricably linked to nature', depends on his interaction with this other reality, the spiritual world. To his great regret, Malaurie was not able to make a return visit to these people, which preyed on his mind. 'Never do I feel as much nostalgia as when I re-read those logbooks, the pages yellowed and greasy with fish oil. One by one I look at the drawings done by the Utkuhikhalingmiut…the itineraries…maps, clothes and other objects, tattoos, evil and ancestral spirits… That people was unique.'

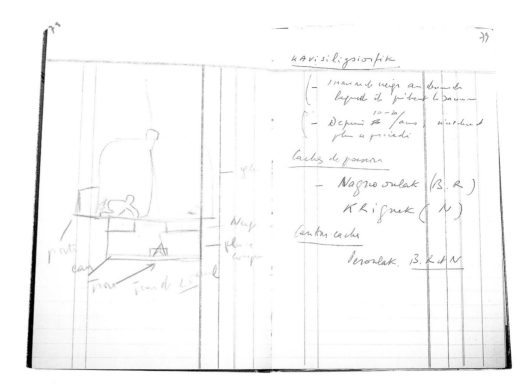

'I gave him my notebook and charged him with detailing information on each of the igloos, identifying its occupants and the place of each inhabitant in the village... I will ask the women to draw the male and female costumes.'

Extract from Hummocks, Jean Malaurie

IN SERTING MY COCK DEEP UP
... I WATCH HER ██ COME. HE
RASPING AND SHORT HER LIPS
HE PINK TIP OF HER TONGUE
MADE LOVE IN BED. THEM
LAY DOWN ON A BED SHE
SHE WOULD FALL INSTANTLY
WHICH IS EXACTLY WHAT HAP
T. SHE UNPLUGGED HER SE
HE NATRAJ LIKE DANCE OF
DESTRUCTION SHE HELD ME
THE HOT WHITE BED ON HE
RED, UNWASHED, SMELLING
G ME THE TOTAL SEX HOURI
E. AND THAT IS HOW SHE
TWELVE HOURS. I REMEM
HING HER FOR A LONG TIME
E WOULD WAKE UP AND FUCK
HINDU GOD IN THE MIDDLE OF
AGAIN

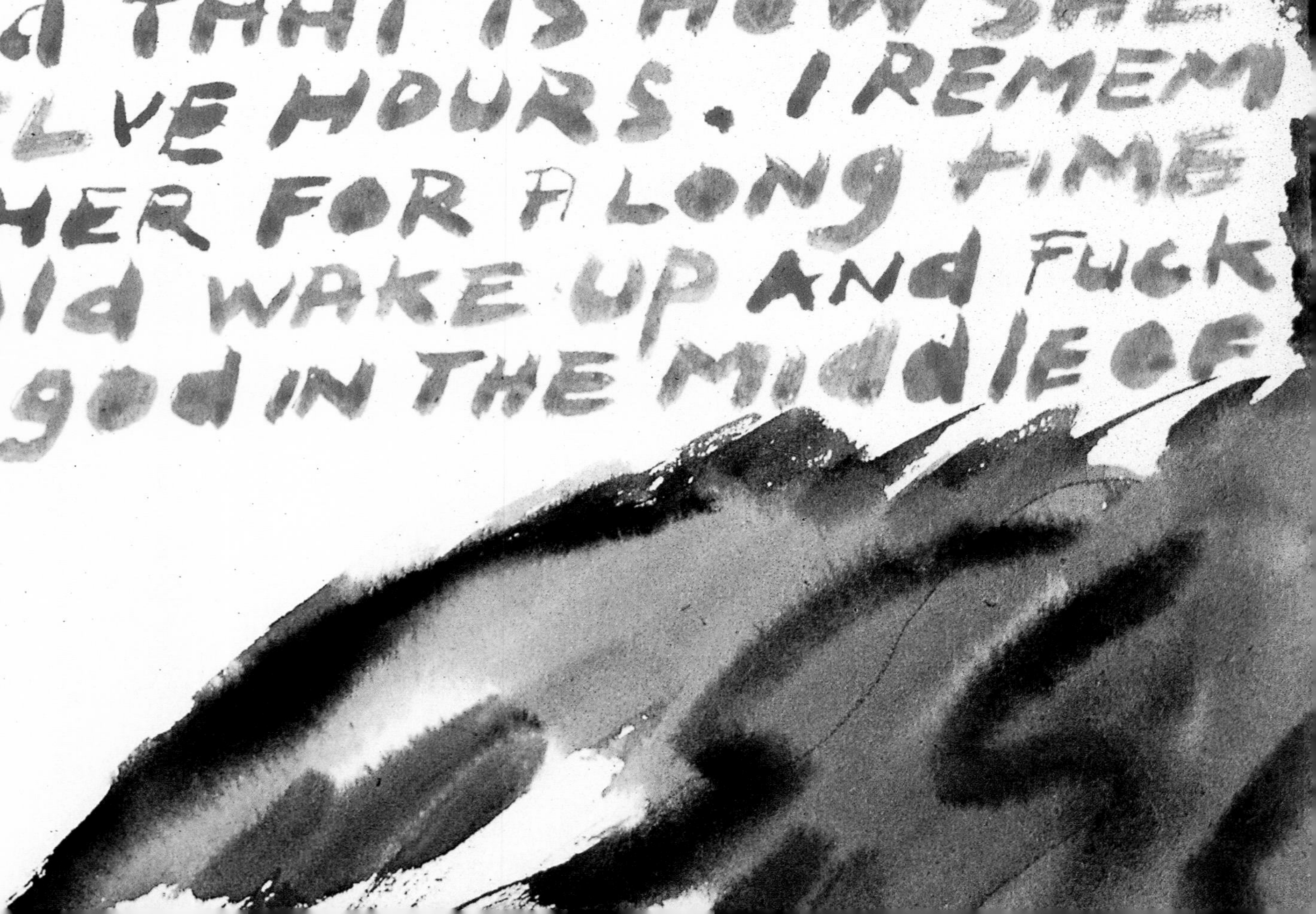

CONTEMPORARY DIARIES

como se llama: *dice:* a-ne-kuh-mina anksuhmeta

2·24. (cont.) will go this afternoon to the jungle for some
pen drawings. Sunset: 6:10. while I draw, here in Andrés open
lodge, childa play—

Yhyanner Territori
Venezuela.

fott 2·24·68

SAM SCOTT
Amazonian Notebooks

It has taken the American painter Sam Scott thirty-five years to reveal the existence of his wonderful notebooks that date from the time of his expedition to Amazonian Indian territory at the end of the 1960s. Scott, sensitive and protective about one of the most important experiences of his life, had no desire until now to show his record of this intensely lived journey to the public.

In search of the 'people of wood and water'

In September 1967, already pursuing a career as an artist, the twenty-seven-year-old Sam Scott agreed to accept the post of illustrator on a scientific expedition to the Amazon. Financed by the US Atomic Energy Agency, the expedition's objective was to analyse possible biological and radioactive contamination (which turned out to be very real) caused by nuclear testing in the atmosphere. It was thought that cameras might frighten local tribe members, so an illustrator was therefore chosen to accompany the trip.

The expedition travelled to the Venezuelan village of Makiritari near the river Caura, a tributary of the enormous Orinoco. Near by they encountered a group of small tribes, known as the Yecuana – 'the people of wood and water'. The territory of these hunting tribes bordered that of the better-known Yanomani people in Brazil. The discovery of the Yecuana affected Sam Scott to such an extent that he decided to stay with them for several months once the expedition's work was over. He felt impelled to stay, feeling intuitively that this people, hidden in the jungle, could teach him something about himself and the world. The other members of the expedition left, having arranged to rendezvous with him three months later, in April. Thus Scott found himself alone among the Indians, far from modern civilisation. He had to learn everything from scratch in order to survive.

A jungle apprenticeship

The first problem Scott encountered was his status within the clan. As he was unable to survive or find his way in the jungle alone, the Yecuana decided, with his agreement, to consider him a man-child. This meant

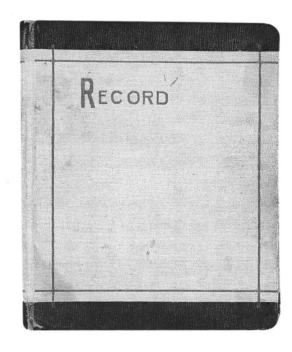

△ **SAM SCOTT'S JOURNAL**, 1968
This hardback notebook and a smaller one with a black cover have been preserved, but other paintings and drawings that Scott completed while in the Amazonian forest were lost when his canoe capsized in the rapids while on a hunting party.
Artist's collection

◁ **THE RIVER AND FOREST IN SONG**, 1968
This drawing was completed on the morning of 24 February 1968, near a river not far from the Indian village of Santa Maria de Erabato, where Sam Scott lived.
He often used to make his way along this stretch of water to observe all kinds of birds, fish, giant water spiders and iridescent butterflies along the mud-covered banks.
This moment of silence and harmony with nature is very much like the peaceful image we have of the first days after the Creation.
Artist's collection

PRECEDING PAGES: MAX PAM IN SOUTHERN INDIA, 2003
This nude in watercolour and pencil was inspired by a dream the artist had during his stay in southern India.
Artist's collection

Redro Antonio, of the
Alto Ventuari.
3·68

that he was not in competition with the men of the village, but a difficult apprenticeship was about to begin. He slept with those not yet married in a collective hut made out of logs and covered with a thatch of banana leaves. This spacious building was guarded by a large boa constrictor that lived on the roof and ate insects and vermin. Scott tried to get beyond the language barrier by using his Spanish to communicate with the two brothers who became his guides on numerous hunting expeditions. He developed a real closeness with these two men, and drew them in his notebooks. These portraits show dignified faces and a dark, direct look in the eyes. Little by little he learnt their language, which originates, he tells us, in the Caribbean. A rough outline of its vocabulary can be found in his notebooks.

Scott had begun filling two notebooks while with the expedition party. Now these notebooks took on an important role in his adaptation to this new environment, serving as an outlet for his thoughts and feelings in the midst of complex and sometimes difficult relationships. They also helped him with the feeling of isolation that dogged him, especially in the cold rainy season when movement was severely limited. He was not predisposed to 'hibernate' like the Yecuana, who occupied their time sleeping in hammocks heated by burning embers. Instead, he spent his time sketching the Indians' way of life. On one occasion, unobserved, he did a drawing of the women surrounded by utensils and occupied with the preparation of a meal.

In spite of the difficult living conditions, he did get used to it, wearing the couco, the traditional loincloth for men, round his waist and learning to walk barefoot in an environment where piranhas and vipers competed with poisonous ants and killer bees. During his three months with the Yecuana, Scott fell ill on several occasions, and doctors were later astonished that he had been able to survive.

Sam Scott, 'White Stork'

Little by little, the young artist forgot about clocks and the other constraints of modern civilisation, and learnt how to live in the forest. He observed what was going on around him, went fishing and hunting, ate and smoked with the hunters during tribal assemblies, and developed deep ties with those he described as 'gentle giants who live in perfect harmony with the universe'. After a time he was initiated into the world of men, the world of the White Cloud. This was a great honour, a sign that the warriors had confidence in him and held him in esteem. Surrounded by spectacular rainforest scenery, he received his spiritual name – 'White

▷△ **WEAPONS USED FOR HUNTING,** 1968
Scott's personal impressions and accounts of excursions are punctuated by ink sketches of tools and weapons.
Artist's collection

▷▽ **MAKING CASSAVA BREAD FROM MANIOC ROOTS,** 1968
The manioc root is about the size of a yam, fatally poisonous if eaten raw and gives off a horrible odour of bitter almonds.
The milky white poison is

extracted with the help of a press, and the wet root is then chopped up and dried in the sun. Once hard, it becomes edible and nutritious.
The Yecuana use it to make a flat bread, which they bake in large dishes in the oven. They also prepare it using a fermentation technique. This makes a sustaining food that can keep the hunters going all day.
Artist's collection

'I spent entire days just sitting on a rock in the middle of the
river watching nature in activity around me.'

1.31 Went through the motions at Ministry of Justice, then out to the airport with Louis. Incredible excitement with Boris as we took off, over brown mountain, the plains, finally over the Orinoco. then from sun to mist and rain flying through clouds, low cover, and then, the jungle. Limitless, infinite. A chrome green. mists and columns of smoke rising from the trees. Touching down finally — 6 hrs. and app. 800 kilometers later. I am now 600 miles into the central jungle. Sta. Maria was hot and sunny — able to wear shorts and tennis shoes. Very little discomfort, really, except for the chiggers. A clearing & houses. about 120 people. The brothers are very nice. The expedition is leaving Saturday, and I am going with them to Cuchimé, about 150 miles by river.

2.1 Went up the river to a Shoshoni village. More dirt, sickness. Very upset when the expedition shot an egret, but Hermano will eat it. The Mahrutari are incredibly strong — Simón is as strong as three men — José as well! The doctors are over here since the Mahr got shotguns. Don't they still wrestle (to test their strength.) Incorrect (6 rifles) (1 spying) no wives.

survival kit.

2.15 On the river for 12 days with the Mackintan. As I write this I am sitting in the great house, at a little distance from the other men. Both feet swollen and hurt like hell with jim rot, and the malaria tablets have knocked me down too! I am happy — The river was an incredible adventure. we left about noon in large canoes, loaded down with blood samples, gasoline, cooking gear, personal belongings, shotguns, small puppys, bananas. sweltering hea

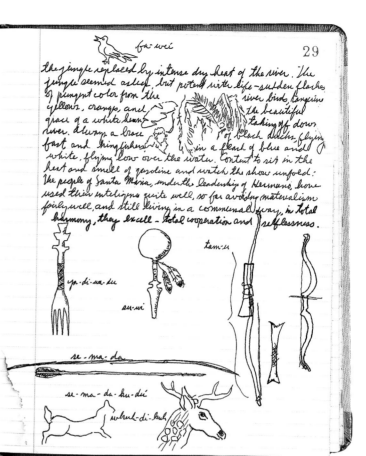

the jungle replaced by intense dry heat of the river. The jungle seemed asleep, but potent with life — sudden flashes of pungent color from the river birds, tangerine yellows, oranges, and the beautiful grace of a white heron, taking off down river. Always a breve fast and kingfishers of black ducks flying, in a flash of blue and white, flying low over the water. Content to sit in the heat and smell of gasoline and watch the show unfold: The people of Santa Maria, under the leadership of Hermano, have used their intelligence quite well, so far avoiding materialism fairly well and still living in a communal way, in total harmony, they excel — total cooperation and selflessness.

ya-di-wa-du

au-wi

tam-u

se-ma-da

se-ma-da-ku-di

wheh-di-kuh

Read: Koch-Grünberg (1923: 3, pp.250-355 and Civrieux. 85

3.1
2:30 Culture of the Mahnitari (con'd)

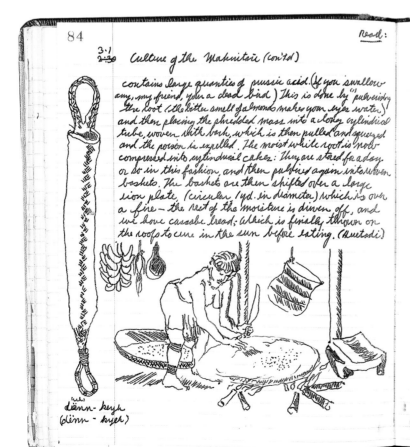

contains large quantities of prussic acid. (If you swallow any, my friend, you a dead bird.) This is done by "pulverizing the root (the bitter smell of almonds makes your eyes water) and then placing the shredded mass into a long, cylindrical tube, woven with bark, which is then pulled and squeezed and the poison is expelled. The moist white root is now compressed into cylindrical cakes: they are stored for a day or so in this fashion, and then pulping again into woven baskets. The baskets are then shifted over a large iron plate, (circular 1 yd. in diameter) which is over a fire — the rest of the moisture is driven off, and we have cassabe bread; which is finally thrown on the roofs to cure in the sun before eating. (huetodi)

dienn-keyh
(dienn-keyh)

in the "winter" when the rain prohibits hunting and fishing the diet is exclusively cassabe, with peppers, and smoked meat.

Monyoco is a more refined form of yuca. Because of its durability it is used on trips as the principal staple. It has a nutty taste, and is served with water. In fact, the greater volume of their food is served in water, and the Yecuana men all drink (eat) in exaggerated quantities, usually 1 or 2 litres per man per meal. Cassabe in water (yucuta) bananas (guaduda) in water (properly plantains,) in water. The meat is principally fish, venado, danta, or birds, such as wild turkey (cadacadi) (pauji), pavo or paya, and with some hunters, monkeys (shiri) or babas (yadija) In the rainy season, when game is difficult to obtain, the diet may change to the large frogs which are important in their mythology (recine, wa-wsh) or the giant worms that live in the clay of the banks of the river. When these are lacking, cassabe and ají (womi) form the diet.

The people of the Yecuana are proud and yet friendly, very strong and yet very gentle. They are laughing most of the time. the men smoking and talking in the great house; lounging around fires, or lying in hammocks. They believe themselves to be the best river-men in the world, and probably they are. (They traverse with poles, against the current, rapids that would be unthinkable anywhere else in the world) They construct canoes with admirable precision, canoes up to fifteen meters in length from one tree trunk — they are the SOTO, "The men."

Stork' – and his personal paddle. Here was proof that he had become integrated into Yecuana society.

As arranged, the members of the expedition come looking for him at the end of April. His return to the United States proved difficult and he suffered from culture shock. He had lost the habit of sleeping on a mattress and continued to spend nights on the ground. He could no longer stand modern civilisation and its plethora of activities, which he judged sterile and too noisy. He stayed shut up in his apartment. The journey into the jungle had marked him for ever.

Looking back

Sam Scott's notebooks stayed at the bottom of his trunk for a long time, and it is only recently that he agreed to show them to a few friends. The first notebook consists mainly of his own drawings and writings, with just a few sketches done by Yecuana warriors. The second book contains only drawings done by the Indians. These artists, holding a pencil for the first time, produced images that resemble neolithic cave-paintings. They show hunting excursions and various animals, such as the jaguar, anaconda and giant alligator. The notebooks thus bring together two artistic aesthetics separated by thousands of years. Indeed, on one page there is 'a drawing of a man looking at the sun, which is as old as mankind itself'.

Sam Scott's initiation into life with the Amazonian Indians was a spiritual experience that convinced him of the existence of a life force pre-dating biblical creation stories. It gave him a deep sense of forces that 'exist beyond the material world' and profoundly marked his life and art. Since then, both have become dedicated to the Creator who gave him awareness. His Amazonian notebooks are stunning evidence of this.

△ **A HUNTER AND THE SPIRITS THAT PROTECT HIM, DRAWN BY A MAKIRITARI WARRIOR,** 1968
The earrings this hunter is wearing are a mark of his status in the tribe. Carrying a bow and arrow, he is symbolically accompanied by the spirit of his animal protector, a large blue heron, which represents the river and all the two-legged animals that inhabit this region. Below the heron, whose beak is open, as if to cry out in warning, is a black panther. The panther evokes the forest, the night and all the four-legged creatures of the jungle.
Artist's collection

▷ **SELF-PORTRAIT IN A CLEARING, AMAZONIAN JUNGLE, VENEZUELA,** 1968
Sam Scott put his Western clothing back on for this self-portrait, made at a key moment in his Amazonian experience. He was beginning to feel overwhelmed by his jungle experience and needed to reassert his own identity.
Artist's collection

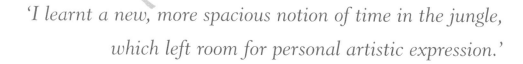

'I learnt a new, more spacious notion of time in the jungle,
which left room for personal artistic expression.'

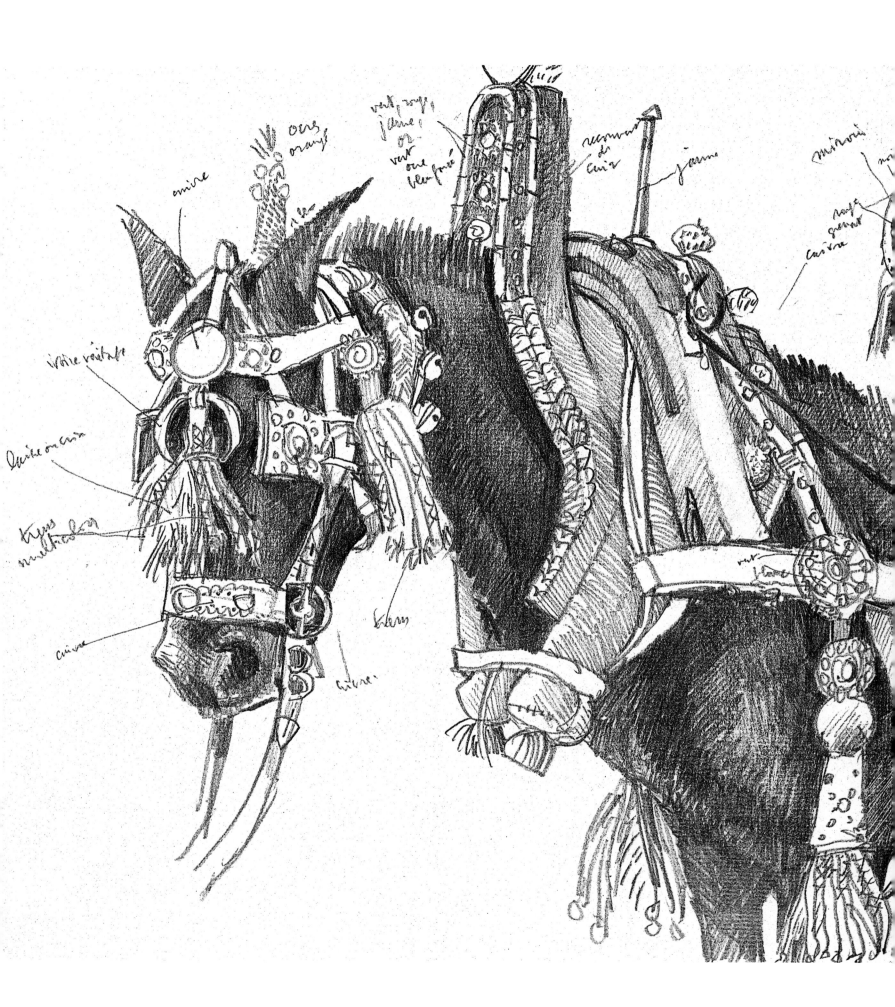

YVON LE CORRE
Journey to Portugal

More than four hundred pages thick, Yvon Le Corre's Portuguese travel diaries illustrate a year-long voyage full of joy and surprises, plus a number of difficulties. Along with his wife Azou and their three-year-old son Yun, the painter-navigator left the Breton port of Tréguier on 4 May 1988 in a sailing boat without auxiliary motor and set a course for the Portuguese coast. Le Corre's diary, in which he intended to capture images of Portugal's maritime heritage, vast natural landscapes and popular traditions, began with a series of water-colours of the Brittany coast.

At the mercy of the wind

The boat the family travelled in, the *Eliboubane*, was a replica of a nine-teenth- century fishing boat on which the sails were lowered at night to make a roof for the cabin. The family spent the first week of the voyage at the Ile de Sein and on the Glénan Islands, where Le Corre did some watercolours of the coastline. Crossing the Bay of Biscay in five days, the boat sailed past La Coruña, then headed due south past Vigo, Porto and Aveiro, finally docking at Torreira. They now decided to cross Portugal by foot in search of its threatened rural heritage.

Le Corre's diary traces this long journey step by step. The family set off on 9 September in temperatures of 40°C, covering about fifteen kilometres a day. Along the way they stopped in villages, stocked up on food in orchards or country shops, and washed in rivers or fountains. When winter came, they rented rooms or found refuge in haphazard shelters. During this time Le Corre earned a bit of money by accepting several artistic commissions, which included painting a restaurant sign and restoring religious and secular images on *moliceiros* (riverboats with a semi-circular prow). To a large degree the journey was dependent on chance, and Le Corre adopted a similar approach to the subject matter for his drawings. 'The pleasure of sketching,' he wrote, 'is in taking the time that is yours and not letting anyone steal it from you.'

He drew regional peculiarities to the quiet rhythm of the family's stride, his drawings taking shape in the diary and gradually filling its pages. Perhaps

◁ **HORSE AT SANTIAGO DO CACÉM,** DECEMBER 1988
Notes on this pencil drawing served to remind Le Corre of the colours (yellow, dark blue…) and materials (brass, leather…) of his subject. Faithful to his principle of completing his drawings while on the spot, he left it as it was. Its incompleteness is part of the aesthetic and nature of the sketchbook.
Artist's collection

△ **A GALICIAN *DORNA* NEAR AROSA,** 1988
Le Corre is a sailor as much as he is an artist. In his magnificent book *Les Outils de la Passion* (Tools of the Trade), 2001, he talks about another passion – boat building. Here again he is inspired by traditional skills and know-how. The *dorna* he draws here with such precision is shown in profile in pencil at the top of the page to give a better sense of its proportions.
Artist's collection

inevitably, it includes a lot of unusual subject matter, such as a stone cross surmounted by a revolutionary star, and a tyre cut in the form of a bird ready to take flight. Le Corre often drew standing up, which required him to be something of a juggler – 'one hand for the paper, the other for the brush, one more for the colours and another for the water'! His watercolours began with just a few pencil lines, and on rare occasions he enhanced them with a dash of gouache. He also used blue and red pencils in homage to the painter and diarist Mathurin Méheut (1882-1958).

Sketching 'on the hoof', he often had to work fast to get down colours prone to being swept away by clouds or to capture objects that might move from one moment to the next. What if the owner of a boat should push it out into the waves before he'd finished? Sometimes, on spotting something he wanted to paint, he would throw his bags to the ground, 'the teeming box of watercolours squirming all over the place like maggots', and an urgency would take hold of him, forcing him to forget practical considerations while he painted whatever it was that had inspired the stop.

'The pleasure of sketching is in taking the time which is yours
and not letting anyone steal it from you.'

'What a thankless task this painting business is!' he commented, perhaps alluding to the pain in one eye that constantly forced him to stop work after only a short period of concentration. This affliction served to increase his hurry, as he had vowed never to continue his sketches and watercolours after he had left his subjects. Sometimes these subjects were cooperative, such as the horseman who waited for Le Corre to note the colours of his mount's head on his drawing. On other occasions, however, bad weather would force him to

◁ **ON THE WAY UP THE WESTERN COAST,**
DECEMBER 1988
The comments in pencil and pen – how things worked, personal impressions, puns – are part and parcel of the drawing. Le Corre even asked passers-by to give him the Portuguese names for the things he was drawing.
Artist's collection

▽ **THE MILL, SERRA DA ESTRELA,**
SEPTEMBER 1988
Le Corre's sketchbook was in fact made up of two books of two hundred and forty-five pages each (forty-five pages are missing from the second). On returning from his trip, the artist bound them both into one hinged volume with a white buffalo leather cover. The Italian format (24 x 60 cm) was ideal for the production of panoramic views and rich compositions, although the thick paper was not originally designed for drawings and watercolours.
Artist's collection

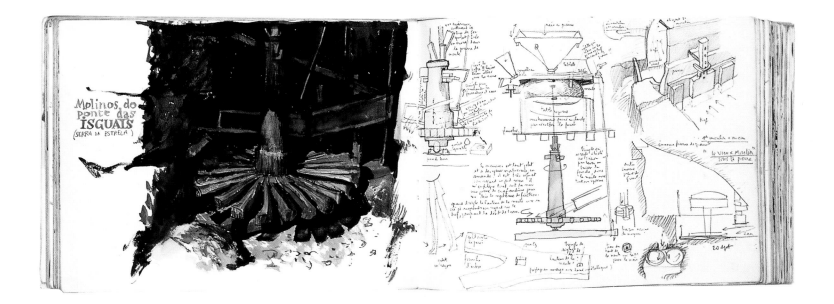

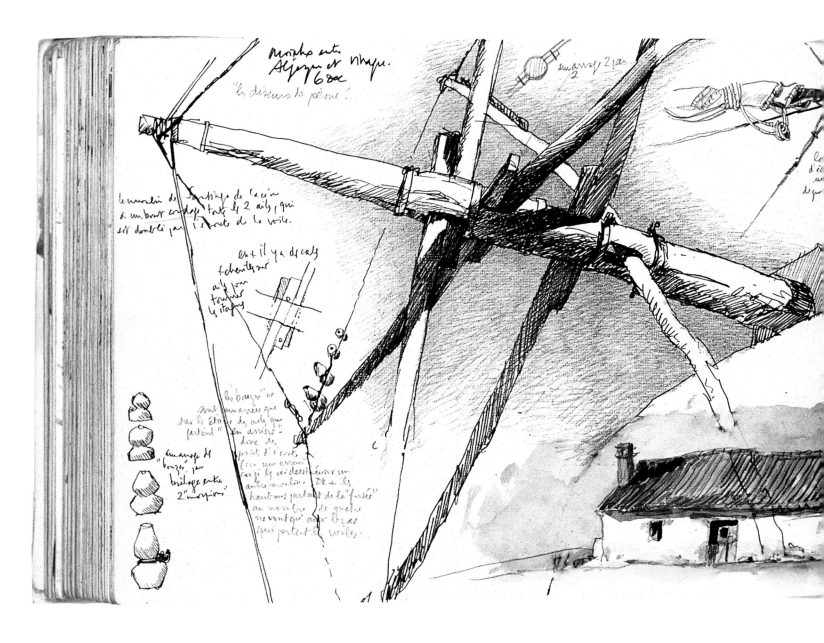

△ **ABANDONED FARMS AND WINDMILLS IN ALENTEJO,** NOVEMBER 1988
Following the failure of agricultural reform in Portugal, many farm buildings fell into ruins. There are several illustrations of windmills in Le Corre's sketchbook. His interest for their workings was linked to his passion for sailing boats – both are made of wood and have sails to capture the force of the wind.
Artist's collection

stop what he was doing before he had finished, the raindrops creating pretty, iridescent haloes on the incomplete page of the hastily closed sketchbook.

Mixed encounters

The sketchbook was a pretext for conversation and a way of getting to know people. Children were always the first to come and see what Le Corre was doing, and old people were often touched by the fact that he was interested in their traditions and were pleased to chat with him. In the Serra da Estrela he spent three days talking with a miller about how his mill worked. Elsewhere, a shepherd gave the family fresh eggs and ham. On another occasion, some shepherds gave the family their house to sleep in while they themselves slept in the stable.

When they crossed the Algarve, however, they were treated with the contempt that the locals have long had for gypsies. The sketchbook now became proof that Le Corre was involved in an artistic enterprise, allowing the family to escape being automatically categorised as thieves and vagabonds. On one occasion it even saved Le Corre from prosecution. Having refused a man's

request to do his portrait because he didn't have the sketchbook with him, he soon found himself battered and bruised and spending the night in a police cell. At the trial a few days later it was the sketchbook brought along by his wife that proved Le Corre was not a criminal.

On reaching Cape St Vincent, the Le Corres didn't get to see the African coast because the weather was too bad. Never mind – they had proved they were 'true people of the road'. They continued walking as far as Lisbon. From there Azou and Yun went back to France, while Yvon tackled a final three-month stage to complete a unique panorama of the northern part of the country. A series of ink drawings and watercolours executed in the sombre and stormy surroundings of granite mountains and villages brings his Portuguese sketchbook to a close. It is a work of unusual sincerity, talent, sensitivity and humour.

'One hand for the paper, the other for the brush, one more for the colours and another for the water!'

Canal Beagle.

TERRITOIRE INDIEN YÁNANA

CANAL BEAGLE

CAP HORN
←

TITOUAN LAMAZOU
Travel Diaries from Cape Horn

Undertaken at the end of 2000, just as the boats competing in the Vendée-Globe race were rounding Cape Horn, this voyage was not a first for Titouan Lamazou. He had already been in sight of Chile's southernmost point on three separate occasions, but always from the deck of a racing yacht. He had never had time to sketch or land on that part of South America known as Tierra del Fuego. With his feet now planted firmly on that ground, he recounted some of the region's early history in his journal: 'Magellan was simply looking for the existence of a passage linking the Atlantic to the Pacific when, in 1520, he became the first to enter the straits that subsequently took his name. From his ship he observed numerous columns of smoke reaching into the sky – signals from one Indian tribe to another warning of the arrival of intruders. Magellan named the country Tierra de Humo (Land of Smoke), but Charles Quint decided that there was no smoke without fire, so it became known as Tierra del Fuego (Land of Fire).

'Theatre of tragedy'

Lamazou travelled to Chile to meet up with an old sailing friend, Yvon Fauconnier. At Puerto Williams, the southernmost town in Chile, they boarded the *Darwin Sound*, a twenty-two-metre ketch, then sailed down the Beagle Channel. In his diary Lamazou wrote, 'How wonderful to have good friends at the helms of beautiful boats in all the ports of the oceans of the world!'

They soon reached the Wollaston Islands, at the southernmost tip of which is Cape Horn, 'right at the end of the end of the world'. Here Lamazou saluted the memory of the men whose lives and fortunes were lost in these seas. On a maritime map in his diary he drew six rows of red ships that came to grief, depicting their hulls half-visible above the waves and their names inscribed below. Above this sobering inventory is a painting in gouache of the minuscule Horn Island Chapel, its steeply sloping roof of corrugated iron and its badly trimmed doorframe indicating its

◁ **WRECK OF A BOAT OFF CAPE HORN**, 2000
The artist has made an ink drawing of a young Indian on this photograph.
Artist's collection

△ **PORTRAIT OF URSULA CALDÉRON**, 2000
In his diary Lamazou recalls the barbarous acts perpetrated by Europeans against the inhabitants of Tierra del Fuego.

Many Patagonian tribes, including the Tehuelches, Ona, Hauch and Yamana, were all exterminated. Using photography and painted portraits, he salutes the grandeur of these extinct people and their culture. In this gouache he pays homage to the last Yaghan Indian woman, whom he met at Puerto Williams.
Artist's collection

Brillante idée d'avoir importé le Castor du Canada... Il es
trié d'inolieu et ne menace pas encore la couche d'oz...

CABO DE HORNOS

ITE MONTES

OCÉAN PACIFIQUE SUD → → → OCEAN ATL

Sens du Vendée Globe

**PHOTOGRAPH OF CAPE HORN WITH
HAND-DRAWN MAP (TOP LEFT); GOUACHE
OF CAPE HORN (BOTTOM LEFT); JOSÉ CATRIN
AT PUERTO TORO (BELOW),** 2000

The photograph of Cape Horn,
on which Lamazou has drawn a
map in ink, was taken in a lull
between two waves. On the
right it looks as if a cyclone has
passed this way, but in fact the
trees strewn on the ground and
the intertwined branches were
the work of 'very active' beavers.
On the gouache of Cape Horn
an arrow indicates the direction
of the Vendée-Globe race.
'During his voyage round the
world, Yvon Fauconnier makes
a stop at Cape Horn and takes
me with him into the canals
of Patagonia,' comments
Lamazou on the photo he took
of his friend at the helm.
 The drawing is of José Catrin,
an old-style fisherman from
Puerto Toro, the southernmost
village in the world.
Artist's collection

*très actif. Sans rien exagérer non plus : le Castor n'a jamais
Petite vallée derrière la marina de Puerto Williams - Titouan 01.01.01*

CALETA LEON

NTIQUE SUD →

Canal de Beagle. 01.01.01 *Tit*

'I like to head off…across continents, a trail in the ocean behind my sail, my bag full of gouache and rolls of camera film.'

hasty construction. A cross, much taller than the chapel itself, is planted in the ground in front of it. Both seem to be holding on humbly but tenaciously in the face of strong winds.

On another page, Lamazou reproduces part of a globe that represents Cape Horn in dark green. An arrow pointing from west to east indicates the direction of the wind and currents. Next to this are some flowing lines of vegetation painted in the same tones of green and looking as if they have been shaped by storms and prevailing winds. Some lichen is also stuck to the page. Looking at these pages one might think that this zone of the globe had been moulded from the clay of some ancient world. In fact, Lamazou is opening our eyes to the spectacular presence of the Andes mountain range, which runs down the middle of the continent. At its furthest extremity the Pacific and Atlantic oceans meet in an awe-inspiring hymn to nature: wild waters, rugged coastline and tempestuous storms.

'Cape Horn and the regions of Patagonia and Tierra del Fuego are firmly inscribed as a theatre of tragedy in our collective memory,' writes Lamazou, and in his painting of 'Cabo de Hornos' he charges the grey and brown-green skies with menace and lays down dark lines 'as far as the nose can see' (his own expression). Although, as a general rule, he does not

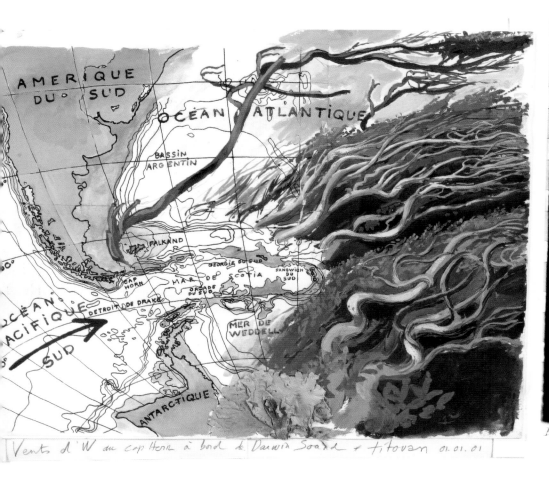

Vents d'W au cap Horn à bord de Darwin Soared + titouan 01.01.01

have any particular affection for landscapes, he shows a strong inclination for this type of illustration in the maritime tradition. Underneath this painting he takes care to note the names of promontories and outcrops of rock and land.

Intuition and simplicity

Being in the habit of compiling a list of contacts in advance of his trips, Lamazou is often able to move from one introduction to the next. At Cape Horn his most important contacts were writers who had written about the region, Bruce Chatwin and Francisco Coloane among them. The note-books or exercise books he takes with him are used only to jot down thoughts that come to him, give an account of his day, set down his impressions in detail and report on encounters that will later help him in preparing text for publication. On returning from his travels he puts these notes to one side, distancing himself from what he has written, and rewrites it later if he feels it necessary. These off-the-cuff texts are, according to him, often unsatisfactory. He professes to be better with images than words, but writing is nevertheless an indispensable part of his work, and he finds he has to resist the temptation to intellectualise his experiences and outlook on the world.

The methodology he uses for his drawings and paintings is very differ-ent. His artistic ouput retains far more of its initial force, although he often abandons ideas he has originally envisaged. In his drawings the

△◁ **THE CHAPEL ON HORN ISLAND**, 2000
The chapel, drawn here in ink, gouache and pencil, is located on a highly symbolic site in terms of maritime history. Cape Horn is where prayers are dedicated to the memory of all the men lost in the seas off this point.
Artist's collection

△▷ **CAPE HORN**, 2000
Lamazou linked drawing and photography together very early in his creative adventure. If he doesn't touch up the surface of a print, he invariably frames it in a white gouache margin that yellows and cracks over time, giving the image a crafted feel and an altogether different artistic status. As he must wait to develop his photographs, it is likely that he partially reconstructs his diary when he gets back to France. However, although he does often add to his photos, they are never new studies inspired by the photos themselves: this is not because of a hard and fast rule but rather because he is never inspired by the idea.
He writes, 'As far as I'm concerned it is a sterile technique that has never attracted me.' Going from three dimensions to two reduces the scope for error or the reinterpretation of eye or hand. When arranging his diaries back in France, memories, paintings, drawings and photos combine to re-create the atmosphere of the journey and the quality of friendships established.
Artist's collection

PORTRAITS OF A GAUCHO, 2000

At Cape Horn, Titouan Lamazou devoted a series of portraits to José Alvaro, a twenty-eight-year-old horseman who looks forty and who hunts wild bulls on the Estancia Yendegaia, a territory of 40,000 hectares. They quickly established a connection and went together on horseback along the coast of the Beagle Channel. This was a lucky meeting for Lamazou, who has ridden horses since his childhood and who laments the fact that 'today there are so few places on the planet where you can ride out as freely as you can there'. These images (two photographs and one gouache) of Alvaro in full gallop with a smile on his face say a lot about the rapport the two men shared on the day they spent together in the Patagonian countryside.

Artist's collection

creative force ebbs away at the end of a voyage, and he has to be on guard to avoid spoiling what are sometimes just the beginnings of drawings by adding inappropriately to them later, an error he has apparently made on more than one occasion. Some sketches seem to be without interest at first, but end up acquiring a new importance after the voyage, when time and distance have had the chance to work on his critical faculties. He often comes to accept errors or incomplete illustrations in the interests of over-all composition, and these illustrations then take on an aesthetic function that is an inherent and fundamental part of his work.

Always on the lookout for natural forms of expression, and determined to keep his work as real as he can, Lamazou tries to give the reader as direct a rapport as possible with the people he meets and the beauty of the regions he crosses. His visual universe is full on and full of colour, consisting of juxtapositions, collage and montage. What's more, he's a publishing success story! Thanks, at least in part, to him and Yvon Le Corre (his art teacher in Marseilles), this type of composition is now setting the trend in the travel diary genre. Titouan Lamazou has indeed made a very real contribution to restoring some of the lost dignity of our planet.

'Whether in paintings, travel diaries or literature,
the task is always to aim for simplicity.
Far from excluding spontaneity and richness,
this effort brings us closer to these things
in an exuberant artistic asceticism.'

MAX PAM
Women of Southern India

At the beginning of January 2003, the Australian traveller and photographer Max Pam left Singapore for India. Pam, who says that several lives would not be enough to discover all of this ancient civilisation, had already travelled across the country more than fifteen times before, taking in its cultural diversity without ever tiring of it. On this occasion he was travelling with his wife on a romantic pilgrimage, returning to where they had first met and the places they had visited together. They had fallen in love thirty years earlier in the south of this immense, multifaceted country. Pam, then a young hippie in search of experience, was already taking notes on his adventures. Now a university academic, he had not visited India since 1992, preferring to make solitary journeys to Africa and Tibet, from which he brought back remarkable travel diaries that were published as Ethiopia (2000) and Kailash (2002).

Pam covers a whole range of subjects in his diaries, illustrating them with landscapes, detailed drawings and portraits in black and white and colour. He generally uses a square format, and surrounds his illustrations with words painted in capital letters. These record his impressions, encounters, disappointments and passing thoughts. He never sets off without taking a notebook along, and never works to commission. He sees what he does as subjective, intimate and introspective. The notebook, which he never lets out of his sight, is a 'faithful companion' that helps him to survive sleepless nights in small hotels in the middle of nowhere. For his most recent voyage to India he equipped himself with a cheap sketchbook picked up in Australia. Within it he created an original artistic work, and previously unpublished sections of it are presented here.

Experiments in imagery

Max Pam and his wife landed at Cochin airport and made their way along the coast of southern India from west to east. Over the course of a month he produced the elements of the work that he later published as South India 2003. He noted everything that happened, recording his

◁ **PORTRAITS OF INDIAN WOMEN,** JANUARY 2003
Max Pam has always had a preference for the square format, and for a long time worked only in black and white. Colour has appeared in his photos only over the last few years of a career that began in the late 1960s. Although his first trip to India was cut short by the third Indo-Pakistani war, his passion for the country had already been established: 'I left England with a Hasselblad and became a photographer in the course of my journey to the east, without really knowing how or when.'
Artist's collection

△ **MIRA DREAMING,** JANUARY 2003
This female nude, whom he named Mira, came to Pam in a dream. He was profoundly affected by the experience, and the images he woke with retained their intensity on the page. Indeed, she became one of the main features of his diary. This fantasy figure adds to what is already a very poetic and sensitive work.
Artist's collection

Pam has a penchant for photos taken 'in the thick of things', showing the fugitive nature of travel impressions.

In the foreground of the image on the right we can see two hands, those of the photographer and his wife, who are returning to the places where they first met.

Artist's collection

▷ **ILLUSTRATIONS OF MATCHBOXES FEATURING INDIAN WOMEN,** 2003
The use of different types of iconography (photos, drawings, reproductions of statues) reinforces the 'kaleidoscopic' effect that the travel diary genre has made its own. The inclusion of common objects, such as matchboxes, makes us think of the everyday exoticism of far-off places.

Artist's collection

▽ **TITLE PAGE OF THE DIARY,** 2003
Painted in red and black inks, this page, like so many passages in the diary, was done with Chinese calligraphy brushes. It has the appearance of being dashed on to the page, the smudges adding to the feeling of immediacy.

Artist's collection

impressions in a single volume. The exercise of writing, he says, helps him to take possession of the smallest details of experiences and everyday perceptions. Since the beginning of his travels he had been inspired by Allen Ginsberg's book *Indian Journals*, 1962–3. The American writer was a pioneer of the subculture aesthetic, which greatly appealed to the Australian. According to Pam, writing is a much more complete form of expression than images because pictures do not surround the reader with the same intensity. In South India 2003 Pam manages to use very different sorts of image production without creating a clash. For example, his version of the Bayeux Tapestry in black ink coexists with other sections done with Chinese calligraphy brushes.

As Pam pursues his journeys, he systematically leaves space in his notebooks for the photos he takes along the way, slotting them in once he's back in Australia. This process allows him to relive his travels all over again, and readers of his books are inevitably drawn into the emotions of his journeys. In his diary of southern India Pam experimented with watercolour, a technique he had not explored before. As a novice, he sketched first in pencil, learning the principles of drawing from a manual. Some of the coloured mandalas (circles representing the universe) that appear in South India are derived from books on Indian art, while others are copied from Hindu sculptures.

'I took a blank notebook and some watercolours with me, and worked on my paintings during the trip. I worked mostly in the evening in my hotel room.'

ON THE RIGHT BANK FINISH
ING A SHIFT. THEY WERE CRO
WDED INTO A CANOE, VERY
LOW IN WATER. 20 OR 30 PEO
PLE, ALL STANDING, PERFEC
TLY BALANCED AND ALL THE
TIME WAVING AND SMILING
AT US AS THE BOAT WAS POLE
D ACROSS TO THE FAR BAN
K BY THE FERRYMAN.
KOLLAM. HOT AND HUMID AT
DUSK A BLACK OUT HAPPENS
AS I STRIDE INTO THE HOTEL
TO CHECK IN. NOTHING CAN H
APPEN. I SIT IN THE DARK AND
SWEAT IT OUT WITH THE RECE

△ REPRESENTATION OF THE TANTRA,
'TO RAIN, TO COME, TO SMELL,
TO DANCE, TO FINISH, TO GROOVE',
JANUARY 2003
Here, in ink, watercolour
and pencil, Pam has
reproduced a traditional
figure of tantric art.
The body of the woman
is an archetype of diverse
symbols showing how
different points on the
spine can become a path
to liberation. On the right
he uses a style of writing
that appears modern but
comes, in fact, from
the Bayeux Tapestry.
Artist's collection

▷ INDIAN NUDE, JANUARY 2003
The original pages of
Pam's diary – twenty
pages of text and thirty
pages of images –
are ivory in colour and
measure 21 x 20 cm.
At Edith Cowan University
in Australia, where he
teaches Art, Pam sets
his students the task
of creating a book as part
of their course. Some
of them go travelling
and come back with
a travel diary.
Artist's collection

Beautiful muse

On this voyage Max Pam was strongly disturbed by the beauty and charm of southern Indian women. However, the naked female called Mira who features so often in the diary is not a paid model or an exotic conquest, but a vision from a dream. She appeared to him one night in a small, hot and noisy town, but, he tells us regretfully, he has 'only met this women once in his existence'. The other nudes in the diary are also from 'highly erotic dreams that I had one night in my hotel room in Allapuzza'.

As for the women in the photos, he had no difficulty in capturing their frank and direct smiles on film. Max Pam has always had the ability to capture the essential humanity of his subjects. The unique attribute of his diary is the way it uses drawings and photography to convey reality and dreams, producing an erotic vision of great finesse. Maybe this is due to his relationship with India that 'is first and foremost a relationship of love, plural by necessity. The metropolis and culture – whether traditional, modern or mass – and the nature and spirituality of this country come together in an indivisible unit. Whether the elements are good or bad, beautiful or ugly, they all had to be lived.' The same goes for the desires and dreams…lived to the fullest!

'The emotional journey that I made was dominated by the beauty and charm of the women of southern India. One of the women in the diary, Mira, is a being from a dream.'

PETER BEARD

Scrapbooks of a Man's Existence

Of all his works, Peter Beard values one above the rest – a self-portrait photograph taken in 1965 called 'Whatever happens, I'll write'. Although there are several versions of the image, in all of them Beard is lying on the banks of Lake Rudolf in Kenya, absorbed in writing a diary. In a trick of the camera an enormous crocodile is shown swallowing him up from behind, his body already in its mouth up to the waist. A small stream of blood (red ink or true haemoglobin?) is flowing from the tip of a pen he is holding in his hand. Behind the humour lies a truth about art and the human condition, which summarises the relationship between this artist and his diaries.

Beard began began keeping a diary at his mother's behest while on holiday at Long Island. Aged eleven at the time, he hasn't stopped writing in the fifty-odd years since. He has covered literally thousands of pages, adopting many different techniques and processes, and allowing his work to evolve over time. The growing status and success of his journals set a trend and developed them as an art form that is now recognised as a discipline in its own right.

To open one of Peter Beard's journals is to open the pages of his life. He uses commonplace year-planner diaries, and usually works in the evening at one of his two principal residences in the United States or Kenya. He records the constant journeys between these two places, gives details of other countries visited on his travels (Japan, Haiti, Denmark, France, England, Bhutan, Egypt...), and glues in images from his published books, portraits of loved ones and encounters with animals photographed in the middle of the savannah. Day after day Beard beats pathways and covers tracks in a world at the heart of which his feelings, impressions and experiences are the constant inspiration.

Adventure and creativity

In 1955 Beard visited Africa for the first time, and it soon became his second home. In 1961 he moved into Hog Ranch in the Ngong Hills, not far from Nairobi. One of his neighbours was the Danish writer Karen

◁ **SCRAPBOOK COLLAGE,** C. 1990
In this pocket notebook, the smallest format of his diaries, Peter Beard has assembled fashion photographs, administrative paperwork, press cuttings and advertisements, then allowed his pen to add flourishes and shading in blue and red ink. The juxtaposition of printed text and image accentuates the feeling that this is no more than a fleeting moment in time.
Artist's collection

△ **SELF-PORTRAIT OF PETER BEARD, DIARY IN HAND,** 1999
The exhibitions and magazine features dedicated to this author, cinematographer, journalist, photographer and artist are now too numerous to count. Two books have been published about him, one in the United States and one in Italy. The exhibition catalogue 'Diary Peter Beard', published in Tokyo in 1993, concentrates on the work in his scrapbook diaries.
Artist's collection

'Whatever happens,

I'll write.'

▷ **PAGES FROM ONE OF**
PETER BEARD'S DIARIES, 1976
The author has used a
leaf, sections from comic
strips, press cuttings and
printed photographs on
varied and unrelated
subject matter with
the aim of accentuating
contrasts and provoking
a series of visual shocks,
going from the general to
the particular. The notes
in his squashed handwriting
are full of personal details,
while the images of dead
animals, an injured foot
and an elephant embryo
are disconcerting.
He took the last self-
portrait in Uganda in
1966, and also used
it in other work.
Artist's collection

Blixen, who read his diaries and played a brief but fundamental role in his life. She died only nine months after their meeting and left him her archives. Numerous homages to her appear in the pages of his diaries and in his works of art. Among the latter are portraits he painted during the last days of her life.

During Beard's first stay in Africa, he began work on a photographic history devoted to elephants and ecological damage, which was published as *The End of the Game* in 1965. Containing over three hundred photographs, the book received enthusiastic acclaim from both the public and the media. It brought together texts censuring the consumer frenzy of modern society and accounts of travellers, explorers, missionaries and

hunters of a time that was fast disappearing. Like a collage, the book combined various elements – articles, images new and old, photos of the artist… Beard borrowed from the aesthetic he had established in his scrapbooks and introduced an editorial line that concentrated on the theme of man's interaction with nature. Numerous drawings and paintings done by Karen Blixen's house steward were also featured in the work. Indeed, Beard often invites friends and acquaintances to leave their mark on his art. Celebrities such as Andy Warhol, Salvador Dali and Tina Turner as well as children and members of the Kikuyu tribe have all contributed.

Beard's technique is to fill his scrapbooks little by little with bits and pieces and 'futile and insignificant details'. Each page becomes a combina-

△ PAGES FROM ONE OF PETER BEARD'S DIARIES, C. 1980

△ **PAGES FROM ONE OF PETER BEARD'S DIARIES,** C. 1980

Peter Beard's fascination for the world of fashion is not unconnected to his artistic aesthetic. What is futile, frivolous and superficial is an important element of modern society. Top models appear like markers throughout his diaries, sometimes in erotic or aggressive poses, like the woman we see here. The author plays with these images, using them to overturn notions of nomenclature and scale, and clashing styles in much in the same way that our consumer and image-based society does.
Artist's collection

tion of lists, quotations, telephone numbers and scraps he has stapled in, photographic collages and sections from comic books, pages torn from magazines, press cuttings, adverts, photocopies, curios and wrapping paper. A huge variety of textures is present, including cloth, plastic, leaves, bark and snake skin. We find mistakes, marks and fingerprints, as well as remarkable drawings in India ink (black, brown, red, green and blue), there are even traces of blood, often representing people whose features resemble doodles drawn during telephone conversations.

Many other elements are collected, assembled and superimposed in diverse methods of montage. Anything that might provoke or wake his memory is included, and the visual shock is an essential element in these subjective archives. They are a sort of personal and archaeological museum that plunges back in time with the violence of modernity. This is achieved with a swirl of consumer society images, portraits of stars, nude

'Photography is a good way to advertise mistakes.'

bodies, giraffes and lions, images of war and advertising slogans. As happens with channel surfing on television, the most disparate images bump against one another, vying for space, just as they do on the small screen. The last vestiges of historic Africa brush up against symbols of capitalism (a far more savage system than the tribal one that came before it). The colossal and daily work that the pages of Peter Beard's diaries represent is at the very heart of his creativity, in which nothing, beginning with his own art, is sacred.

In 1996 Beard was seriously injured by an elephant in Kenya's Masai Mara reserve, and only just escaped with his life. Escape he did however and, fortunately for us, this master of the mix continues to create diaries that embody his life.

▽ **PAGES FROM PETER BEARD'S DIARY,** 15 AND 16 JUNE 1976
Empty space is rare in Beard's diaries. Here the repetitive motif of expanding spirals drawn in fine lines is used systematically to fill any areas of blank paper. A piece of plastic, a Kenyan stamp and cinema tickets add themselves to the eclectic inventory of items that make his diaries such unique objects.
Artist's collection

List of diarists

General Index

Bibliography

Alaoui, Brahim (ed), *Delacroix in Morocco*, Flammarion, London, 1994.

Ayala, Roselyne de and Guéno, Jean-Pierre, *Les Plus Beaux Récits de voyage*, éditions de la Martinière, Paris, 2003.

Ayala, Roselyne de. and Guéno, Jean-Pierre, *Brilliant beginnings: the youthful works of great artists, writers, and composers*, translated from the French by John Goodman, Abrams, New York, 2000.

Banks, Joseph, *The Journal of Joseph Banks in the Endeavour*, with a commentary by A. M. Lysaght, Guildford, 1980.

Battesti, Michèle (ed), *Images des mers du Sud: le voyage de la corvette la* Coquille, *1822–1825*, Le May, Boulogne-Billancourt, 1993.

Beard, Peter, *The End of the Game: The Last Word from Paradise*, Chronicle Books, San Francisco, 1996.

Boch, Julie, *Ingénieur Duplessis, Périple de Beauchesne à la Terre de Feu (1698–1701), Une expédition mandatée par Louis XIV*, foreword by Marie Foucard, Transboréal, Paris, 2003.

Brettell, Richard R. and Darragon, Éric, *Edward Hopper, les années parisiennes, 1906–1910*, Le Passage, Paris, 2004.

Brosse, Jacques, *Great Voyages of Discovery: Circumnavigators and Scientists, 1764-1843*, Facts on File Inc, New York, 1985.

Carelli, Mario (ed), *À la découverte de l'Amazonie: Les carnets du naturaliste Hercule Florence*, Coll. "Album Découvertes Gallimard", Gallimard, Paris, 1992.

Charcot, Jean-Baptiste, *Le Pourquoi-Pas? dans l'Antarctique*, Arthaud, Paris, 1996.

James Cook, *The Journals on His Voyages of Discovery*, Vol 1, 2 & 3, The Boydell Press, Woodbridge, 1999.

Cuisenier, Jean, Delouche, Denise and Lossignol, Simone, *Un carnet de croquis et son devenir, François Hyppolyte Lalaisse et la Bretagne*, 2 vol., éditions de la Cité, Paris, 1985.

Edwards, Jim and Peterson, William, *Sam Scott, Drawings, Watercolors, Oil Paintings*, Fresco Fine Art Publications, Albuquerque, 2003.

Fournié, Pierre (ed), *Aventuriers du monde, les grands explorateurs français au temps des premiers photographes, 1866–1914*, L'Iconoclaste, Paris, 2003.

Fox, Michael D. and Fox, Suzanne G. (ed), *Meriwether Lewis and William Clark: the Corps of Discovery and the Exploration of the American Frontier*, PowerPlus Books, New York, 2005.

Fulton, Pamela Jeanne (ed), *The Minerva Journal of John Washington Price. A Voyage From Cork, Ireland, to Sydney, New South Wales, 1798-1800*, The Miegunyah Press, Melbourne, 2000.

Gauguin, Paul, *Ancien Culte mahorie*, René Huyghe (ed), Hermann, Paris, 1951.

Gauguin, Paul, *Noa Noa: The Tahiti Journal Of Paul Gauguin*, translated by O.F. Theis, Chronicle Books, San Francisco, 2005.

Goncourt, Edmond and Jules de, *Notes sur l'Italie (1855–1856)*, Coll. "Les Chemins de l'Italie", Desjonquères, Paris, 1996.

Paul Hogarth, *The Artist as Reporter*, Studio Vista, New York, 1967.

Hugo, Victor, *Correspondance familiale et écrits intimes* (2 Bde), Jean and Sheila Gaudon and Bernard Leuilliot, with a foreword by Jean Gaudon, Coll. "Bouquins", Robert Laffont, Paris, 1991.

Hugo, Victor, *Récits et dessins de voyage*, La Renaissance du livre, Tournai, 2001.

Hugo, Victor, *The Memoirs of Victor Hugo*, Indypublish, New York, 2002.

Jacobi, Dominique, *Pascal Coste, Toutes les Égypte*, éditions Parenthèses, Marseille, 1998.

Keeler, Mary (ed) *Sir Francis Drake's West Indian voyage, 1585-86*, Hakluyt Society, London, 1981.

Knight, David, *Scientific Travellers, 1789-1874*, Routledge, London, 2003.

Knight, David, *The Naturalist on the River Amazons: Henry Walter Bates*, Routledge, London 2004.

Lafon, Marie-Françoise, *Philippe, duc d'Orléans (1869–1926), explorateur, navigateur, naturaliste*, Boubée, Paris 1999.

Lamazou, Titouan, *Coffret Lamazou 2000 (Carnets de voyage, 2 vol.)*, Coll. "Nouveaux Loisirs", Gallimard, Paris, 2000.

Lamazou, Titouan, *Kinshasa*, Coll. "Nouveaux Loisirs", Gallimard, Paris, 2001

Lamazou, Titouan, *Titouan en Haïti*, Coll. "Nouveaux Loisirs", Gallimard, Paris, 2003.

Le Corre, Yvon, *Les Outils de la passion*, Le Chasse-Marée, Douarnenez, 1998.

Le Corre, Yvon, *Les Tavernes d'Alcina, voyage au Portugal*, Gallimard, Paris, 1990.

Levin, Gail, *Edward Hopper, The Art and the Artist*, W.W Norton & Company, New York-London, 1996.

Malaurie, Jean, *Call of the North: An Explorer's Journey to the North Pole*, Abrams, New York, 2001.

Monod, Théodore, *Magic Desert*, Arpel Graphics, Santa Barbara, 2002.

Moulton, Gary E. (ed), *The Definitive Journals of Lewis & Clark*, University of Nebraska Press, Lincoln, 2002.

Pam, Max, *Indian Ocean Journals*, Scalo, Zurich, 1998.

Récamier, Docteur, *L'Âme de l'exilé, souvenirs des voyages de Monseigneur le duc d'Orléans*, librairie Plon, Paris, 1929.

Rice, Tony, Dr., *Voyages of Discovery: Three Centuries of Natural History Exploration*, NHM Publishing, London, 1999.

Rübesamen, Hans-Eckart (ed), *Georg Forster, Reise um die Welt mit Kapitän Cook*, Lamuv Verlag, Göttingen, 2002.

Savary, Claude and Perrois, Louis (foreword), *Le Gabon de Fernand Grébert, 1913–1932*, Coll. "Sources et Témoignages", éditions D et musée d'Ethnographie de Genève, Geneva 2003.

Sillevis, John (ed), *Jongkind, aquarelles*, Bibliothèque de l'image, Paris, 2002.

Warrell, Ian, *Turner, Le voyage sur la Loire*, éd. de la RMN, Paris 1998.

Zug, James (ed), Ledvard, John, *The Last Voyage of Captain Cook: With Ledyard's Selected Letters and Siberian Journal*, National Geographic Books, London, 2005.

Acknowledgements

The author and publisher would like to thank all those involved in the making of this book with special thanks to :
Gabrielle Baglione, Laurence Bascle (Museum images),
Peter Beard, Amélie Bélanger, Pascal Blanchard, Jacques Brosse, Jean-Marc Durou, Étienne Féau, Pierre Fournié,
Jean et Michèle Gaumy, Svetlana Guilbot, Pascal Heurtel, Titouan Lamazou, Azou and Yvon Le Corre,
Isabelle Le Toquin, Vincent Lyky, Jean Malaurie, Marie-Isabelle Merle-des-Îles, Ambroise Monod,
Cécile Morand, Max Pam, Bernard Plossu, Sam Scott, Nicolas Texier and Ulrike Leitner from the Berlin-Brandenburgische
Akademie der Wissenschaften for their helpful advice with Alexander von Humboldt's Reisetagebücher.
Our special thanks to Gregor C. Falk who contributed the chapter on Alexander von Humboldt.

Picture Credits